ACTING

AT THE SPEED OF

LIFE

For Deb!

With love, gratitude and affection!

Thanks for everything!

ACTING AT THE SPEED OF LIFE

Conquering Theatrical Style

By Timothy Mooney

Acting at the Speed of Life; Conquering Theatrical Style.

Copyright © 2011 by Timothy Mooney.

Manufactured in the United States of America. All rights reserved. No part of this book may be reproduced or transmitted in any form or by any electronic or mechanical means including information storage and retrieval systems – except by a reviewer who may quote brief passages in a review to be printed in a magazine, newspaper, or on the Web – without permission in writing from the publisher. For information, please contact

TMRT Press
P.O. Box 638
Prospect Heights, Illinois 60070
(847) 757-3648.

Although the author and publisher have made every effort to ensure the accuracy and completeness of information contained in this book, we assume no responsibility for errors, inaccuracies, omissions, or any inconsistency herein. Any slights of people, places or organizations are unintentional.

First printing 2011.

ISBN 978-0-9831812-0-0

Library of Congress Control Number: 2011923288

Cover photos by Brian McConkey

For more information, visit www.timmooneyrep.com.

ATTENTION CORPORATIONS, UNIVERSITIES, COLLEGES, AND PROFESSIONAL ORGANIZATIONS: Quantity discounts are available on bulk purchases of this book for educational, gift purposes, or as premiums for increasing magazine subscriptions or renewals. Special books or book excerpts can also be created to fit specific needs. For information, please contact TMRT Press, P.O. Box 638, Prospect Heights, IL 60070; ph 847-757-3648.

To receive free e-mails about the "Acting at the Speed of Life" project, or the Timothy Mooney Repertory Theatre tour and ongoing performances of *Molière than Thou*, *Lot o' Shakespeare* and *Criteria*, please drop a note to info@timmooneyrep.com.

Dedication

To the memory of Dr. William Morgan.

Acknowledgements

I pause to acknowledge the many brilliant directors and teachers that I have been honored to work with… especially those who (as much as I may have rebelled at the time) wouldn't let me get away with my "bag of tricks." The feedback you gave and your relentless attentiveness honed my skills and kept me reaching beyond the easy reading, the safe positioning and the pat answer.

I'd like to thank not only my theatre teachers and directors, but those who touched and inspired me to study English, Aesthetics, Rhetoric, Philosophy and Life, including James and Shirley Mooney, Sister Susan, Mrs. Markert, Bernice McCarthy, Mark Anderson, Brother Robert Ruhl, Joe Proctor, Chuck Pascoe, Meredith Taylor, Judith Lyons, Christopher Moe, Martin Platt, Rex McGraw, Tice Miller, Lindsay Reading Korth, Marcia Douglas, John Dillon, Larry Shue, Douglas Hughes, Dan Sullivan, Tom Bullard, Deb Pekin, and Jeff and Sue Paige. Each of you, whether director, mentor or collaborator, drew more of "me" out of myself.

The lessons I absorbed from you all breathe through these pages, even when I somehow manage to avoid quoting you directly. Your voices, still very present in my head after many, many years, comment on, correct, and sometimes dictate the words that wound up on these pages.

This project would also not have been possible without the advice and support of my good friend and assistant, April Peterson, encouragement from my editor-friend, Forsyth Alexander, timely information and feedback from my web master and advisor, Bruce Cantwell, ongoing support from my good friend, Kirsten Moomey and ideas from my author/illustrator/friend, Lee Rushton Howard (quoted at length in Chapter 49). Thanks as always, to my constant inspiration, my son, Isaac Mooney.

Tim

Advance Reviews:

What People are Saying About the Book

Tim Mooney calls us back to the basics, and it's about time! *Acting at the Speed of Life* communicates with clarity, wisdom and practicality. This text belongs in every theatre artist's bookbag. *Jeff Barker, Northwestern College Theatre Chair*

I have been reading your text with unmatched enthusiasm. It unquestionably fills a niche that needs filling. As a product of "the 1950's era Method," I feel that this easily read text redresses some of the excesses of that Brando dominated era. How little attention was paid to the art of playing as so deftly defined by you in this book. You are right on in your analysis here. What you say is applicable to all manner of plays—modern as well as those from the classic past. Bravo! *David Deacon, Theatre Professor, Texas A&M University-Kingsville*

I really like your book. I can hear you speaking. All the examples from your own acting or teaching experiences really help to make it an easy read. I think this would go nicely into a classical acting class/ Acting Styles class. The advanced students are really hungry for this kind of information and can relate to what you are saying. I felt like I was sitting in one of your workshops again. NO other book I've read captures these simple tasks that are so important. I would recommend every acting student to have your book.
Janice Fronczak, University of Nebraska-Kearney Theatre Chair

Thank You!!!!!!!!! I applied the acting advice in your book to an actual debate, and it worked! I was up against an opponent tonight with better name recognition, more experience in our union, and known as a good speaker. And I took him out! Your tips helped me feel prepared and more relaxed, and helped me keep the focus on the members, not on getting votes. *Julie Blaha, Teachers Union Organizer, Minneapolis, MN*

[It] shed a huge beam of light on some things in my life. You have a gift. You make acting accessible — hard work, yes, but quite within the realm of possibility. I definitely am no expert. However, I do know how much I'm reacting to your honesty. I don't think I'd be alone. *Kelly Crandall, Theatre Student, University of Wisconsin-Milwaukee*

The book for me is now a series of master-classes framed as a storyteller would relate them to me. In a way it reminded me of *An Actor Prepares* when I thought about how I use that book. I leaf through it [and] can read whatever chapter seems most compelling at the time. I see it as a sort of conversation with you, intended as much for directors as actors.
Jim Ryan, Norman North High School Fine Arts Chair

Provocative... Many of its ideas are valuable for any one in or considering an acting career... What was striking was your errant disregard (shared by me) for psychology and the American Method! *Sanford Robbins, U of Delaware Professional Actor Training Program Chair*

I stayed up until 3 am yesterday reading your book! And I have a very short attention span. I just love how passionate you are about the craft and how human and sensitive and honest and funny your writing is. I am all inspired... also you have chosen some of my favorite monologues to prove a point and teach great lessons to actors. *Alina Mostov, Actress*

I have begun delving into the text [and] am anxious to get back to it... It seems like a important work that is what is needed to get back to storytelling in an effective way. Thank you so much for the opportunity. *Cameron Jackson, Florida State University, Theatre Chair*

Reviews:

What People are Saying About the Author

The audience is enthralled... Timothy Mooney is the real deal... A very tight performance indeed, which should be seen by any aspiring actor who wants to tread the boards.
George Psillidies, nytheatre.com

A must-see for aspiring drama students and a pleasant experience for the rest of us... Men like Mooney were born for the spotlight and he relishes every character he takes on... every unique voice he takes on fills the room. *The Vue Weekly, (Edmonton)*

Sparkling eyes, infectious grin and elastic face... the consummate over-the-top showman.
Robin Chase, The Jenny Revue (Winnipeg)

Mooney needs only a trunk of costume pieces and his superior histrionics to turn himself into any number of vivid, irreverent, fast-talking characters straight from the pages of the author's greatest works. A well-trained and appealing performer... a skilled impersonation of one of the theater's most gifted and important creative spirits. *Al Krulik, Orlando Weekly*

A consummate story-teller. I left the theatre with the feeling that I could listen to him tell a story about almost anything... *Stacy Rowland, TheatreSeattle.com*

Molière has never been more accessible... *Marie J. Kilker, aislesay.com*

Electrifying. I've never seen young actors from different schools so mesmerized by a single performer. *Dennis Wemm, West Virginia Theatre Conference President*

The variety of voice and stature any actor should posses. How much you can do with nothing but talent. *Michael McGiveney, America's Quick Change Artists*

I heard, with a great deal of excitement, from students that the masterclass was "[expletive] mindblowingly awesome"... *Mike McFerron, Art Series Director, Lewis University*

I wished all of my movement students had been there... I was so impressed by how in control you were that you could get a laugh with your knee or with a raised eyebrow.
Matt Chiorini, Artistic Director, Arkansas Shakespeare Theatre

The most energetic, exacting and dynamic actor I know.
Yvonne Conybeare, Fairfield University

I can't remember when I've seen an audience so engaged.
Katie Pearson, Theatre Coordinator, Auburn U-Montgomery

A consummate performer and an amazing teacher. He has truly motivated my students to seek higher standards. His workshops were inspiring for all who attended, be they neophytes or veterans. His influence will be felt long after his curtain call. Tim's physical dexterity is amazing, not only in gesture, but in total physicality. His "instrument" is finely tuned to play the music he wants us to hear. *Nancy Jo Humfeld, Director of Theatre, Howard Payne U*

His diction is so clear they understand his rhyming translations without difficulty. His "Stop thief" from "*Les Precieuses Ridicules*" rang in my ears for months, testimony to his ability to capture the essence of the characters and the engaging cadence of his voice.
Jacqueline Thomas, French Prof, Texas A&M U-Kingsville

You de-mystified Shakespeare in a mere 90 minutes. Rather than weeks and weeks of preparation and all this reverential build-up, you just plunged right in, enabling each actor to find confidence in their own voice and rhythmic style... *Tony Osborne, Gonzaga University*

Book This Fellow! I strongly urge you to contact him regarding working with your cast, and those taking Acting Period Styles. He is an invaluable asset regarding text, voice, movement, and helping students discover connections to the material that are alive and inspiring.
Fred Gorelick, North Eugene High School

You were soooo helpful! We advanced yesterday with high praise from the judge, he loved us! AND, we won a ton of individual acting awards also! *Daisy Payne, Lake Travis High School*

I got nothing but very positive comments all day. I was amazed at how still and attentive our ADD kids were, too. I think they were spellbound... Your visit was one of the highlights of my teaching career. *Kathy Wilson, Melbourne Central Catholic*

Actors are only as good as the best performer they have ever seen, so it was an inspiration and motivational challenge for them to witness your truly amazing interpretation... They will all remember an enlightening morning when they met Molière and his friends and saw firsthand how a talented, trained actor can bring them to life.
Anne Poyner, Theatre Teacher, Summit HS

Last night I met with the students for the first time since you were here. Your ears should have been burning! Each student there had something wonderful to say about the experience. Our Harpagon was especially moved. His mother wrote to make sure I knew how much it meant to him. *Lynda Sharpe, Middleton High School, Madison, WI*

A completely accessible performance from beginning to end... He is clearly an entertainer at heart, and worth seeing for that alone. *Katelyn Coyne*

The man is a chameleon. Enraged, excited and electrifying, he is all over the stage and a joy to watch! *Naomi Stauffer, Auburn University of Montgomery Alumni*

I have been going to theatrical productions for over 60 years (I counted up so I could say that) and I have never been to one where the audience was as enthusiastic, as caught up in the spirit of the show. If you had sent us out to storm the Bastille I think we would have tried. *Martha Hull, Roanoke, VA*

I am thrilled that [my daughter] had the wonderful opportunity to work with you...She went home and wrote everything she could remember you said down... it was magic for her... She was radiating. *Parent, Harley School*

Brilliant!!! So much [educational value], the expressions, the power of enunciation. Everything I saw inspired me to push more in my career. Thank you!!
Jonathan Breitkrautz (Actor/Student)

Every one of his movements... from his broad sweeping arm movements to the twitches of his face were purposeful and exact... *Rian Slay, Jr. (Student)*

If only, we, as actors, could be so bold and so individually inspired as his performance was... an amazing and eye opening performance. *Joshua McFadden, Sr. (Student)*

Not only was he the master of wordplay and how to say every line with perfect comedic timing, he was definitely the master of movement! His creativity amazed me! I learned that, as an actor, I need to be bolder. *Tiffany McFadden, Jr. (Student)*

Table of Contents

PART IV: PLAYING WITH DISCIPLINE

PART V: OUTWITTING YOURSELF

PART VI: PUTTING IT TOGETHER

Introduction: Who am I?

...the little voice in the back of my head was clarifying issues of presentation and staging that had been so elusive.

There comes that dreaded moment in my Acting Workshops when the hosting professor asks, "So tell us a little about your career? How did you get started?"

(It's not that talking about myself is not my favorite topic… but usually I've got two hours or less to work with, and making sense of my own story sucks a good 10-15 minutes out of our available time.)

Quite often my response is to offer up a view of my career as an example of "what *not* to do!"

Actually, I don't regret the many choices I've made. Without them I wouldn't have gotten here, now. And Being Here, Now is the perfect place to be.

But certainly, along the way, I have often wished that I might Get Somewhere Else, Faster.

This book is the product of a number of entirely un-anticipatable series of twists and turns I never might have expected life to take. In the process, I have found myself helming a series of projects which have given me a unique view on a particular area of the theatre. And, it has become my particular avocation to share it.

But traveling briefly, back in time …

I was evidently an actor by the time I reached the age of six. You can see it in the home movies my dad took. The fourth of four boys in the family, I grew up desperate for attention and struggling to differentiate myself from the pack.

Years later, I played Marley's Ghost in the Fifth Grade Christmas Play, and performed in the children's choruses of *Oliver* and *Fiddler on the Roof.* Usually my fellow students would be cast much better than myself, so I never thought much of acting as a career move.

Getting better roles in high school, I enjoyed, not so much the art of performance, as the society of performers. (I attended an all-boys high school, and the "sister school" imported boys to perform in their shows.)

In college, I found myself spending my extra time in the theatre, and felt no inclination to do anything else. I am perhaps the most stubborn (or, "determined") man I know, and was insistent on forging my own way in a field that was nothing like my father's or my siblings'.

Eventually, looking to make my avocation feed the college credit that I could be earning, I unilaterally changed my major to Theatre, and plunged into the deep end of the pool.

I've never kept track of how many shows I've done, but a good estimation might figure about five per year from college, forward. As we've passed thirty years by now, this suggests 150 shows or so.

Rather than let my mind fester, during the summer following my freshman year (spent working at the Taco Bell) I set my sights toward reading all of Shakespeare's plays. The next summer, I attempted all of Strindberg and Shaw (though I must confess I never quite finished *Man and Superman*).

Reading Shakespeare seemed natural to me. Perhaps I had become accustomed to the "thee" and "thou" style of *Thor* comic books as a child. But later university classes in Shakespeare built my affinity, and an internship with the Alabama Shakespeare Festival followed.

Upon graduation, I was one of a thousand actors of my exact same type, auditioning for all of the same roles in the Big City. I decided that learning to ***direct*** would be my ticket to steady work. This provided sufficient cover to return to academia, working on my Master of Fine Arts.

The MFA was completed with a directing internship at the Milwaukee Repertory Theatre, where I had the pleasure of working with the amazing Larry Shue.[1] Larry was to die in an airplane crash about a year later, but his ability to write as well as act had a profound impact. (I saw him off-Broadway, performing the title role in his own production of *The Foreigner.*)

As a youthful professor, I taught acting at Northern Illinois University for two years, but I had an uneasy feeling that I was simply parroting the acting texts planted in my hands. The material I was teaching didn't speak to the work I was *actually* doing, or the way that my brain was thinking about that work in practice. I didn't know how to come clean with what my inner voice was telling me, and I may have even been a bit embarrassed that that little voice wasn't saying the things that it "should." And so, I silently felt a little bit phony about the whole thing.

At the Seattle Rep I interned in Literary Management as well as Directing, and found myself reading through the stacks of unsolicited scripts piled up in the office. I was assistant director on a production of *Tartuffe*, which was eventually to affect me much more deeply than I could have imagined.

Reading through the slush pile of scripts, I realized that these manuscripts (a couple of which I recognized from my time at the Milwaukee Rep) were making the rounds through the offices of theatres across the United States. Artistic Directors and Literary Managers, occupied with "putting theatre on," were letting them pile up, and I envisioned a newsletter that would disseminate this information to theatres across the country, enabling theatres to target works that responded to their needs.

I created *The Script Review*. For seven years I wrote about manuscripts, with twenty reviews in each newsletter, distributed to theatres nation-wide. It was ambitious, challenging, fun… and never made any money. What I *did* learn over those years was how to articulate a point in a limited space. The expense of paper,

---

[1] Author of *The Foreigner*, *The Nerd* and *Wenceslas Square*.

toner and postage taught me to tighten my prose. I found that there is a perfect word waiting which might describe the very particular, idiosyncratic notion twisting its way through my head, which might effectively underline the dramatic action in the imagination of the reader.

I became Artistic Director of Stage Two, a small theatre in Chicago's northern suburbs, and made use of the many excellent plays that I had been reading for *The Script Review* to assemble Stage Two's season.

Any artistic director will tell you it is difficult to develop an audience exclusively through new work but (stubborn) I persisted, only occasionally compromising with the production of a familiar title. The summer months were the leanest of times, and during these we focused our efforts on more familiar work.

I stumbled back over *Tartuffe*.

Among the theatre staff, there was an energy and excitement in support of *Tartuffe*, and the brilliant Seattle Rep cast from nine years prior was vivid in my memory. Here was an opportunity to pursue our stated mission while still producing a familiar title. I had been exploring verse, of late, as a newfound proliferation of verbal chatter (*The Internet*) was suddenly unleashing a stream of unimpeded creative writing. I decided to try my hand at a new variation on *Tartuffe*.

Many (myself included) scoffed at the notion, particularly as Richard Wilbur's version of the play was, and remains, quite popular. I did not expect I would actually finish the project.

Yet, one line of dialogue led to a rhyming line of dialogue, which led me to another, and yet another couplet, and on through the opening scene, and through the first, second, and third acts.

I paused for auditions, and the first couple of actors to show up left me disappointed at my apparently lackluster writing. The rhythms and stresses were all off somehow. Dialogue that I imagined to be knock-down, drag-out hilarious, was coming out dour, ponderous and witless.

It wasn't until a very talented actress read the role of Dorine that the play came roaring back. There was a life in the thing, and it simply needed actors who could see that life, bubbling just beneath the formal structure of the verse, who were equipped, in turn, with the vocal apparatus to make those bubbles of wit "pop" where the audience could see, hear and enjoy them.

I dove back in, writing acts four and five in record time. The play worked on more levels than I imagined, and I got off the treadmill of running a theatre to concentrate on what was now a "writing career." I tested this theatrical magic repeatedly, eager to know if this was an ability that lived reliably within me, or was the product of my special relationship with *Tartuffe*. I explored new versions of the plays of Molière: *The School for Husbands, The Doctor in Spite of Himself, The Miser, The Precious Young Maidens*… seventeen plays in all, so far.

Occasionally, a theatre would produce one of these. Or sometimes I would rejoin my old theatre company to work on one of them. I might well travel to see a production in the exotic lands of Ohio, Colorado, Michigan. Sometimes actors would recapture the life, wit and zest, much like that early audition for Dorine. And sometimes, the thing would fall flat: dour, ponderous, witless.

Sub-consciously, I isolated differences between successful and less successful performances. Some actors would struggle, while others picked up the style with ease. Occasionally, I would see a video of a show to which I was unable to lend direct support, and now and then, I would quietly be grateful to not have been present.

Shifting from the role of director to that of actor, repeated coincidences found me playing the roles that Molière had originally performed. As Molière had carried the bulk of the responsibilities with his theatre, I found I could likewise lead by example: establishing a performance style, speaking through the voice that I was already hearing in the back of my head: the voice that had been there back when I was choosing one word, rather than another.

Simultaneously, I was doing the "luncheon circuit," speaking to the Kiwanis, the Rotary, the Eagles... And one engagement with the Canadian Womens' Guild planted an idea in my head. They didn't want a lecture ***about*** Molière; they wanted a performance ***of*** Molière.

I resisted this notion, indignantly assuming that fragmenting the work of Molière would violate his spirit, disturbing his delicately structured layers of plot. Or more likely, I was embarrassed by the arrogance of a one-man performance which would contrive to manipulate my own ego front and center. And yet...

And yet, having generated these words, and played many of these roles, I was living a strange, parallel life to my favorite playwright. Most of Molière's translators were French language experts or poets, and very few of these authors would have the inclination, much less the ambition or theatrical instinct, to play these parts.

Molière than Thou was created and memorized within six months, and although it only saw a moderate success when performed at my home theatre, the minimal simplicity of its design made it easily transportable. I established bookings for the performance, slowly at first...

Before long it had transformed itself into the preoccupying thrust of my career. Within two years, I was driving around the States, performing for some ten thousand students a year, and running acting workshops which gave me the opportunity to develop and explore acting theory in practice.

Along the way, and through the course of writing this book, the tour has continued (nine years as of this printing), while adding four more one-person shows in the process. (*What a megalomaniac!*)

My plunge back into Shakespeare, with the one-person show, *Lot o' Shakespeare*, arose when I was already a dozen or so drafts into the composition of this text, and while I've slipped in a number of observations from that experience, there will be more to come, either in future editions, or in some unconceived book yet-to-come.

Fifteen years prior, I was teaching somebody else's acting theories, and they were never quite a good "fit." But now, as the author of these works, the little voice in the back of my head was getting more specific and insistent about issues of presentation and staging that had been so elusive.

I was discovering issues that had been left un-articulated: Students are not always getting the "straight stuff," and acting theory has fragmented into a million different schools of thought.

Well, now I'm making that a million and one.

Theatre practitioners get into elaborate arguments about "being true" to Shakespeare or Molière, and gradually I've developed an opinion on that subject. Having written most of my work in verse, I listen for the musicality of that verse in a particular manner. I imagine Shakespeare and Molière listening in a similar manner, and I would like to imagine that they might underline certain passages in this book.

This is not intended as the only acting text in an actor's library! A strict adherence to these notions (without any corresponding internal exploration) would leave the actor significantly imbalanced in favor of external performance study.

While working on this, I continued to revisit the work of Stanislavsky and remind myself of the brilliant study to which so many of us owe such debt, and with whom I will seem to be in such conflict.

Lurking behind Stanislavsky's work is the context of an era that celebrated bombast… broad, stylized declamation, exaggerated to such a degree that it had lost touch with an internal spirit of truth, emotion or communion.

Stanislavsky was a rebel of his time, leading actors out of that particular desert, much as Shakespeare placed words in Hamlet's mouth to rail against his contemporary actors who were "out-Heroding Herod." In either instance, these men would likely be shocked at how very far we have come from the context of those times.

Perhaps I am the Bizarro-world Stanislavsky… his evil twin nudging you back toward a sense of theatricality that got thrown out with the bathwater, as it were… the other side of a coin which may turn out to be the same.

Or, perhaps I like to think of this as the acting book that Molière would write, had he suspected that his assumed, often stylized and external manner of performance would not be self-evident.

Or … not.

Preface

We all want to know just why the author has called us all here tonight... And the modern actor runs interference between us and the playwright.

What are the actors' two most fundamental responsibilities?

I like to kick-start each workshop with this question, if only to startle actors out of their passivity. Responses fly back at me:

"Being in character."

"Memorizing your lines."

As a playwright I like that answer.

"Feeling the emotion."

"Understanding the play."

"Communicating the meaning of the play."

As answers go, this one is actually pretty close, but too elaborate for our needs. I encourage them:

Think simpler. Much more basic.

"Pursuing the objective."

"Connecting with your fellow actors."

"Connecting with yourself!"

All these are great answers!... None of them happen to be the specific ones that I am looking for, but they're great answers ...

They're not done yet:

"Listening."

"Telling the story."

"Having fun."

"Entertaining the audience."

There is a moment of silence.

No more guesses? All right, here are my two, and as soon as I say the first one, you're going to guess the second one: Are you ready? The first one is "BEING SEEN." And the second...?

"BEING HEARD."

Exactly.

Now, if I was talking to a group of *Med Students*, and asking them about what the most fundamental responsibilities of a Doctor were, they would all, pretty much, come up with the same two things: Something to do with "First of all do no harm..." and second, "Save the patient."

If I was talking to a group of *Law Students* about what the two most fundamental responsibilities of a Lawyer were, they would all pretty much agree with "Don't incriminate your client," and "Win the case."

But when I talk with a group of *Artists*, and especially *Actors*, the answers that I get are all over the map!

First of all, acting is an incredibly subjective experience... an art form in which the "canvas," as it were, is one's own body, one's voice and psychological makeup. The actor lives perpetually on the inside, looking out from the work that he is creating.

Beyond this, though, acting study has splintered into a myriad of "schools of thought," and each teacher has their own school from which they have emerged, and their own reaction to that school, to the extent that they are rebelling against it, or promoting it. They also have a wide variety of practical applications of this material, as each individual student has their own very specific needs, which leads the teacher to impress the importance of different *elements* of the system to *different degrees*, so that multiple students of the same teacher will come away with a variety of impressions about the relative importance of those fundamental responsibilities.

"Being Seen and Being Heard." Everything else... yes, everything else needs to build on top of this.

You say you've got the most textured, detailed, nuanced, passionate inner life ever witnessed on stage? Great. Bring it on. Use it. But if you aren't being seen or heard, nobody will be able to penetrate the wall of incomprehensibility enough to care.

Why isn't this simple assertion the most important thesis of our acting textbooks? Maybe it's just so damn obvious, and we feel like we've got to have something more subtle to write about, or to teach about. Perhaps there's a prejudice against such "external" methods. Maybe we've grown so accustomed to television or film acting that we think of this as the editor's job. Somewhere along the line, we forgot, and the virus is spreading. Actors are infected with the disease of invisibility and inaudibility, and plays, especially classical works, are losing meaning, swallowed up in the incomprehensible garble that actors mumble.

Ask any theatre-goer, one who attends, but does not actually work in the theatre: "What is the biggest problem that you encounter when you see a show?" Without hesitation 95% of them will tell you:[2] *"I can't hear what the actors are saying!"*

[2] This statistic, like all statistics in this book... are made up.

Ask "Who among you has ever missed the most important moment, or speech, or scene of a play?" and they will all raise their hands. We all want to know just why the author has called us all here tonight. We may have shown up simply because our friends are in a show, but once we're in the seat, our natural curiosity gets the best of us, and we want to know what the *author* has to say. And the modern actor ***runs interference between us and the playwright***.

"Being seen and being heard" is even more fundamental than our character objectives. This is a responsibility that lies beneath any character discovery we may layer into our performances.

Think it's too obvious? Too easy?

I spent two hours of an afternoon with actors, expressing the nature of this great responsibility. They nodded, laughing and agreeing throughout. I went to dinner, came back, and watched these same actors in rehearsal, continuing to mutter their lines looking down into the floor, being neither seen nor heard.

There are psychological factors in the way, as well as internal arguments to which the actor gives precedence, time and again. These things are both persuasive and pervasive, and it takes training and practice to counter them.

At the risk of sounding alarmist, I have adapted a well-known quote from Benjamin Franklin for our use:

> For the want of a consonant, the word was lost,
> For the want of a word, the line was lost,
> For the want of a line, the scene was lost,
> For the want of a scene, the act was lost,
> For the want of an act, the show was lost.

Acting happens "at the speed of life." Once that one word has slipped by, there is no picking it up again. And subsequent lines will be lost in the cacophony of "What did he say?"

This has a domino effect. It is the simplest of responsibilities, and yet the responsibility least fulfilled. We think of ourselves as artists. We arm ourselves with "concepts" and "methods," but we thumb our nose at the people for whom we are supposedly performing.

Part I

BEING SEEN

Chapter 1

Getting Yourself Seen

> *To be an actor is to be conscious of being looked at and, seemingly, judged. To know that people "out there" are looking in introduces a strain of self-awareness in which every movement which once might have danced unconsciously across the body, becomes a conscious choice, and a basis for celebration or, more often, self-loathing.*

"Being seen" is generally the easier of our two responsibilities. And it is also a shared responsibility in which people such as the director, the lighting designer, the set designer and the costume designer take on a significant part.

Yet the actor is responsible for his or her own body in space. And a million notes from the director to "turn out," "open up," "stop upstaging yourself," are often lost on an actor who does not recognize the fundamental nature of this responsibility, or, more likely, feels intrinsically uncomfortable in a position of availability to the audience.

To be painfully clear: There are actors out there who are *intrinsically uncomfortable in a position of availability to the audience.* They work at cross-purposes with their fundamental responsibility. They would rather hide, because in hiding there is security. Or, perhaps, there is self-righteous artistry. "We're not going to *pander* to the audience, are we?"

Unfortunately, there are directors who feel this same way.

An Analogy:

Here we are at auditions. You've prepared your monologue in which your character talks to his or her scene partner. You walk into the space, a space where you have never been before. What is the first thing you are going to do?

"Introduce myself."

"Say hello."

"Introduce the piece."

"Act."

"Smile."

"Shake their hands."

I demonstrate. I walk into the "theatre." I walk along the periphery of the stage, finding the one spot on the stage the lighting designer has *not* seen fit to light.

> Hi, my name's Tim Mooney, and I'm going to be doing a monologue from...
> *"We can't see you!"*
> *"Find your light."*

Some actors have this like an instinct. If you don't have it, you'd better develop it. Practice it. Walk into a room and find out if you can be seen or not.

Being *under* a lighting instrument does not mean you are lit! Lights are focused and have "hot spots" And we need to drift into them comfortably and easily, without anyone noticing us doing it. And there is a world of difference between having that light directly overhead, and having it 30 to 60 degrees in front of us, where it will illuminate our eyes.

Because it is our eyes that everyone wants to see.

AN ASIDE

Need I point out that this is crucial in performance as well? We can rehearse the thing for ages, but once we get into tech rehearsals, and we see where those lights have been focused, are we going to remain locked into our previous positions, or are we going to drift into the spot where the audience can see us better?

Or must the director hold our hands, leading us through every step and position we are expected to maintain? Our "sixth sense of light" should be a natural foundation upon which we overlay our character's purposeful movement, and every bit as fundamental as motivating whatever the script or production may place in front of us.

"Motivating whatever the script or the production may place in front of us." This is a radical notion for actors who see the universe of motivation as limited. "Motivations" are guilty until proven innocent, and the contrarian actor responds with "My character would never do that." Such is an actor I may mistakenly cast once, but never twice.

Assuming that, by this time, we have found our light in our imaginary audition, we then turn to performing the monologue.

A chair sits on the stage, and I set it at profile to my workshop audience. Looking at the chair, I note in my most matter-of-fact voice…

> Of course, you all know the practice of creating your imaginary partner on stage with you and addressing the monologue directly to that partner...
> "Because one loves the glories of the Lord..."

If the actors aren't laughing already, then I know we've got problems.

> *"No, you want to look out this way!"*
> That way?! But I've got to **connect** with my scene partner!
> *"Place him out this way!"*

But he would never be out there! That's just not very... **realistic**, is it?

"But for this that's okay!

Why is it okay?

"Because they want to see your face!"

Why would they want to see my face? Don't they want to see if I can be believable?

"No!"

"Yes!"

"They want you to be believable, but they need more information to know if they're going to cast you!"

So I should... **pander** to them just to give them more information?

"No!"

"Yes!"

"You need to show them what you can do so they know if they can use you!"

Well why would I want to do that?

"So you can get cast!"

And why would I want to get cast?

"So you can make money!"

If you haven't figured it out by now, I am, of course, pulling your legs. *Of course*, you want to set your scene partner out in the audience. That imaginary scene partner *doesn't even exist!* Why would we imagine that an invisible scene partner is any more real when we put them next to us than in front of us?

And do not turn the director for whom you are auditioning into that partner[3], but set that imaginary partner just up above the head of the director, so that he or she does not have to play a role along with you, and yet they get the benefit of looking up into your eyes.

Because the eyes are everything.

Just look at the difference between a monologue performed in profile to one performed looking toward the audience. The monologue is *geometrically* improved, because the inner life of the actor/character is immediately available to the audience. Audition monologues are not about reciting a set of words (even though that is part of the experience). Audition monologues are about exposing yourself at your fullest depth and texture to the auditor. The subtle nuances that play upon your face (assuming that you are even slightly involved with your character's desires) will be evident. A million bits of information are expressed, and the greatest challenge that

---

[3] Newsbreak: There is a new school of thought in which it is "okay" to make the director your scene partner. I tried this recently and could feel the auditors getting *very* uncomfortable... and I have not heard a word from that theatre since! My suggestion: know when you are breaking the rules and proceed with awareness and calculated risk.

you can take on as an actor in this moment, is stripping away the affectation and allowing complete transparency of your own emotional life.

> Think of this as 'available information.' When I am turned out, like this, to you, let's call this "one hundred percent of available information." Now, when I turn profile to you, like this, what percentage of available information are you getting?
>
> *"Fifty percent." (Ninety percent of the students sing this out.)*
>
> *"Forty percent."*
>
> *"Twenty-five." (They've started to re-think this position.)*
>
> *"Twenty."*
>
> Yes, more like twenty percent ... maybe even as little as ten.

We understand faces not just by the more overt movements of smiling or scowling, but through the subtle interplay of one side of the face against the other. There are muscles of incredible texture, detail and subtlety surrounding the eyes and the mouth. The slightest flash of emotion will "play" upon the tiniest of these muscles, all the way down to the widening and contracting iris of the pupil. That level of subtlety and depth is simply not available in profile.

Looking at the surface of the average face seen from directly in front, you see perhaps 45 square inches (assuming a face that is nine inches tall by five inches wide). Of that area, perhaps ten square inches above the forehead, mostly covered with hair, is not expressive. In profile, the amount of space that remains expressive (from the cheeks forward) is reduced to roughly 10 square inches. The expressive portion of the face is now a slight sliver, compared to the much larger mass behind it.

> Consider this: You are taking a picture of a group of friends. What is the one thing that will cause you to delete that photo from the memory of the camera and take another?
>
> *"If their eyes are closed!"*
>
> Exactly. You might have the perfect picture. Everybody's smiling... the framing, the positions, the lighting... perfect. But someone's eyes are closed! A photograph with closed eyes is worthless to us. We delete it from our camera without even checking to see how anything else in the shot came out. 'The eyes are the mirrors of the soul' is not just a cliché.

The eyes are the most vulnerable parts of our body. Revealed, they are not only exposed to wind and light and weather, but they give away, to the curious onlooker, your naked emotional life, and a piece of your soul.

And in our audition scenario, it is that pure, unshielded emotional life which will tell the director whether or not he wants to work with you. It forms the clay with which the director will work for the next six weeks. Together you will bring shape to the being. You want that collaborator to know that you will be supple, and *available* clay.

In performance we want to give our audience the same experience! We want to be just as available to the audience's view. They want to see our eyes as badly as the director did. And more often than not, *we want to hide them.*

Just as we started our audition setting up a chair and staring at it, we "lock in" with our acting partner, as if he or she is the only other object in our universe, and play at the game of "eye contact." We think that this will make us "more believable."

People don't maintain eye contact the way that *actors* maintain eye contact! We love eye contact on stage; we hate it in real life. On stage, more often than not, it's phony, and a product of our fears and anxieties rather than the desires of our characters.

I approach four actors, looking them square in the eye, and ask in sequence:

What did you have for breakfast this morning?
"Eggs, and... um... toast."
What did you wear yesterday?
"Jeans and a t-shirt..."
What does your boyfriend look like?
"I don't have a boyfriend."
What are you going to do tomorrow?
"Go to class."

Notice that three out of the four people that I looked at just now, in order to recall the meal, clothing, or person, *looked away*. They were unable to maintain eye contact while answering the question, even though they already know that my approach to them was a demonstration that *had something to do with eye contact*! And once they looked away, even for less than a second, the answer came to them!

Even when the answer to the question was "I don't have a boyfriend," the subject still looked away, to a neutral space where she could see that file marked "boyfriend" in her mind, notice that the file is *empty*, and only *then* came back to report "I don't have a boyfriend."

Eye contact is a "now" phenomenon. When we are dealing with our past or our future, we have to create an "image." That image, flickering on the "screen" of our imagination, cannot live inside the eyes of someone looking at us. Instead, we find a neutral space, which we treat as though it were a blank picture screen, and we project the image of what we are trying to see.

Watch how life *really* happens. You may be very much surprised.

As I explain, I pick a single person out and speak directly to them:

We hate eye contact in real life! We love it on *stage*, but we hate it in *real life*! You ever get those situations when someone locks eyes with you, and seemingly refuses to look away? Suddenly, we get very uncomfortable. We start to wonder what it is that they want from us. It gets kind of creepy, and we start to wonder if there's some sort of *relationship* that this person is looking to create. We want to look away, but we seem stuck somehow, and fear that we'll insult the other person. But still they keep looking! It's like an *eye contact vortex*... a kind of a tractor beam that sucks out from us every secret we may be trying to hide... "What is he thinking? Is he trying to tell me something? Is he, like, trying to come on to me or something?"

With a push against my jaw, I "unlock" myself from the gaze of this person.

We hate eye contact. Unless we are in an especially intimate situation, we avoid eye contact like the plague!

So what do we really do? We "check-in." We find a starting point for a conversation, and look to make sure that we are "on the same page," as it were, and then look away. We address alternate objects of attention as we generate ideas and build arguments. We conjure images on the wall, we build cases and scenarios, occasionally glancing back to see that our image of the experience we describe is shared, or at least understood. Or we may simply distract ourselves with interesting patterns on the wall, a mirror where we can assess ourselves (often just as uncomfortable), or perhaps our eyes light upon a window and the infinity of life that lies beyond it.

So why, if eye contact is to be so avoided, do actors make it such a dominating part of their vision and scope?

The Rehearsal Process.

Cast as Hamlet, I work side by side with Horatio for six weeks or, better, eight. We read through the script together. We are "blocked" into the scene together, we uncover details of plot, psychology, character traits *together*. We develop the through line of the action together, knowing and sharing the rise and the fall of each moment as we give shape to what we understand is the emotional roller coaster of this play.

We are in *agreement*. We wear similar costumes. I look at Horatio, and I *get myself* as Hamlet. He looks at me, and he *gets himself* as Horatio. We reinforce each other, and remind each other of who we are and what's coming next. He fills my need to "Hamlify" myself. My presence helps to "Horatioize" him.

And then I look "South," out in the direction of the audience.[4]

And suddenly I don't get "agreement" any more.

---

[4] I will use "South" as an ongoing reference for "the direction toward which the audience is sitting."

Who am I looking at now?

"The audience."

I get that. But who, specifically? Who are some of the individuals out there?

"Friends!"

Good, and if there are friends, there must also be ...

"Enemies!"

Good! Who else?

"Teachers!

"Family?"

"Strangers?"

"Critics!"

Yes! People with notebooks and pens who are studiously occupied in writing down certain notes about my being! People who love me. People who hate me. How about this one: The actor who was also up for this role!

"Oooohh!"

And so, whereas looking in this direction, towards my fellow actor, I get "agreement," when I turn in this direction, I now get... "*judgment*!" People who may be questioning *whether I am Hamlet enough!* People judging the quality of my Hamlification!

To be an actor is to be conscious of being looked at and, seemingly, judged. To know that people "out there" are examining my being introduces a strain of self-awareness in which every movement which once might have danced unconsciously across the body becomes a conscious choice, and a basis for celebration or, more often, self-loathing. The public is looking, and from that direction, "South," out there where the audience is, comes tension, insecurity, and mistrust.

In science, this is the well-known "observer effect:" The very act of observing a phenomenon alters the object being observed.

Observe anyone giving a speech who doesn't speak in public often. In the midst of the most everyday gesture, they will catch themselves, suddenly seeing their own action as if through alien eyes, and interrupt that gesture and replace it with another one. A gesture which might previously have employed a single hand is now clumsily executed by two hands in perfect bilateral symmetry. (Bilateral symmetry exists almost exclusively in *conscious* gestures. If your left hand is mimicking your right hand exactly, you are probably thinking too much!)

Gestures which once thrived are now analyzed, criticized, found wanting and eliminated, replaced by other, "safer" gestures, which are then repeated endlessly.

Because when we look to the South, we see those many eyes, looking back at us. They reinforce our insecurity. Perhaps they frown, or look away, or even sleep. We are launched, hurtling, out of the situation in which we wish to be immersed. In the attempt to create a separate reality, we face eyes that are not a part of this reality: judging, probing, questioning, reacting. I am attempting to create Hamlet-the-character, but I see eyes watching Tim-the-actor, and I strain to manipulate Tim-the-actor to seem less distinguishable, or to disappear inside Hamlet the character.

Five feet away from me, to the "east," stands a friend in the same situation, another pair of eyes on the same ride that I am taking. When I look at these eyes, I see Horatio, or perhaps Ophelia looking back at me. These eyes will not take me out of my fictional, invented being. They will not laugh at my paltry attempt to be someone new. They will not judge the fiction of my being, because it is my being which also, in turn, enables their eyes to sink deeper into their *own* fiction. And thus we hang onto each other in our mutual death grip. "As two spent swimmers, that do cling together and choke their art."[5]

In his discussion of "Concentration," Stanislavsky described "circles of attention." We focus our attention on those limited areas in which we can generate a belief. Sometimes, even the distance from you to your partner's eyes is too great, and we contract the circle further, finding, for instance, a dust mote on a piece of clothing that needs removal. As we zero in on that dust mote, or pull out that loose thread, or rearrange that vase of flowers, our world is wholly absorbed by our attention to that single point, and there we recapture belief in ourselves, enabling us to gradually widen the circle once more.

This is a terrific technique… at least on those occasions when we have the time to establish the being of our character in such an insular fashion. And if the audience has somewhere else to focus (like on our scene partner) while we work our character back into a state of belief.

But here once again, we find the character abandoning the audience, escaping, and failing the first responsibility of the actor. Which is…?

"Being seen."

None of this is to say that the occasional communion with dust or thread or flowers is not appropriate, or even helpful. It may well enable the audience' focus to leave oneself and work its way toward the character who happens to be speaking: as part of an understood ebb and flow to the work of art that is being created.

---

[5] Shakespeare, *Macbeth*, Act I, Scene 2.

Chapter 2

"Real Life"

"Just why did this playwright break the great silence of the universe to write this play?"

A thesis to which we will repeatedly return: There is a work of art that is being created.

It is not "real life."

I am addressing the same argument on two separate levels. I acknowledge that eye contact, for instance, happens with far greater regularity on the stage than in "real life." *Ergo*, eye contact is largely artificial.

I am also suggesting that even if eye contact were a more regularly occurring phenomenon, we would generally want to eschew it *anyway*, because it takes us away from the audience.

What does it mean to create a work of art?

First and foremost, a work of art is *selected.* Out of the wealth of possibilities that the universe holds, a work of art is filled up with items chosen and placed in a particular order for an audience to study, consider, appreciate, enjoy, delight in, get outraged at, make decisions about, gain new perspective on.

A play begins at 8:00, and lets out around 10:00 or so, and in the course of those two hours, an audience is "moved." While 8pm may find them arriving as an oddly assorted mass, over two hours they come together amid a mutual appreciation, delight, disdain, distress, excitement, awe… and collectively, they "move" to a different place than they were when they came in.

Words like "acting" and "moved" are not coincidental. They are born of the experience that is created through a performance in a public forum. When we "act" upon something, it "moves."

The playwright has a reason he or she has brought these people together. He or she has a notion about the world and the progression of life, which compels him or her to take pen to paper. My favorite director, Dr. William Morgan,[6] used to pose the question as follows: "Just why did this playwright break the great silence of the universe to write this play?"

Under that great question, the art of the theatre realigns itself. A play is not about me and my little circles of attention. A play is about a great possibility of the universe. My character is a collection of ideas and traits, set into motion to compete, combat and cooperate with other conflicting and agreeing ideas and traits. Whether or not this is a work of "realism," we present those notions to the audience for their

---

[6] Dr. William ("Bill") Morgan, 1922-1999, Professor, University of Nebraska (1959-1984).

consideration. We postulate on their behalf, "What if life were like this?" And we play out the results for them to understand and observe.

In the context of that, which is more important…?

- My subjective belief in myself: a tunnel, where, subject to my anxieties, I crawl within until I establish that it is, once again, "safe" to come out?
- Or my responsibility to the wealth of experience that the playwright has collected, whereby I contribute to or facilitate the movement that these people take from 8:00 to 10:00?

We look East, and North, and West, reinforced in the knowledge of our onstage world. We look up and we look down, perhaps seeing lighting instruments and a stage floor. And then we look "South," and see all our personal foibles, mistakes and uncertainties on trial. And so we argue: "There are all of these other directions to look! Why should 'South' be of such special importance? Why not use all three dimensions and all 360 degrees of life? Why must I be so… artificial!"

Because what we are doing here is *not* life; it is art. And art is artificial. And filled with artifice. And it is so because it is *selected.*

And just as Shakespeare selects Hamlet from the billions of possible peoples, and sets him in Denmark, and confronts him with a ghost and tests him with a quandary that is unique and textured and explosive, and places words in his mouth that are selected down to the very syllable or vowel or consonant sound… so are we compelled to embrace this artificiality, and live within its context.

It is time that we stopped running away from that.

It is time that we got comfortable with presenting who we are to the audience.

It's time that our "circle of attention" embraces the audience, widening, ever widening.

To co-opt Gandhi's oft-quoted vision: "We are the center of a circle, the circumference of which is determined by our own self-imposed limits."

It's time for us to widen the circle. Be seen.

Chapter 3

Asides & Soliloquies

Everything that we think of as being theatrical style, drawn from a period that is distant and seemingly unrelated to us, has its parallel in the modern world.

There is an added level of Being Seen, which lives in the universe of stylistic presentation. This universe is clearly outside the realm of reality, and unapologetically so. It lives in the spirit of a time in which theatre's proper role was more than a forum for thought and ideas, but also a source of news and understanding, in a time in which there were no television serials, news programs, movies, nor 500 channels of cable TV. Scripts were largely copied out by hand, and rarely available to the public at large.

Papermaking, introduced by the Chinese, was not widely used as a medium for writing until the third century, and Johannes Gutenberg did not invent the movable-type printing press until 1439. How rare would the possession of an actual book have been for those first few centuries? How expensive?

The theatre served a role similar to the church, but in a secular frame of reference. It confronted the same big questions of man's existence, but without the guidance of a central text or bible supplying the "right" answer. The script became the central text, and the performers became the priest/shaman/ interlopers between the audience and the knowledge of that bible.

No wonder actors were repeatedly condemned by the church, simply for being actors (which is not to suggest that actors did not effectively earn their bad reputation on occasion). They sacrificed their being to a text that was secular, and not sacred. They allowed themselves to be possessed by something outside of themselves.

The farther back we trace the performance style of previous ages, the more we find that the material was "presented" rather than "represented."

In the representational theatre, I let you, the audience, in on a representation of the life of my character, all the while pretending that you, the audience, are not there. In the presentational theatre, I present to you, the audience, an expression of what my character is about, with full awareness and even acknowledgment of your presence. I take my aim at you every bit as much as I aim at my comrades on stage.

> New Question! What's the difference between a soliloquy and an aside?
>
> *"The soliloquy is to yourself; the aside is to the audience."*
>
> *"The aside is to a character other than the one you're talking to, while the soliloquy is to the audience."*
>
> *"The aside is short; the soliloquy is long."*

You're all dancing around it. In a **soliloquy**, I am alone on stage. I may be talking to myself, to the audience, to God, to some manifestation of my moral conscience, or to some imagined other party. It doesn't matter. The two keys to a soliloquy include me being alone, and me talking.

In an **aside**, someone else is on stage with me, but when I speak, they do not "hear" me, no matter how close they may be, nor however distant the most distant audience member (who hears me perfectly) may be.

Soliloquies

In a soliloquy the actor, alone on stage, delivers an extended monologue. The soliloquy's usual intent is to work out the solution to a problem: A scene has left me filled with conflicting ideas, and I must work through this complicated tangle. The audience may remain present in my mind, and I may be working through my thoughts with their assistance, looking to them for reassurance or direction, or I may fight this battle alone, but always available to their sight and hearing.

Representational actors may still find a way to motivate that speech from within. "I'm just thinking out loud," they may suggest, but with that mindset they may well end up muttering the words to themselves, looking everywhere *but* at the audience.

Shakespeare never wrote the word "Pause" as a stage direction and any occasion for me to work out my thoughts in my own head, as part of my own internal work, or "subtext" or "inner monologue" would be extremely rare. A soliloquy is not a meditation. The discoveries are happening even as my lips continue to move. It is brimming with action. Shakespeare was always writing for an audience, an audience which feels itself in the active role as witness to an event.

Asides

While actors generally have little trouble "getting" a soliloquy, the aside might still trip them up. The actor who truly "gets" this is extremely powerful.

The aside most often enlists the audience to take sides against an opponent.

In the midst of a scene, I deliver a line that is not heard by the other performer(s) on stage. Actors are sometimes disoriented. "You mean I have to look out there and talk to them?"

If the aside is this uncomfortable, that is a fairly good sign that the actor hasn't got the sense of the style to begin with. The aside is the most self-evident use of the presentational style, which lives and breathes at the heart of the play.

We deliver asides in "real life" all the time.

Let's imagine I'm talking on the telephone, but that I'm in a conversation with someone I don't really like very much… who won't stop talking. And somewhere in there my best friend enters the room. I attempt to wrap up this conversation:

"Okay, well, thanks for calling; I'll see you at the…"

(The party at the other end interrupts; I roll my eyes to my friend.)

"Okay, great. I'll do that. And then I'll catch up with you when..."

(Another interruption. I widen my eyes, shrug outrageously, and open and close my hand like it is a flapping mouth.)

"Got it. Got it. So then let me get back to you when..."

(Again! This time I cover the mouthpiece of the telephone. "This guy just won't shut up!")

"Uh-huh! Uh-huh..."

(Covering the mouthpiece, "He goes on and on ...")

"Right... yeah..."

("I hate this guy.")

"Okay... well..."

("He's such an ass...")

This is the exact way that an aside works. We have "covered the mouthpiece," accepting the convention that the other party cannot hear what we are saying, as we bring the audience into our confidence. They are, almost without exception, our "best friends" and neighbors. They are on our side, as far as we are concerned, even if we are the villain in the play. When we speak an aside, we are looking for and, almost universally, get their support.

How do we know when something is intended to be delivered as an aside?

"The actor talks to the audience."

No, I mean before that. As an actor, how do you know ...?

"It says so in the script!"

How does it say so in the script?

"Well, in... parentheses, it'll say, 'Aside.'"

Yes, and how did it get there?

"Somebody put it there."

Who?

"Um ... the playwright?"

No...

"The stage manager!" (Someone else pipes in.)

Keep going...

"The publisher!"

"The editor!"

Yes. Keep in mind that Shakespeare wrote almost no stage directions. They didn't have photocopiers back then. They couldn't just run off a copy of the script for all twenty of the actors participating. He was probably writing out a series of 'sides' by hand, and may well have been coaching the performers personally. These actors also lived and worked in the same stylistic universe that Shakespeare lived in. He didn't actually *need* to explain things.

Somewhere in the process of preparing the script for publication for our modern reading audience, someone figured out that this was originally intended to be delivered as an aside, whereby (even though the audience may be able to hear the actor perfectly clearly from as much as 150 feet away) another character, also on stage, perhaps within arm's reach of the speaker, cannot hear it.

So how do you suppose that the Editor knew that this was intended as an aside?

"The actor looked at the audience."

No, before seeing it performed, looking at the unedited text, how did the Editor know?

"He noticed that the other character doesn't react."

Yes! Contextually! The editor is reading along, and Character X says something really outrageous. And yet, Character Y doesn't react at all! And so the editor knows, "This statement should have sent Character Y through the freakin' roof!" And yet, Character Y doesn't go through the freakin' roof. Therefore, this comment must have been...

"An aside!"

And so, what did our editor do?

"He put in the word 'Aside,' in parentheses."

Great! And how do we know when Character X is done with his aside?

"The Editor puts in 'To Character Y...'"

Great. You're with me so far. Now comes the important part:

Just because some Editor, somewhere, does not put the word 'Aside' into the text, does not mean that the speech is not intended to be delivered to the audience.

There's a triple negative in that sentence, so it's a little tough to follow, so I'm going to say it one more time:

Just because some Editor, somewhere, does NOT put the word 'Aside' into the text, does NOT mean that the speech is NOT intended to be delivered to the audience.

Our assumption tends to be that these asides and soliloquies are somehow the exception, that they're intrinsically different from the rest of the speeches of the play. But performers were *always* talking to the audience, sometimes even in the middle of direct address to other characters onstage! These occasional asides and soliloquies are simply the most obvious manifestation of their vision of "what theatre is meant to be." *They were the tip of the iceberg!*

When Rosalind in *As You Like It* says "'Tis such fools as you make the world full of ill-favored children!" a dry look out at the audience casts all those attending the play as "ill-favored," and gets a boisterous laugh each time.

It was not an either/or, black/white, on/off situation. Actors didn't flip, schizophrenically, from face-to-face dialogue to aside, pivoting ninety degrees in one direction, and then back again. They address the audience, AND each other, ***AND explore every degree of connection in-between!***

When Arnolphe (in Molière's *The School for Wives*) wants to present his ward, Agnes, with examples of wicked men or evil coquettes, a simple glance at the audience before him would give him plenty of living examples for his argument. The audience, feeling itself cast in the role of these townspeople, would participate more actively, hating Arnolphe all the more, or sympathizing the more emphatically with Agnes.

When we rethink these plays in that light, they come alive. It becomes impossible to treat them as "museum pieces." A "museum" implies some level of uninvolved one-way observation, a neutral and pristine examination of a culture defined and separated from our own by an implied velvet rope. But when that play demands *my* participation, then Arnolphe's outward sneer keeps me from placing these characters "under glass."

Even when I consciously know that Arnolphe lived more than three hundred years ago, the live actor's sneer in my direction is an immediate indictment of me, here, now.

I don't need a "director's concept" to make the play "relevant" to me. As human beings on stage are looking at and sharing with other human beings in the audience, the matter is relevant already. If it wasn't, then this play would not be available to us now. It would not have stood the test of time.

I cannot overemphasize the power of the difference between an argument that is "represented" behind the fourth wall, and one that is "presented," laid directly before us for our participation and reaction. In the first instance, we, the audience, are peeking in, almost through an unseen window, or a one-way mirror. We are distant observers, much more judgmental, and *we* don't even know who *we* are!

Once the actors begin to speak to us directly, we see ourselves as confidantes, judges, witnesses, lovers, enemies. We play a role in the action, and in the process, it matters to us much more just who should happen to come out on top. If I am "John Smith," from the year 2011, observing an action reenacted from the 17th century, I am not particularly likely to care about the success or failure of the protagonist. But if I feel myself somehow akin to the family of Orgon (in *Tartuffe*), having been "cast" as a fellow townsperson, simply by the virtue of the actor's inclusion of me in the conversation, then I will care whether or not the family is destroyed by the charlatan, because when they get evicted, Tartuffe may well set his sights on destroying me!

And once we have made that leap, we begin to question much more actively, "Are there, in fact, any "Tartuffes" around me now? How might I prevent such a rogue from taking my wife, my home and my reputation?"

An Exercise

This exercise works best if we don't reveal its name until the second half, so resist looking ahead for a moment:

> Let's get two female volunteers. (There'll be another exercise for the men, later.) We're going to cast them in a scene from *The Misanthrope*[7], as Arsinoe and Celimene. We might suggest that Arsinoe is "sanctimonious," and that Celemine is a "coquette." It might make more sense to say that Arsinoe is "uptight" and Celemine is "loose." Or, if all else fails, Arsinoe is a "prude," and Celemine is a "slut." (In a hastily-assembled exercise, I cut to the chase.)
>
> All that we really need to know is that these two characters are fond of the same man, and as a result, mostly hate each other. Their supposed "support" of each other, through their great "friendship" is entirely fabricated.

For now, in my workshop setting, I give them the first few lines of the speech of each character, just to test the waters. I ask them to play the scene as best they can. And there may be some chuckles from the audience over the evident conflict, and the characters' abilities to mask their true intentions inside a rather twisted rhetoric. But mostly, the actors play it "straight."

ARSINOE
Madame, the best friend's one who gives support
In matters of the weightiest import.
And we both know there's no subordination
To matters which might touch our reputation.
As such, I've hurried here upon a mission
To tell of talk which threatens your position.
I had a talk last night with just a few
Upstanding folk when topic turned to you...

CELIMENE
Oh, Madam, I could not miss your intent
And I instinctively knew what you meant.
This information gives such inspiration,
I am reminded of your reputation.,
And think that I might repay you your due,
By telling of what people say of you!

[7] Borrowed from my own adaptation of Moliere's *The Misanthrope*, available through Playscripts, Inc., www.playscripts.com.

Exercise, Part Two

Okay, great. Terrific reading. We could understand the words, the characters' intentions, some of the subtext and innuendo. It was a nice, serviceable, believable recitation and interaction.

Notice how you, the audience, responded: There were a couple of chuckles of recognition, but largely no huge guffaws. You responded to it mostly as a "drawing room comedy" or a "comedy of manners."

We're going to repeat that scene, but this time, we'll perform both monologues in their entirety, following each through to the end.

And this is the point where I give you the name of the exercise. As soon as I do, you're going to have a sense of how this exercise is going to go:

"The Jerry Springer Show"

The winner of an argument on *The Jerry Springer Show* is not the one with the most thought-through, logical, intellectual, philosophical, balanced, nuanced position. It is not about me having an argument with you, and building a conclusion through a succession of logical points. It is about me winning the emotions of the audience over to my side, in opposition to you, and you, subsequently, trying to win them back.

If I can win people over to my side, I become a much more powerful character. If I can insinuate things about you that will make the people "out there" call out, chant, catcall, shout, and drown you out, then I "win." (Logic and intelligence have little or nothing to do with it.)

Now! ***You***, the ***audience*** of this scene, *are playing the audience at the Jerry Springer show!*

You can take sides with one character or another, as the mood takes you. Or, side with both, in turn. Maybe you side with one character for a while, but then the other wins you over every bit as strongly. In other words, you can flip 180 degrees from the convictions of your previous position!

And, just to give a heads-up to our performers, the winner of this argument is generally the one who is better able to get her face up and off of the piece of paper, and the one who manages to punctuate her lines with a RISING INFLECTION, while clearing a space for the audience to respond.

All right, are you ready?

"Yeahhh!"

Okay, how do we warm things up on *The Jerry Springer Show*?

"Jerr-REY! Jerr-REY! Jerr-REY!"

Okay, take it away!

The Misanthrope, Act III, Scene 4

ARSINOE
Madame, the best friend's one who gives support
In matters of the weightiest import.
And we both know there's no subordination
To matters which might touch our reputation.
As such, I've hurried here upon a mission
To tell of talk which threatens your position.
I had a talk last night with just a few
Upstanding folk when topic turned to you.
And though, you know, I instantly defended,
I fear your actions were not well commended.
The looseness of your ways and the parade
Of men who visit you weren't well portrayed.
Your coquetry, I fear's, notorious,
And they spoke in a tone censorious!
I was astounded at this sharp attack,
And in your fair defense I did not lack.
I spoke of your good spirit and I mentioned,
You only have the finest of intentions.
And yet some things I couldn't quite gainsay,
With issues that I can't explain away.
And ultimately, I made the confession
That your behavior gives the wrong impression.
And that your actions may well be the source
Of gossip and conjecture rather coarse.
And that you wouldn't be so oft mistook
If you took greater care for how things look.
It's not that I'm suggesting you're to blame
For deeds the like of which we mustn't name!
But people's minds do tend that way to go,
And we must guard 'gainst vice's slightest show.
I know you know my purity of purpose,
Intending only to do you great service,
I share these thoughts to help my dearest friend,
And have in mind no other hoped-for end.

CELIMENE
Oh, Madam, I could not miss your intent
And I instinctively knew what you meant.
This information gives such inspiration,
I am reminded of your reputation,
And think that I might repay you your due,
By telling of what people say of you!
I'll follow the example that you've set
Reporting of the good folk I have met:
I stopped the other day at a soiree
And there, some people, tasting the buffet,
Had launched a conversation that regarded
Where pious folk from piety had parted.
Alas! I fear the prudery you savor
Was not regarded with all that much favor.
The pious face you manage to contort
The way you talk of virtue and distort ...
Most notably, the twisted way you measure
The nature of one's inoffensive pleasure.
"Why does," they asked, "she keep this pious show
When everything she does belies it so?
She says her prayers as much as would a nun
But cheats her maids of wages they have won.
She shows her piety all through the parish,
And yet she paints her face all thick and garish.
On naked statues she would place her ban,
And yet she wouldn't mind a naked man!"
Of course, I told them they were being vicious
And that your nature wasn't that malicious.
But still, I couldn't shake their new conviction,
And they suggested I make interdiction,
To tell you to leave off their moral health,
And rather worry more about yourself!
I know you know my purity of purpose,
Intending only to do you great service,
I share these thoughts to help my dearest friend,
And have in mind no other hoped-for end.

DEBRIEF

So, let's talk about the difference between the two types of performances! Pretty vivid, weren't they?

First of all, who "won" this argument? Let's vote by applause...

Why did you choose that one? Did she have the more persuasive argument? Was she more logical? More thought-through? Do we prefer her philosophy? Do we see ourselves as "uptight" or "loose" variously, and choose based on our own preference?

What did she do?

"She looked at us!"

"She looked up from the piece of paper!"

"She paused to let us shout out!"

"She waited for us to finish shouting to start her next line!"

"She made her voice go up at the end of the lines!"

"She walked downstage and interacted!"

Do we respond more powerfully to the one who knows how to work us for a reaction? How much are we, the audience, willing to shift our sympathies or our priorities simply based on the charisma, or the timing or the "presence" of the actor? How much of theatrical power is tied up in the actor's ability to work the crowd?

Celimene is clearly the sentimental favorite, as the modern audience, and probably Molière, agree more readily with her liberated attitude (Molière does, after all, give her the final word, here), and yet, perhaps one out of every five times, the audience may be brought to side with Arsinoe, *if* she has the stronger ability to "work the house."

Keeping in mind that nowhere in this script does it contain the word "aside," how much of this material works when played directly to the audience? After hearing our initial teaser, what was the difference the second time around?

"I felt like I was a part of the scene!"

Whereas the first time through, how did you feel?

"I didn't feel anything. I was just watching."

Why was the feeling stronger the second time?

"I knew who I was. I had a relationship to them."

That's right. This time around we actually "cast" you in this play. I told you that you were the audience at the *Jerry Springer Show*.

"But even if you hadn't told us ..."

You still would have felt the urge to respond?

"Well, yeah. The way they were talking at us. They way they paused for us to respond. I think it would be hard to not start shouting things."

That's a great point. Even when you, the audience, have not been informed up front about the role you are playing in this scene, you will instinctively feel the part, based on the way you are treated. With enough clues and enough permission, you will go from a state of passive judgment to involved participation.

Audiences love the opportunity to go that extra mile with us. They just need clear instructions about what direction to set out in.

"So, is this the way that you would direct 'The Misanthrope?'

Actually, no! There are a multitude of character traits and gestures and side-trips that go with *The Jerry Springer Show* which would take our audience out of the scene, and have them laughing at stuff that has nothing to do with '*The Misanthrope*.' But would I use the overall style and strategies of *The Jerry Springer Show*: The roaring defiance, the one-upsmanship, the direct address of the audience, and the extra split-second's invitation for the audience to jump in with their reaction? Absolutely.

This presentational delivery of the material takes the experience from being abstract and hypothetical, to being live and tangible. The audience's engagement is *geometrically* increased.

"Geometrically" being an important word, here, because the communication has gone from being a "line" from Character A to Character B, to a "triangle," as Character A's attack of Character B passes through the audience on its way across the stage.

But also "geometrically" because the audience's engagement in the scene has not just doubled; it has increased by a factor of several multiples. The audience is probably about five times more engaged than they were before!

Note, also, the impact in the opposite direction. The *audience* influenced the *performance*! What happened to the actors as they realized that they had to surmount an opposition that included, not only their acting partner, but an entire audience? What happened when they felt that audience rushing to their side in their support? Was their energy reinvigorated? Were they thrown off? What's the difference in the feeling of a one-on-one argument vs. an argument that is now *one-hundred*-on-one, as the audience chooses the one that they believe?

We feel "acting power" coursing through our veins.

The audience now senses that they are a part of the world of this scene. They will moan and laugh and sneer in ways that they would never have imagined when they set out to attend a "classical play."

That's because their presence has been acknowledged. Their voice is requested. They are valued as an intrinsic part of this world. Even though they may have been born more than three hundred years after all of these characters were dead, they "*get themselves*" in a new way, as a part of this world.

And with a stake in who wins.

How often, in reality, do we have "audiences" to discussions and debates? How natural is it to play a series of points off of an audience, or to talk to someone *through* an audience?

Did the first version or the second version of the scene actually feel "more real?"

Is it possible that the parameters of reality broadened to encompass a different type of relationship that acknowledges other people who are present?

Everything that we think of as being theatrical style, drawn from a period that is distant and seemingly unrelated to us, has its parallel in the modern world, be it the telephone "aside," or the *Jerry Springer Show*.

Chapter 4

Perfect it and Forget It

When the relationship gets lost in the delicate manipulation of foreign objects, then we are no longer fulfilling the playwright's vision.

A professor meets me for breakfast as I pass through town. We chat briefly about Molière and my tour, as well as some of her challenges directing a classical play. Once we hit this topic, she has an urgent question:

"When the people back then greeted each other, and bowed, how did they execute them? What kind of choreography went into them?"

My response:

"*Which **week***?"

Attempting to recreate a bow (or any ritual that might be impacted by fashion and practice)[8] with photographic realism would be the equivalent of someone from three hundred years in the future attempting to recreate with exactitude a ritual gang handshake performed between street thugs.

Consider the personal and social influences that might impact a bow that two men might perform upon greeting each other:

- The fashion of this particular era, this year, or even this week.
- The relative status of the two (the lesser bowing the more deeply).
- Each man's opinion about the relative status of the two.
- The relative modesty or arrogance or "masculinity" of either party.
- The ongoing changes in the relationship.
- The events of the day, and the activity that either is trying to get to.
- The mood of the moment.
- Perceived or actual slights one may have performed toward the other.
- The plans or strategies that either may carry toward influencing the other through flattery or other means.
- Any physical impairment that either man may have.

I think back to a recent performance as Alceste in *The Misanthrope*, who has been approached by Oronte, a terrible and obvious flatterer and sycophant, who "kisses up" to Alceste with some thinly disguised end in mind. Alceste, who is, after all, a "misanthrope," is immediately suspicious, and as Oronte fawns with a series of

---

[8] The 5-volume series, "A History of Private Life", Roger Chartier, Ed., Belknap, Harvard, 1989 (notably Volume III, "Passions of the Rennaissance") is a particularly valuable resource.

three bows, each broader and fuller than the one preceding it, Alceste performs the most minimal bow that he can possibly get away with without overt insult.

On each of his bows, Oronte makes a grand flourish, sweeping his arms in front of his face before extending them, palms up, out to either side, extending a foot forward, and bending almost perpendicularly from the waist, dropping his eyes to look at the ground, first saying:

ORONTE: I cannot be the first here on that score;
The world must beat a path to your front door!
ALCESTE: Sir!

In response, Alceste, backs away a step, which leaves a foot extended forward (a reflection of Oronte's extended foot, but much more passively executed), while bending slightly from the waist, perhaps 20 degrees forward, extending his arms forward with palms up. Oronte resumes his flourishes, eventually saying:

ORONTE: There shines light no brighter in our nation
Than your great merit by my estimation!
ALCESTE: Sir!

On his second bow, Alceste places a hand upon his heart, backing up yet another step, while this time his bow is a much slighter nod, not from the waist but from the shoulders, inclining only the head, perhaps 45 degrees forward. Oronte reinvigorates his sweeping bow with even greater flattery:

ORONTE: No, sir, none here match your noted worth!
Here in this state, perhaps upon this earth!
ALCESTE: Sir!

With the third bow, Alceste signals Oronte to stop, raising his hands, palms outward, while taking yet another step backwards, dipping his head forward, only as an afterthought, ending with hands clasped in front of his waist.

No one "bow" would communicate these evolving complexities of the personalities or the relationship. Oronte's very inclination to repeat the bow drives Alceste into suspicion and resistance, changing the fullness, the degree and the very nature of his "bow" in each response.

And, indeed, there are "bowers" who would take this over the top: a more foppish character would extend the flourishes by holding lace handkerchiefs, and rotating the hands from the wrists, or elbows, and waggling the head side-to-side before extending the arms widely, and plunging into a deep bow with the leg extended excruciatingly far forward. The ending position might find the bower practically kissing his own knee and straining to get back up.

The Stuff

Actors (and directors) like to get caught up in the "stuff" that represents the period to them. And so they fixate on the elaborate language of bowing, of handling fans or snuff boxes, or they strap on swords, which clank against the furniture throughout the course of the play.

I admire the commitment to research and accuracy, and I encourage it wholeheartedly. Research it. Learn it. Execute it. Perfect it.

And then forget it.

There are books with detailed descriptions of bows, many based on fencing positions and ballet attitudes. (Classes in ballet give the actor an excellent discipline, organizing muscles into positions and gestures that were fashionable three hundred years ago.) Keep in mind that any individual source which you may find is generally a "snapshot" of what was performed in that day. The bows of 1667 may well be different from those of 1666… (And you have little way of knowing how wistfully sentimental the author was for the "old days," when people *knew* how to bow!) And learning the resulting end position of any activity may be as effective as learning a dance by following footprints laid out on the floor. The thing lives and thrives in the action, not in the details of the position.

Playwrights of the 16th and 17th centuries were not writing about fans or foils. ***The play itself is always about the relationship between the people.***

When the relationship gets lost in the delicate manipulation of foreign objects, then we are no longer fulfilling the playwright's vision. Don't get lost in the *accoutrements;* get inside the action underlying the extra "stuff."

The one thing they were NOT likely thinking was "how am I supposed to execute this bow?" (…unless it was Monsieur Jourdain from *The Bourgeois Gentleman*, a clueless imitator of fashion).

Take a good look at the reason the character might have for manipulating a fan, or brandishing a sword. And never do anything without a reason. If the answer to the question is "Because that's how they did things back then," dig deeper.

Imagine we have time-traveled forward, three hundred years into the future, and are watching the performance of a historical play first produced in the twenty-first century. Actors who have never owned the collection of toys that we carry with us spend their time manipulating cell phones, I-pods, purses, pagers, cigarettes, pill bottles, Gameboys, guns, car keys, wallets, and pens. They take classes on the proper manipulation of eyeglasses, and the secret messages spoken through the eyeglasses and sunglasses of this prehistoric time (before all eyes were surgically corrected at birth, or genetically preprogrammed). And the actors eat it up, working and reworking their performances to master the manipulation of these foreign devices.

And they overlook about what the plays were originally about! How many contemporary plays do we have that are actually "about" the use and manipulation of cell phones, purses or pens? These are merely tools that we use to pursue things that we really want. In this same way: fans, swords, handkerchiefs and snuff boxes were merely tools that the 17th century character used to get the things that he or she really wanted. And those things are the same things that we want today: Love, power, attention, affection, acknowledgement, money, security, superiority…

The tools change. The action remains the same. Which is why some plays mean just as much to us today as they did four hundred years ago.

Chapter 5

The Link Between Sight and Sound

Part of being heard is, in fact, being seen.

Consider that being heard and being seen are closely connected. Since most of us have been seeing at the same time as we are hearing for all of our lives, we are little aware how much verbal comprehension is dependent on visual input.

Even in the hyperlinked universe in which we live, we still find ourselves watching news interviews from remote areas of the planet, where the uplink is not immediate. We hear the foreign correspondent's voice, and then we see their lips move a moment after the fact. How difficult it is to actually understand what they are saying! And how quickly it becomes evident that the face and the voice are inextricably linked in our ability to "hear."

While watching a play, we seem to hear a lot better than we actually do. We seem to hear about 90 percent of the words being spoken. But placing a recording device in the auditorium, we go back to listen to the sounds that were actually recorded. Suddenly, the audibility of a play that seemed to hover around ninety percent now drops below twenty-five percent! How much of that play were we actually "getting" through the positions and the faces of the actors?

There was a director who would hold a trick in reserve. During the final rehearsals of a comedy, he would leave the lights just slightly below their full intensity, just a little bit darker than they "ought" to be. At the final dress rehearsal, the producer would approach him: "I don't know, Tom, it's just… it's just not funny. Can't you have them talk faster or something?"

Rather than return to his actors with the generalized note to "speed up," he would, instead, go to the lighting designer, and tell him to nudge the lights up a little brighter. Faces that were simply a shade too dark became more evident, etched and clarified for the audience. The opening night audience laughs with hilarity. The producer approaches the director: "Wow, you really did it! I can't believe how you pulled it all together in just the last twenty-four hours!"

I can recall several performances in which, making my entrance, I suddenly discover that the lighting level established in the technical rehearsal is no longer the level that we're experiencing on stage. (Mine is a one-person show, and that one person, Molière, who never knew of this thing called electricity, cannot fix this problem without breaking character.) And suddenly, surrounded by this gloomy atmosphere, Molière's giddy comic antics feel brooding and sinister.

Part of being heard is, in fact, being seen.

And, by the way… comedy plays better in bright light.

Chapter 6

The Tim Mooney Three-Second Rule®

This, however, was something concrete, a living reminder of what he was expected to do, and a continuous check on when he was actually not living up to that expectation.

So, there I am, directing *The Imaginary Invalid*. I wrote this version myself, so I have a pretty good feel for how I want it to go. In fact, I'd already written many of the chapters of this book by the time I was working on this, so I've got a substantial "bag of tricks" pretty well developed by now.

In fact, I have choreographed the action "to within an inch of its life" as one reviewer suggests, and the stage positions effectively set up lazzi, and put the focus on whichever character has the focal moment, again and again and again.

And there, in the middle of Act II, we hit "the monologue," where one character holds court in front of the other characters for a good two pages. There are perhaps a dozen people on stage, who toss in the occasional mocking one-liner, before this character resumes holding forth, giving an unintentionally bad impression of his son, the very character he is trying to commend.

I have cleared out the stage for him, and my blocking of this scene has left the other ten characters on stage in a semicircular arc, with a large clearing down center. My actor can weave his way through this semicircle, passing upstage and downstage of his fellow characters, and he can occasionally take over that large area down center and "own" the space.

There's a problem.

He hasn't an instinct for this.

Again and again, his attention and his delivery will drift to a performer upstage of himself, or sideways, to a performer who is across from him, placing himself in profile to the audience.

Two or three times, he and I mark our way through the scene, and he understands, consciously, what he is supposed to be doing, and when. He "gets" the concept of opening up to the audience. But bring the rest of the actors back onto the stage with him, and he gives it all upstage to them again, with his back or his profile to the audience.

This is a presentational play, with words that carry shades and multiplicities of meaning, which are now getting lost in the actor's instinctive realism, or perhaps his instinctive neediness, as he turns to his fellow actors for reassurance or reinforcement.

We have come back to this scene for a third time, and each time we have come back, we spend an hour trying to inject the scene with a sense of the style that the rest of the play carries. Unless we figure this out, the actor will end up looking bad next to the others who are comfortable with this style. And we are quickly running out of the rehearsal time that has been scheduled for this particular scene.

I get an idea.

I send the other actors out of the rehearsal hall, on a half-hour break.

With only myself, the stage manager and this performer in the room, I suggest the most outrageous acting exercise I have ever put together.

The three-second rule.

Anyone who follows the game of basketball knows the three-second rule. That's the rule that the defender cannot remain "in the paint" for more than three seconds at any given stretch, without getting whistled for a "technical foul."

There is a particular prop in the show: the tiny bell which Argan rings to summon the maid, Toinette, all while shouting "ting-a-ling!" after her.

> Here's the deal:
>
> We are going to create a "three-second rule." You are welcome to look left or right, or even upstage as you act, but you must open up to the audience, looking downstage, at some point during the course of any three seconds of this monologue.
>
> If I find that three seconds have gone by, without you looking downstage, I will ring this bell, as a reminder that you have not been sharing this material with the audience.

Another actor might have been offended by the crass, unforgiving nature of this very mechanical measurement of his acting success. This actor, however, was eager for something that would give him a handle on this (or perhaps that would get me off his back). Theories of positioning and placement were abstract to him, and went out the window when he found himself working to carry the scene alongside his fellow performers. This, however, was something concrete: a living reminder of what he was expected to do, and a continuous check on when he was not satisfying that expectation.

It started out rough at first, with me ringing the bell again and again. Each time he would mutter a quiet "damn!" and adjust his position, and soldier on.

Within twenty minutes, he was performing with "style." He had mastered the art of turning out to the audience and felt, in his bones, the "rightness" of being out there, for the audience, rather than giving it all upstage to his fellows.

In this most outrageous and, literally, Pavlovian fashion, the little bell had become a reminder that nudged him away from the wings and out toward the house.

For a play of a slightly different style, our measuring standard might be much longer (five seconds… ten seconds…), or as little as a single second. Or a given stylistic convention might demand that whichever character is speaking *never* looks away from the audience! Whatever the choice, we in the audience feel it indelibly fused with the vision and the style peculiarly embracing this particular universe.

"Wasn't that kind of... crass and manipulative?"

Yes.

"Was his performance better?"

Much.

"Could the audience hear and see better?"

Yes.

"Did he survive opening night?"

Quite well.

"Could you have gone about this a different way?"

With all the rehearsal time in the world, yes, of course.

All I can say is that it's better than the electrified fence.

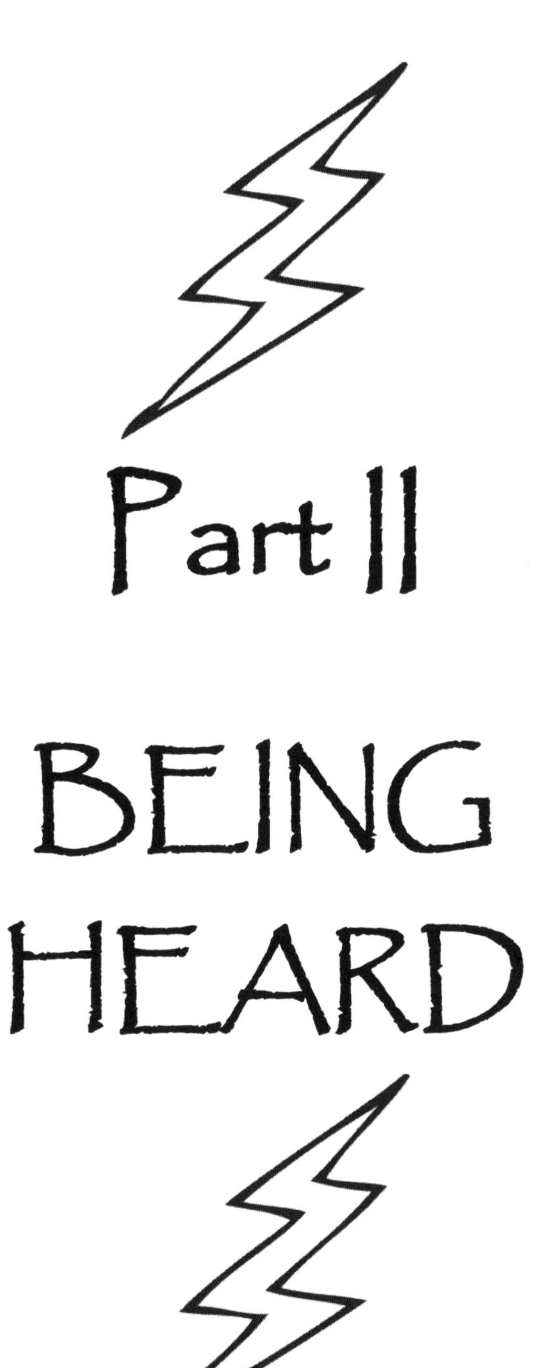

Part II

BEING HEARD

Chapter 7

Classical Performance

Everything that we need to perform Shakespeare lives inside the words that are intended to be spoken aloud.

What makes classical performance so special? Or, to be more specific, what makes the plays of Shakespeare so special? Why have they survived for four hundred years?

"They're still relevant today."

"Great plots."

"Exciting action."

Yes, yes, yes, all true... keep going.

"It gives us a window into that time."

Well, yes, but wouldn't **any** play from that time give us a window into that time? Let's not confuse the *age* of the play with its *quality*. Assume that they had as much crap on their stage as we do today. The plays that have survived, however, have done so as the result of some level of quality.

"Great words."

"Hard to understand words."

"Funky words."

Ah. What is the nature of those words?

(...)

When you look at the page itself, a page out of Shakespeare, what are you looking at? ... Do you see a lot of stage directions there?

"No."

So what are those words?

"Verse."

Yes, but what is that verse? What is meant to be done with it?

"Performed."

"Recited."

"Dialogue."

Yes! They are words intended to be spoken aloud. Dialogue. Speeches. Monologues. Soliloquies. All that we have from Shakespeare are those words he intended to be spoken aloud. The play does not open with a long stage direction. Nothing says "Hamlet enters, wandering distractedly. He moves to the mantelpiece. He is troubled. Something is gnawing at his mind. He scratches his neck. He lights a cigarette ..."

Whatever we get, we get from what is spoken. Whatever has survived these four hundred years has survived by means of the sounds that are made when actors open their mouths and shape these phrases into existence. Everything that we need from Shakespeare lives inside the words that are intended to be spoken aloud!

All else is interpolated. Directors, designers, actors, everyone takes their inspiration from the speech itself. How many times do we see, in a Shakespearean play, "Ah! Here we are in Verona!"? Which tells us? ...

"We're in Verona!"

That we are in Verona! No scene designer stayed up late painting a "Verona" for Shakespeare. Because, you know what? Five minutes later, somebody else is going to walk on stage and note, "Ah! Here we are in Padua!"

The Verona and the Padua that an audience is capable of creating in their imagination is much more detailed and "real" than any backdrop that a painter can create. But more to the point, all of the information about these locations that we might want is here in the words themselves.

Likewise, all character information, and the entire emotional lives of these characters, can be generated out of the words they speak.

As we look at Hamlet, we may see an overriding burden of "sadness" darkening his attitude. Or, we might also make an case for "anger," "melancholy," "frustration," "resentment," "fury," "cynicism," "ambivalence," "desperation," "hysteria," "manic-depression," or all of the above. (There have been endless books written about any of these, and more.)

But let's say I tighten my grip on this "sadness" notion, and like the good method actor that I am, I go back in time to remind myself of my own saddest moments: The day the dog got run over by a car, the way that my girlfriend broke up with me, or how my parents weren't there for me when I needed them most. (*Hypothetically speaking, Dad.*)

It's pretty likely that before long I will, indeed, start to feel very sad. But…

A) This "brand" of sadness probably comes with *baggage* that has nothing to do with Hamlet.

B) Fixating on this single emotional trait probably leads me away from the ten options listed above, thus reducing the variety and texture that I might bring to each moment and…

C) While I am off in my own indulgent emotional exercise, the audience, with a mind of its own, is probably working out whether the car is parked securely, wondering whether it will still have wheels, given the bad neighborhood they parked in, or if it may be getting towed away at this very moment, given the uncertainty of the parking regulations of that particular block...

Such side trips into other uncharted waters lie outside the great wealth of material that Shakespeare (and other such playwrights) have given us.

Such side trips are actually, probably, destructive to the play. And when we learn how to fully commit to the words that we have been given, the emotional life of the character rises, overwhelming us like a tidal wave.

Everything that we need to perform Shakespeare …

Chapter 8

Articulation, Volume and Projection

The fact is that you probably gave up on speaking the final consonants of words long ago.

When an elbow is bending, when knees fold, when fingers dance across a keyboard, we are articulating those joints. We are taking the appendages from straight, unbroken extensions of our body, and bending them. We give them shape. We give them visual interest.

In the same way, we take an unbroken stream of air that is escaping from our lungs and we give it shape. We form words out of it. We articulate it through the motion of our lips, teeth and tongue. Just as a joint may bend further or lesser, just as the muscles extending that joint can stretch longer or shorter, so do we have the ability to give greater or lesser articulation to our words as we give them aural interest. Just as muscles may atrophy, and the joints may develop arthritis (which sounds suspiciously like "articulation"), so do the muscles of the face, and the sounds therein, suffer from lack of use.

Perhaps the greatest enemy to good articulation today is the microphone.

And its evil spawn, the body-mic.

For thousands of years, actors performed in large arenas, and were heard from the first row on back to the last. I don't recall ever reading a report of a play from the 17th century suggesting that this or that actor was too quiet or unintelligible. There must have been a few hard-to-understand actors, but either reports of their work have gone the same path as the manuscripts of mediocre playwrights, or there was a basic threshold level of vocal competency to which actors were scrupulously held.

Without a voice that would carry to the back row, and without an articulatory mechanism which would clarify each word, these same performers would never succeed in the profession. They knew already that the play was all about the words, and they put all of their energy into speaking them well. A mumbler or a mutterer would get weeded out early.

Today, mumblers and mutterers are the rule, more than the exception.

That's the bad news.

The good news is that if you take this seriously, and really work at it, you can win the casting battles in contemporary and in classical works. Your clarity of speech can give you a head start over 90% of your competition.

Mumblers will continue to overrun our performances until we stem the tide of the practice of attaching microphones to our performers for everything.

It starts in the grade schools. Well-meaning teachers, under pressure from moms and dads who want to showcase little Jimmy's talents, attach a crutch to Jimmy's lapel which will blast Jimmy's voice out of the speakers, suspended twenty feet above the stage floor, to the left and the right of the stage.

If Jimmy ever did anything so pointless as to project his voice, he would blast the parents out of their seats. And so, he learns to swallow his words.

But here's the rub: Mom and Dad only *think* they are hearing little Jimmy better because, well, they know these lines already! They've seen the script! They've heard Jimmy working these lines for the last five weeks! If you trained a camera on them through the course of the performance, you'd see them forming the words with their lips, probably with greater clarity than Jimmy does.[9]

In the course of the performance, Jimmy learns nothing about articulation or projection, and so he carries all of his lazy habits with him through high school and on to college, where the professors are also thinking more and more about maybe working microphones into the show, because after all, Jimmy's dad is an alum.

Microphones don't make your words any clearer.

Microphones only make bad speech louder.

One single concession to this: Amid the ever-louder, electrified orchestras that accompany musicals, the actor needs weapons in his arsenal to balance the otherwise overwhelming music.

(Although, nobody seems willing to acknowledge this, but at least 50% of the time these microphones fail, are ridiculously out of balance with the orchestra, or with each other, or contribute to more distracting noise than they are worth… and by the way, the Emperor has no clothes.)

In my theatre universe, microphones are forbidden for "straight plays."

As an audience member, I come to the theatre, not to admire the technical wizardry of the producer, but to participate in the time-honored ritual of engaging in a public forum, observing humanity in action, contemplating the choices that an individual, caught up in a conflict, might make, understanding better what it means to be a human being.

I come to the theatre and I look at the mouth of the actor, speaking what the playwright has given him to say, and from a speaker, some thirty feet from his mouth, comes the actor's voice.

That very same actor may well walk offstage, away from the action– he may even walk down a long staircase, placing him some supposed fifty feet or more from the stage – and when he tosses a line back in from his offstage position, that line will be heard just as loudly as when he stood downstage center, and every bit as clearly as those who stand immediately before us.

---

[9] High school theatre directors from privileged schools whisper their secret agreement with this. The more exclusive the campus, the more that the technological tools at the director's disposal are crippling the actors. (Not to mention the fact that these kids are *way* too cool to be bothered with emotional commitment.)

We see the human qualities of the performer/character. We contemplate the choices and the actions that that character performs. And we wonder what we might do in the same situation. If the character is a protagonist, we will likely begin to "identify" with him or her. The process of identification gives a play its emotional power. If we cry, it is because the action has touched something in ourselves which has set off our emotional current. We see ourselves rising to greatness, or falling to ignominy.

Removing the voice from the throat of the protagonist and placing it thirty feet from its source inhibits identification.

It also reminds us that we are not in reality, but in a world of "techno-reality." We are emulating the television or the cinema, where it doesn't even matter if the actors are speaking clearly! (If there are problems, the editors can fix it in post-production!) Every concession towards techno-reality suggests to that growing band of video/movie/TV/game-watchers, that this is not real life here before them, and thereby, behavior that is appropriate in front of the television (which includes but is not limited to: talking, texting, eating, sleeping, taking phone calls(!), unwrapping candies, necking, taking notes, sleeping…) is perfectly appropriate here. Because after all, it is not real, the characters are not people, and no one who is "up there" can see or hear me "out here," or might possibly care what I do.

Or, as one brilliant performer[10] confided: "The microphone only gives them permission not to listen."

Good stage speech can be heard in a whisper.

The Issue

The issue is almost never volume.

The issue is speaking the entire word.

Who here has ever tried learning a foreign language?

(All hands go up.)

Great, everybody! You listen to those endless tapes of "native speakers?" They repeat at length with crisp articulation the words that we need to learn... our teachers drill proper pronunciation into us, and after a year or two we start to feel pretty competent about our ability to actually function in a foreign country, right?

And then we have our first encounter with an actual native from that country. How did that go for you?

(Faces darken.)

Right! Those people do not sound a bit like the tapes!

The same thing happens to them when they try to learn our language. They come here, expecting all of us to speak like we do in the tapes that they have been

[10] Charlie Ross, author/performer of *The One-Man Star Wars Trilogy*.

studying. And then they too realize that they've been duped. They can't understand a word that we're speaking.

And we think that it's about them. They're obviously of diminished mental capacity if they can't make out what is, to us, perfectly clear.

By virtue of the fact that we live where we live and speak the way that we speak, we have no idea of the poor quality of our own speech. We can make ourselves understood to those people around us, who speak back to us the way that we speak. As such, we come to know the language in a particular way and we don't notice that we have made this adjustment.

We get so much information from context: a look, a shrug, a nod, an eyebrow, a pursing of the lips, a previous conversation… that *we have long stopped the practice of speaking entire words!* And we don't even know it. We gave up speaking the final consonants of words long ago, just as those speakers in foreign lands let go of their final consonants long before we came along.

This disease is not confined to consonants! Depending on our background, we almost certainly have replaced the word "to" with "tuh." The word "for" is "fer," while "your" is now "yer." "Get" has become "git." "Can has become "kin." (These are all vowels that make our mouths stretch further than is comfortable.)

Our multi-syllabic words bubble with land mines: syllables race by at such a clip that we don't recognize how badly they're mangled. "Did you" becomes "didja," "protection" becomes "protekshin," "intended" becomes "intindid" and "important" (with a final schwa or an "uh" in the final syllable) shifts to "imporin."

But even among people we've known all of our lives, what context of familiarity is going to help the audience know and understand the very unfamiliar phrasings of Shakespeare? Our traditional speech is not going to make us intelligible. We need to take that speech and overwork it, until *every letter and syllable* is being sounded.

An Experiment

Once again, set up a recording device in the back row of the auditorium. Then go back up on the stage and play out a Shakespeare scene you've been working on. Speak as well as you can. Then go back to the back row and play it back. Surprised? Try this again during the average rehearsal of an average play, when the performers *are not aware* of the experiment. The results will probably shock you.

Do this with an audio recorder. We are so image conscious that once a video is displayed, we cannot "hear" ourselves any more. We are too busy looking at the stupid look on our face, the silly way we stand, the position of our hands. Just what are we doing with our hands!?!

But with an audio recorder we can isolate the voice. And more often than not, we hear nothing but white noise. Overhead fans blow, the air conditioner hums. In the background, we may actually hear "voice." We notice a musicality, a rise and a fall of intonations. We may catch a clear word or two, or be able to identify the speaker by intonation or inflection. But I would be willing to bet we do not understand one full sentence from the beginning to the end.

Not one full sentence.

We can blame the quality of the recording equipment, such as it is. As we know, the audience gets messages from the face, the eyes, the physical silhouette, the tone of the voice or the inflection. An audio recorder is not a record of the entire information stream. But these only slightly mitigate the problem; it is not an excuse for neglect.

This is a disease that's probably keeping you from getting cast… at least in plays where words make a difference… which is just about all of them.

We begin rehearsals in a state of not-knowing, and we gather in a circle to read this work aloud. As we read, we also see. As the words pass through our ears, so do they also pass before our eyes. And while we may or may not hear the specific words emerging from our fellow performers' mouths, we still understand the ongoing thread of the plot, the cleverness or passion of the dialogue, and the developing idiom or motif of the playwright. And we laugh/cry/respond in a manner responsive to the playwright's intent.

We look forward to performing this play and we go away to memorize.

We return for subsequent rehearsals, at first holding scripts in hand, and later tossing them aside. But always in the company of those who were in attendance at that first rehearsal! We develop socio-emotive-articulatory shorthand in collusion with our comrades, who already get the jokes and the intent, and along with us, seek to improve upon them.

Opening night is generally the first time that someone from outside of this process is present to hear (or not hear) us reciting these words.

And that audience perfectly reflects that non-native language student: The audience was not present for the first read-through, and never saw the script and never got the many discoveries and in-jokes that we developed along the way. Likewise, the language student was never there, absorbing the language from birth, nor to observe the many short cuts, gestures and tonal differences which mean so much to the native speakers.

We may choose to feel superior to these people. We get it and they don't.

But their very ignorance should be precious to us. They have the power to reveal where we are not communicating, if only we might have the power to listen past our insecurities to hear them!

A woman with a thick European accent came up to me after a performance almost in tears. She wanted to thank me. For the first time since coming to America, she was able to understand every word that I had spoken in the play she'd just seen. In twenty years of attending plays in the United States, this was the first time she had understood everything.

I have a deaf friend who has told me the same thing.

The joy and the gratitude these folks express is something that every actor should experience.

Chapter 9

Getting Heard

Those great consonants, which are your obstacles, give you all of the emotion you need, if you will only allow yourself to do battle with them.

In "Building a Character," Stanislavsky suggests:

"If vowels are the rivers, then consonants are the banks."

"You need them both."

To which, I add: "Or else all you have is a muddy swamp."

Most audibility issues come from actors' failure to enunciate consonants or to sound vowels. Some have one problem, some have the other, and both are just as destructive.

We may hear from one actor:

"H, mst wckd spd! t pst wth sch dxtrty t'ncstsshts!

From another actor, that same line comes out:

"O, oss wigi pee! do oas wi sudg desairidee oo insedsoousees!"

If we could somehow combine the skills of these two actors, the reading that we might get would sound something like:

"Oh, most wicked speed! To post with such dexterity to incestuous sheets!"

Audiences don't have the words memorized already. And if they did, either of the above readings will probably upset them even more.

As acting happens "at the speed of life," we get just one opportunity to say something clearly and effectively. Once it's gone, we're on to the next.

A S I D E

As the director, I have to pull these two actors in two different directions. The direction I give one actor will not help the other, nor vice versa. Telling both that they need to "project," or simply "I can't hear you!" is *not specific enough*. The actor needs information that will help him or her actually fix the problem. Which means the directors among us need to listen more carefully.

Also, "projection" is not as crucial as you probably think. My *Tartuffe* monologue (explored in Chapter 16, "A Date With Tartuffe") is delivered in my lowest possible tones, but as long as I am clear in the enunciation of each consonant and vowel, the audience hears it, even in an auditorium of 900 people, with no microphone!

I think of vowels as "pure" emotion… an impulse that wells up inside of us, so clear and rich, that none of the articulators: the lips, the teeth, the tongue, will move to impede it.

When you lean on that hot stove by mistake, without even an instant to think of your response, what is the sound that bursts from your mouth?

"Aaaaaooowww!"

The class answers in chorus. (The joker in class will inevitably, toss in a curse word.)

Let's say it's the fourth of July, and this big, gorgeous firework explodes into a bright GREEN! BLUE! PURPLE! GOLD! SILVER! GLITTERY! GLITTERY! GLITTERY! What sound comes out of your mouth?

"Oooooohhhh!"

And then?

"Aaahhhhhh."

Always in that order, too! The first being amazement, the second, appreciation!

Let's say there's this little six-year old boy, and he's been digging in the garden, and he's got a dozen roses, and he carries them up to his mother and says, "Here, Mommy, I got these for you because it's Mother's Day, and I wanted to tell you that I love you."

"Aawwwwwwwww."

And when the insult is really low and uncalled for, and the anger flashes in the recipient's eyes, everyone around will murmur a low …?

"Woaoaoaoaoao!"

Language has its roots in these instinctive expressions. These sounds are made the same way in the United States as they are made in Asia, in South America or Africa. It is genetically inside of us. The cavemen and women, hundreds of thousands of years ago, made all of the same sounds. They are a part of our biological make-up… like a bark is to a dog or a meow is to a cat!

Since the caveman days, as our crude humanoid brains grew in size and neural texture, we added consonants around these vowels to clarify subtle distinctions of meaning. And then we added prefixes and suffixes and distinguished nouns from verbs, all the way on down to prepositional phrases that reflect more intellectual distinctions, articulating more complex nuances of thought. Humanity may have started out with onomatopoetic words, such as "woosh" or "buzz," but as time passed, words grew more complicated, removing them further from the initial emotional impulse. But sometimes the best way to get back to the emotional root of a word, is to speak it aloud and pay attention to how it makes us feel *now*.

For instance, as we add more and more consonants, we generate a state of *emotionus interruptus*… a desire placed in check, clipped off. King Lear rages at

"Servile ministers that have with two pernicious daughters joined your high engendered battles 'gainst a head so old and white as this!" Lear is bristling with rage, wanting to roar his unfettered anger and every ending consonant stops him time and time again, reining in the sound that wants to howl from his lips, until this line at last gives way to the open-ended vowels of "Oh! Oh! Tis foul!" (The effort expended on the line itself is so enormous, by the time Lear arrives at his final roar, there is little air to give it voice, and this final desperate moment is filled with the anguish of an old man, overwhelmed and losing his mind.)

ASIDE

Love your obstacles.

Vowels are pure emotion… emotion that is interrupted by consonants. If all King Lear had to do was to roar out "Oh! Oh! Tis foul!" then this would not be one of the greatest speeches of all time. The consonants introduce conflict into what might be an easy or self-indulgent expression of emotion. The process of that conflict, biting into Lear's words, frustrates Lear furiously. Relish that frustration. It will feed you with emotions you might never imagine.

In other words, the interruption of one emotion stirs *another* emotion. The consonants that interrupt Lear's release of pure, howling pain or screaming rage, stir frustration. And frustration redoubles anger.

An Exercise

I turn to Shakespeare. I pass out the soliloquy that I quote below.

Who can tell me the situation of Hamlet that leads up to this scene?

"Hamlet's father died under suspicious circumstances. His mother was remarried in record time to none other than his uncle."[11]

Yes. Those are the only five points that we need to know to make sense of this scene:

1) Hamlet's father is dead.
2) He died under suspicious circumstances.
3) Hamlet's mother, Queen Gertrude, has gotten remarried.
4) She has remarried in an extremely short period of time.
5) The man she has married is Hamlet's father's brother.

The plots of Shakespeare tend to feel distant or remote to us. And largely unmoving. They sound like fairy tales: A prince, a queen, a king in a distant land, far away and long ago. They might as well be characters in *Cinderella*.

We're going to do a quick internal exercise now… I rarely do anything internal, so, when I do, I always like to point it out, if only to make you realize

---

[11] Okay, no one actually answers quite this succinctly, but by now you get the give and take of these sessions.

that internal processes are still crucial to our work. It just happens that we're not dwelling on that, largely because our external work brings a sizeable portion of our internal lives under our conscious control.

But take a moment to just get the gist of the situation. Don't make a big emotional exercise out of it. I want you to apply Hamlet's five circumstances to yourself. I'll say them again, slowly, and as I say them, just think of them in terms of yourself and your own family. This is almost the entirety of the "internal work" that I'm going to ask of you today.

1) Dad is dead.
2) He died under suspicious circumstances.
3) Mom has gotten remarried.
4) In an extremely short period of time.
5) To Dad's brother.

So what feelings come up for you when you think of this?

"Anger."

"Resentment."

"Disgust."

"Hurt."

"Sad."

"Upset."

Okay, all true, but I suspect there's one feeling that you're glossing over. Let's run through it again.

I repeat, more quickly this time, ticking the circumstances off on my fingers, but pausing and emphasizing the final line:

Dad is dead... he died under suspicious circumstances... mom has gotten remarried... in an extremely short period of time ...

The man mom has married is ***Dad's brother!***

"Yuk!"

"Gross!"

"Ick!"

"Disgusting!"

"Ewwww!"

There it is. That's the feeling you were holding back And that's another one of those pure emotional responses that lives in a single vowel: "Eeeeeeewwww!" Just saying it forces you to squinch up your nose.

That's good. Don't dwell on it, and don't torment yourself with gross feelings about your own family. Just notice that it's there.

So now we turn to what Shakespeare has to say, or what Shakespeare has Hamlet say aloud.

A S I D E

I share this as class exercise, largely because I expect no amount of coaxing and cajoling can get you, the reader, alone in your room, to do it with the full array of vocal and articulatory effort that the exercise demands. If you are reading this without a coach to hold you accountable, then the responsibility is all on you to be relentless in your effort to drive yourself. The only one who can make this work for you is you. A dorm room, a library, or a cafeteria probably won't give you the privacy you need to let yourself go. Get some space either within the secure four walls of a classroom or, better, a theatre. Actually do this. Don't read in silence, because that will have no impact on you. It will remain stale and distant.

This will change the way you look at dialogue.

Forever.

First, check in.

Stand up.

Breathe for a few moments. We're going to take ten seconds of silence.

Here comes our second (and probably last) internal exercise:

In this silence, examine your frame of mind.

Your blood pressure.

Your mood.

The electricity of your brain waves.

The feeling in your face.

Your sweat glands.

The state of your awareness.

The pulse in your throat. In your heart. And at the top of your head.

Do you have any sensory awareness of your hair follicles? No? We'll check back on that later.

How about your mood? Are you bored? Excited? Curious? Annoyed?... It is what it is. Just be honest with it, and don't try to get it to fit some imaginary "correct" response.

You can't actually know where it is that you've gone, unless you happened to notice where you were when you started. So, this is just our moment of noticing. And so, ten seconds in silence ...

(...)

Good.

Now, we're going to read this piece out loud. I realize we haven't said word one about iambic pentameter, or classical speech, or scansion, or pronunciation. This will be a bit of a train wreck at first. But we will do this chorally, as a group, so that we can make the same discoveries at the same time, and drive each other forward. We'll probably fall into a pace that works to greater or lesser degree for everyone, so we'll likely start and end at the same place. If we don't, that's entirely fine... even better, actually. Some will pause more at the punctuation than others. Don't worry about it. Just read aloud, as effectively as you, individually, know how... whatever that might mean to you right now. (And for now, ignore the asterisks.)

HAMLET
Oh, that this too, too solid flesh would melt,
Thaw, and resolve itself into a dew,
Or that the Everlasting had not fixed
His canon 'gainst self-slaughter. O God, God,
How weary, stale, flat and unprofitable
Seem to me all the uses of this world!
Fie on't, ah, fie, 'tis an unweeded garden
That grows to seed. Things rank and gross in nature
Possess it merely. That it should come to this:
But two months dead, nay, not so much, not two,
*So excellent a king, that was, to this:
Hyperion to a satyr, so loving to my mother
That he might not beteem the winds of heaven
Visit her face too roughly. Heaven and earth,
Must I remember? Why, she would hang on him
As if increase of appetite had grown
By what it fed on; and yet within a month –
Let me not think on't; frailty, thy name is woman –
*A little month, or ere those shoes were old
With which she followed my poor father's body
Like Niobe, all tears, why she, even she –
*O God, a beast that wants discourse of reason
Would have mourned longer – married with my uncle,
My father's brother, but no more like my father
Than I to Hercules. Within a month,
Ere yet the salt of most unrighteous tears
Had left the flushing in her galled eyes,
She married. *O, most wicked speed, to post
With such dexterity to incestuous sheets!
It is not, nor it cannot come to good.
But break my heart, for I must hold my tongue.

Very good. You got through it. No major derailments. A couple of odd-sounding words. Some of you were throwing yourselves into it more fully than others.

Things to notice: How much are you forging your own way, throwing yourself into the reading, and how much are you holding back, *not* wanting to draw too much attention to yourself? Is your point of concentration on the feel, the meaning and the impact of the words, or on your need to pass unnoticed?

We could stop here, if we wanted, to discuss meaning or pronunciation, but for now, let's just continue.

1) Rattle the Lights!

We're going to do it again, but this time, I'm going to give you a little bit of an adjustment: I noticed from that last time through that you were worried about making sense of it all, and were a little bit tentative. Let's cut loose of all of that. Continue to stand. Let the breath fill up your lungs to the point that the diaphragm is depressed and the stomach actually pooches out. Test it. Put your hand on your stomach and make sure that you can make the stomach expand when you take a deep breath. Good.

Now, take a look at those lighting instruments up there over the stage. I want you to imagine that whoever attached the lighting instruments to the battens didn't quite tighten the bolts completely, so that they're just a little loose.

I want you imagine, as you speak your lines, that your voice can actually ***rattle those lights!*** Imagine that your voice has the power to shake that light fixture loose to the point that it may very well come CRASHING to the floor! Fill the room with your voice and vibrate the room. Don't give up. Use every ounce of breath to shake the rafters.[12]

Now, in order to accomplish this, we have to remind ourselves that voices do, indeed, have power in the physical universe. Since a voice is essentially invisible, it remains amorphous to us, intangible, unreal. We forget that our voices have the power to actually, physically vibrate an object. Here's a quick exercise to demonstrate:

Take that piece of paper that has this monologue on it, and hold it about three inches from your mouth and make about five seconds of random noise.

---

[12] Obviously, if we are exploring this in a traditional classroom, we adjust our focus to the ceiling tiles, or somesuch.

"MMM-AAHH-OAOAOHH-BRRRRR-EEEE-NNNNGGG" Do you feel the piece of paper vibrating between your fingertips?

(Everyone nods.)

Voices seem ethereal, effervescent. This is not in any way mystical. Your voice moves the air and vibrates that which it touches. It is only by your voice vibrating objects in the physical universe, that you are ever actually heard. Your voice reaches out and vibrates the eardrum of anyone who is within "earshot" of you.

So, what is it we're going to do?

"Rattle the lights!"

I'm sorry, I couldn't hear that... You're going to do what?

"Rattle the lights."

WHAT?

"RATTLE THE LIGHTS!"

You absolutely have to believe in the possibility of this. You don't have to believe that it "will" happen, so much as you believe that it "can" happen. How many of you are willing to believe that? Let me see your hands.

(All hands go up.)

Alright, I am a witness. You have all signed on for this exercise, and I will hold you accountable to that agreement. If I see that you are not believing in the possibility of rattling the lights, I will come up to give you a little bit of gentle encouragement by reciting the monologue directly *into your face!*

I can hear the voice in your head: "How can he possibly know what's in my head? If I'm believing it or not believing it?" I'll tell you how I'll know:

- Your mouth will not open very wide...
- And your face will remain buried in the piece of paper.

This time, we'll cut away a portion of the speech, and pick it up about halfway through, at the first asterisk. Are you ready? Remember, you are going to do what...?

"RATTLE THE LIGHTS!"

Great! Take in a deep breath and ...

> *So excellent a king, that was, to this:
> Hyperion to a satyr, so loving to my mother
> That he might not beteem the winds of heaven
> Visit her face too roughly. Heaven and earth,
> Must I remember? Why, she would hang on him
> As if increase of appetite had grown
> By what it fed on; and yet within a month –

Let me not think on't; frailty, thy name is woman –
A little month, or ere those shoes were old
With which she followed my poor father's body
Like Niobe, all tears, why she, even she –
*O God, a beast that wants discourse of reason
Would have mourned longer – married with my uncle,
My father's brother, but no more like my father
Than I to Hercules. Within a month,
Ere yet the salt of most unrighteous tears
Had left the flushing in her galled eyes,
She married. *O, most wicked speed, to post
With such dexterity to incestuous sheets!
It is not, nor it cannot come to good.
But break my heart, for I must hold my tongue.

Excellent! Powerful stuff! As we move on, remember that this is an additive exercise. We add things to it, and never let go of what we've learned. Use that strength. Always fill the room.

Number one is always what?

"RATTLE THE LIGHTS!"

2) Make Ugly Faces!

Okay, now! Here's the next step. I want you to oVeRaRTiCuLaTe eVeRy WoRd oF THiS SPeCH. I WaNT You To CheW aLL oF YouR CoNSoNaNTS iN The MoST eXGGeRaTeD MaNNeR ThaT You CaN, To The PoiNT THaT You aRe aLL... MaKiNG uGLy FaCeS!

iN FaCT, i WaNT You To MaKe SuCH uGLy FaCeS THaT iF a PHoToGRaPHeR WeRe To WaLK iN HeRe aND STaRT SNaPPiNG PHoToS, You WouLD Be So HoRRiFieD THaT You WouLD SNaTCH The CaMeRa FroM HiS HaNDS, RiP THe MeMoRy CaRD FRoM THe CaMeRa, DaSH iT To THe GRouND aND CRuSH iT uNDeR YouR HeeL!

NoW HeRe iS THe BiGGeST PRoBLeM THaT i See WiTH YouNG, TeeNaGe aCToRS. You'Re aLL... MoST oF You... *Too DaMN PReTTy!*

Seriously. I work with actors whose faces look like they will break if they were to actually flex or contract a muscle. Or if their lips should move. They've chosen role models who they believe they should look like. And *their faces freeze* in the positions of the images that they've chosen for themselves. The way that seems "pretty" to them.[13]

Here, for once, we are going to determine your success on how UGLY you can get. In fact, we deduct points for being pretty: It's limiting your

---

[13] More about this in the chapter on "Being Cool."

emotional responsiveness! This time, as I walk amongst you, when I see your frozen porcelain or granite faces, I will come up to you and holler, "You're... too... pretty!" until such time as you stop clinging desperately to your shockingly good looks. So, goal number two for us is to: "Make ugly faces!" Say it with me; you're going to do what?

"Make ugly faces!"

What?

"MAKE UGLY FACES!"

Shakespeare gives you some pretty exciting consonants to chew. These are gifts to you from a man who lived four hundred years ago. Accept them and take advantage of them. Make the muscles in your face work much, much harder than you otherwise ever would!

So, number one, we're going to do what?

"RATTLE THE LIGHTS!"

And, number two, we're going to do what?"

"MAKE UGLY FACES!"

And remember, we're making ugly faces not just for the sake of making ugly faces, but in service of the consonants! Taking it from the second asterisk! Take in a deep breath, here we go!

> *A little month, or ere those shoes were old
> With which she followed my poor father's body
> Like Niobe, all tears, why she, even she –
> *O God, a beast that wants discourse of reason
> Would have mourned longer – married with my uncle,
> My father's brother, but no more like my father
> Than I to Hercules. Within a month,
> Ere yet the salt of most unrighteous tears
> Had left the flushing in her galled eyes,
> She married. *O, most wicked speed, to post
> With such dexterity to incestuous sheets!
> It is not, nor it cannot come to good.
> But break my heart, for I must hold my tongue.

Great! Fantastic! You eased up on rattling lights as you exaggerated consonants, but you're really starting to heat up those words. But, I gotta say, some of you are still SUSPICIOUSLY PRETTY!

3) Spit!

Okay, you're doing great, but you're still holding back in one area. Just *one major thing* keeping you from being fully self-expressed.

You're still holding a little tension here in your lower lip, in the sides of your cheeks, your jaw, your tongue and along the lower ridge of your gums and your soft palate. As you've been speaking, there's been a tiny puddle of saliva gathering behind your lower ridge of teeth.

And you have been working very, very hard to keep that little puddle of wetness inside your mouth, because for all of your life, people have taught you that it is "not nice to spit!"

This time you have my permission to let it go!

Number one was what?

"RATTLE THE LIGHTS!"

Number two was what?

"MAKE UGLY FACES!"

Number three?

"SPIT!"

That's right! Now this is going to be a problem for those of you who are standing in the front row, so those of you behind them, will want to place the piece of paper you are holding about 6 inches in front of your mouth. At the end of this exercise, you should be able to feel just how wet it has gotten. If your paper is wet, you get an "A" for the day!

Now, need I remind you, that if I see that you're not diving in all the way on this one, that I'm going to come up there once again and speak these words right in your face? And this particular exercise is one in which you *really don't want me doing that*, so you're going to really want to let it go without any further encouragement from me.

Okay, ready? Take in a deep breath and let's go!

> *O God, a beast that wants discourse of reason
> Would have mourned longer – married with my uncle,
> My father's brother, but no more like my father
> Than I to Hercules. Within a month,
> Ere yet the salt of most unrighteous tears
> Had left the flushing in her galled eyes,
> She married. *O, most wicked speed, to post
> With such dexterity to incestuous sheets!
> It is not, nor it cannot come to good.
> But break my heart, for I must hold my tongue.

Wow! Can you feel the difference? Check your pages. Are they wet?

4) Words that Drive the Speech

All right, here's where we get down to it. We're going to cut away everything that remains except for a single sentence. At the center of all of this is the phrase "O, most wicked speed, to post with such dexterity to incestuous sheets!" Can you feel the meaning behind that? Can you hear the climax in the speech?

Here's the change, though. We'll do this sentence five times! Speak the thing five times out loud. I'll count it out on my fingers so nobody has to suffer the embarrassment of starting the line a sixth time when everyone else has gone silent! Don't give up, but get louder, uglier, and wetter with each repetition!

Number one is what?

"RATTLE THE LIGHTS!"

Number two?

"MAKE UGLY FACES!"

Number three?

"SPIT!"

We don't get a chance to speak amazing words like this aloud very often. Take in a deep breath, here we go!

O, most wicked speed,
To post with such dexterity to incestuous sheets!
O, most wicked speed,
To post with such dexterity to incestuous sheets!
O, most wicked speed,
To post with such dexterity to incestuous sheets!
O, most wicked speed,
To post with such dexterity to incestuous sheets!
O, most wicked speed,
To post with such dexterity to incestuous sheets!

Beautiful.

5) Two Words

Okay, one more piece! We're deconstructing this huge soliloquy down to two words, and I don't believe you will have any problem at this point guessing which words those are?

"Incestuous sheets!"

Exactly right. The two most beautiful words in all of Shakespeare!

Not because of what they describe, but because of the way the very act of speaking them makes your face turn red with anger, and forces your tongue, your lips, your teeth, your cheeks, your nose to work overtime. It also underlines everything that's going on for Hamlet throughout this speech. All those words that led up to this? That was just tap dancing... This is the moment where what's really going on for Hamlet comes roaring out of him, and the very difficulty of speaking the words underlines and reinforces the emotional action.

Notice that these are "hard" words to say. Your mouth has to work overtime. There's an "s" at the end of the first word, and at the beginning of the second. Say them both!

Every once in a while, an actor gets words like these to speak and his first instinct is to go to the director and say, "You know, I'm not sure if I can speak that quite right. What do you suppose we simplify it? What if I said "messy sheets?" Or "sweaty sheets?" Or "rumpled sheets?"

To which I remind the actor, and everyone else: "Love your obstacles." If everything was easy, then we wouldn't have a play. Those great consonants, which are your obstacles, give you all of the emotion you need, if you will only allow yourself to do battle with them.

A S I D E

I had an actor once who, in the midst of a furious exchange, had the innocuous-looking equation "4/5" in his script. Try pronouncing that aloud: how does it come out?

"Four-fiss."

That's right, "four-fiss" is how we usually say it. But this actor put everything he had into every consonant, and said: "FouRR-FIFF-TH-SSS," enunciating, and "ploding" all three of those final consonant sounds in succession. He absolutely stole the stage out from under me every night. I was on stage with him, and it was nearly impossible to keep a straight face.

But he might well have gone to the director at some point and said to him, "You know, *"four-fifths"* is kind of hard to say... what if I just said *"eighty percent*?"

This is how most actors kill their most exciting moments.

Okay, ten times this time! Are you ready? What is it we're going to do? Number one?

"RATTLE THE LIGHTS!"

Number two?

"MAKE UGLY FACES!"

Number three?

"SPIT!"

Okay! And make it get rattling-er, uglier and *wetter* with each successive repetition! Take in a breath! Ten times! Let's go!

Incestuous sheets!
Incestuous sheets!

Incestuous sheets!
Incestuous sheets!
Incestuous sheets!
Incestuous sheets!
Incestuous sheets!
Incestuous sheets!
Incestuous sheets!
INCESTUOUS SHEETS!

Now! COMPLETE SILENCE FOR A MOMENT! It's time to check in! Quiet, please. Quickly, before you lose the moment. What are you feeling? What is going on inside you? How hard is your blood pounding? Where is your breath? Where are your emotions? Are you conscious of the follicles of your hair? Tell me. Speak it out loud.

"I feel lightheaded."

"I feel angry."

"I feel icky."

"I feel disgusted."

"I feel the hairs on top of my head!"

"I'm pissed off!"

Yes. perfect. All of that lives in the words. Remember our initial summation of the situation? We generally assessed the thing as having a high-icky-factor. Well we found "icky," and it lives in our voice; our face physically winces and sneers as we speak this, and that ***physiological*** action, creates a dramatic ***psychological*** shift in our hearts and minds.

The emotion comes on with a rush, every time I come to this line. "Incestuous sheets" has been lingering in the dark recesses of Hamlet's mind as he talks about everything BUT the deepest, most nagging source of his disgust.

And at last, having released this darkest, ugliest thought in a climax of emotion, the genius of Shakespeare follows this line with twenty one-syllable words, sixteen of which end in a hard consonant sound!

It brings the speech to a dead stop, like a set of rusty brakes, decelerating one step at a time: "It is not nor it can not come to good, but break my heart for I must hold my tongue."

Speaking it aloud, the emotion washes over my face. And I am moved. Transported. I feel Hamlet in the very hairs on the back of my neck.

We didn't force that. We didn't say, "*this* is what the speech is about and let's make it fit *this* inner emotional life." All we did was push the accelerator on the mechanics of the speaking: we took the dials of the components of speech and turned them up to "11." You generated a vision of the way in which your voice fills the room; the way your emotional life resonates in your face; and you shook loose of the inhibitions that were limiting your full self-expressiveness.

And there we found all of this emotion waiting there for us. Isn't it compelling? Gripping? The audience will sit up and feel this right along with you!

You will not be able to read this speech again the way you read it at the start of this exercise. The wealth of emotion that lives in these words will sneak over you in a rush, even without you realizing it, so that by the time you get to "To post with such dexterity to incestuous sheets!" you will feel a wave of heat wash through your face, the hair of your arms standing up, a lump in your throat, and a shudder of emotion shaking your lungs.

The dead hand of Shakespeare reaches out to you from four hundred years away and points you to this page. "Look here," he says. "Speak this." "Stop killing your dog and speak."

I'll say it again, perhaps not for the last time: Everything you need to perform Shakespeare lives inside the words that are intended to be spoken aloud.

Chapter 10

The Perils of Pausing

They were participating in a work of art that was larger than they, as individuals, could ever be.

On first glance, we tend to resist the consonants in that *Hamlet* speech. We look at them and say, "Oh, that's just too hard. Lemme see if I can get through this." And we whip through it, gliding as quickly across the consonants as we might. Skirting the difficult passage of "To post with such dexterity to incestuous sheets," and concentrating on the pause that we are going to take right before the final "But break my heart, for I must hold my tongue." Ah! During that pause, all will be revealed! The depth of my torture, the anguish of my struggle, the strength of my revulsion.

Well, that's just wrong.

The text itself is the content.

You are the vessel for the content of the play. It passes through your lips. Once you make your job as an actor about what you are going to do to embellish that content *in lieu of the text itself* then you are disassembling the play.

Take a look at any printed edition of a classical verse work. Notice the spots where characters deliver short, three or four-word speeches. What happens to that text? Does the publisher run it all along the left margin, like we would today? Like I just did… two paragraphs up?

No, the text does this little stair-stepping routine as the lines work their way across the page, each picking up where the other left off, until the line of the verse is complete. Only then does a "full return" start a new line line back at the left margin.

Shakespeare (or whomever was signing his name as "Shakespeare" 400 years ago) wrote this exchange as a single line of iambic pentameter verse. But why did Shakespeare bother? If the actors were caught up amid an exchange of lines anyway, why was he so… *persnickety* as to maintain this arbitrary ten-syllable form? Isn't that a bit (as we would say) "anal?"

It is a modern invention to consider that a play is an exchange of dialogue in a "realistic" situation, where two people trade their thoughts at a "contemplative" pace.

The theatre was an event. There was no television or newspaper. There was the church, the theatre, the public bazaar and the court. The opportunities for open discussion of public matters, the availability of a forum for the dissemination of thought, was limited and they made every syllable count. The theatre was where one went to understand the world and the one's actions within the community.

A play was not an "entertainment option." The play was the central hub for great ideas to be explored and declaimed. In Greek times, it would mean standing on enormous shoes ("*kothurni*") to make your figure taller, wearing a mask to emphasize your features whereby you might be seen by an audience up to two hundred yards away. And, of course, speaking fully.

The theatre was the delivery vehicle for the greatest poetic work of the day. And the poetry became more interesting when shadings of contrary opinion in the poem were addressed by more than one performer. Thus, dialogue was born.

In Shakespeare's age, the play was still an elaborate epic poem, acted out by a collective of characters. They were contributing individually to a work of art that was larger than they, as individuals, could ever be.

The great relentless engine known as iambic pentameter steadily drove the action through the course of the evening, and performers would tap into this source of power whenever they would step up to take their moment.

Lack of realism is not a *failing* of these plays; *It Was Never Their Intent!*

When we see dialogue jumping from one character to another within the course of a single line, we realize that we are participating in the expression of something beyond the particulars of who we are and what we may be thinking, remembering, feeling, doing, playing with, or contemplating. We are, in fact, sharing that line with our partner, and the rhythm continues… the play absorbs us into its workings.

This is alien to modern thinking. We are obsessed with the image of this or that individual actor: their look, their style, their quirk, their inflection, their mumble… to the point that characters are intertwined with actors, and actors have replaced the text as the primary vehicles of modern theatre.

To coin a phrase: "There is no *I* in Cast."

The particular layout of the stair-stepping exchange of dialogue as traded from one character to another suggests that the lines are read as single parts of a large epic poem, which means…

No pausing.

Some graduate student[14] once did a thesis, counting up the time that would be added to a given play if every actor simply took a single second before each line of dialogue.

This added about twenty minutes to the average play.

That would be twenty minutes of… what?

Nothing.

This is just the estimate for a single second of silence per line of dialogue! How easy is it to fall into that languid rhythm where we take two seconds (or three!) to absorb the intent of the line that has reached us…

…think about our response,

…work up the desire or the will to deliver it

---

[14] This may well be an apocryphal story, passed along by the aforementioned Dr. Morgan.

…and, thereupon,

…to speak.

This is how we end up with productions of *Hamlet* that don't get out of the theatre until Midnight!

Of course "in the moment," from our side of the footlights, it seems like a lot more than nothing! We are thinking!

We are reacting!

We are contemplating!

We are remembering how this event reminds us of the breakup of that relationship, or the failure of our parents, or the death of our dog.

But to the audience?

They're thinking, "Boy, that babysitter is going to kill me."

Or, "I wonder where we should go for a drink afterwards?"

Or, "Okay, the tickets were twenty bucks each, ten for parking, dinner was fifty-five, I had to tip that *maitre 'd* a five just to get a good table, and by the time this show is over, this girl I'm with is going to be half asleep… that's a hundred-thirty bucks, and be lucky if I get a good-night *hug* out of it!"

They are not as 'into' you, as *you* are 'into' you.

Give the audience the respect of having their own thoughts, too. It is our responsibility to shape the direction of the pattern of thoughts we are leading them through, so that they can become *engrossed*. So that they can be *occupied*. So that they can *think along with us*. They would actually rather not think about money or the babysitter, or how well their date is going! They want you to take them somewhere else! They want *their* acting to happen at the speed of life, too!

"Well, when it comes to dialogue, just what is 'the speed of life?'"

Well, even though I'm speaking now, I suspect that your brains have not shut down. As I deliver this lecture aloud, you do not simply absorb these words as they fly past. You test them, consider them, counter them, dismiss them, strategize about them… And if this situation were in any way urgent, crucial or important, you would be dying to get a word in edgewise!

One of the great plagues of memorization is that, rather than listening to the words coming out of our fellow actors mouths, we are simply listening for the silence, alerting us that it is now our turn to speak. If we have waited that long, then we have lost already.

The live stage bubbles with situations that are urgent, crucial or important. We don't invite people to come observe us from the opposite side of our desk at work, and if we did, we wouldn't expect applause at the end of the day. We invite people to see events to which we have given an aesthetic shape.

While we are wandering off, into our "thinking time," we are loosening the edges of that shape; we are giving ourselves over to some incidental quality, as we discover that, hey, this moment on stage is analogous to one of mine, this pain is similar to what I am feeling, this desire is like mine, this character is somewhat like me, but not me!

That's not good enough. We start the play at 8:00, and end at 10:00. For those two hours we have the ability to give shape to something, to lead the viewer from one event to the next to the next, to fix a shape that we have chosen to mold, so that when that viewer walks back out the door, he or she will be somehow different. He or she will have been "moved."

Every time we pause we leave that audience to wander off and hit the reset button. They go back to zero. They rethink. They drift. We're now facing a lot of heavy lifting to get them back to where they were.

SOLILOQUY

Spending a summer as an intern with the Alabama Shakespeare Festival many years ago, I carried banners, juggled, fought and danced, and we had a sort of company policy: we were not to pause through the course of a performance. We would jump on that train every night at 8pm, and not get off until 10.

As speaking parts were rare that summer, the policy had little impact on me. As the Attendant to Theseus in *A Midsummer Night's Dream*, for instance, I would appear at the very beginning of the play, and not return until the final act, ninety minutes later. In the meantime, I would return to the green room, beneath the stage. There I would get out of my stylish Theseus Attendant jacket, loosen my shirt, roll up my sleeves and do what actors do during time off. I would play backgammon or cards. I would flirt with the attractive seamstress. I would write letters. In the background, the intercom would play the dialogue as it was rolling along upstairs. It became a sort of a constant hum in the background, and we rarely paid any attention to it, unless we had an entrance approaching. At that time we would rearrange the costume, button, tuck, unroll, fasten. We would climb the tall staircase which doubled back upon itself, working its way to the stage level, hunt down the props, be it a banner or a halberd or a pike, and get into place.

And then there were those actors who had not quite "bought in" to the company philosophy (or didn't see how it applied to *them*). And, every now and again, over the speakers, in the green room in the bowels of the theatre, a silence would descend.

(…)

Of course, we were in the midst of our various preoccupations, and no one was really listening to hear precisely the context from which that silence had sprung. And our assumption was that we had missed our entrance! Somehow ninety minutes had flown past, feeling like no more than a half an hour, and here we were playing backgammon, a good three minutes from any possibility of making any appearance on the stage!

Collectively, we clutched. We leaned forward. We held our breath, replaying the last few scenes in our minds. They couldn't possibly have gotten to the end already! I would have at least had to hear… this or that incident or laugh line... Or had, perhaps, someone else missed an entrance? Had we jumped? Was there a prop missing, that brought the show to a dead halt? We looked at each other.

And there was always one actor who had been there many times, over several seasons of this style of performance, who recognized the antics of the performer who was on stage, "taking his moment." He would remain, comfortable in his chair with a superior smirk on his face, taking us all in. When the initial shock of concern had diminished to simple curiosity, we would turn to the one bastion of calm in the midst of our panic, and he would note, in his most smug, languid tones: "Oh, they're just… *acting*."

And in this theatre, you never wanted to be accused of "acting."

"Acting" suggested that you were bringing something *else* to the play that *wasn't there already*, or, worse, that in your own act of self indulgence, you were leading the play out, away from itself, somewhere into yourself, before wandering your way back.

And I mention this largely because it points up one thing. That when we were doing the thing up right, you noticed the pause!

Does this mean that we can never pause? No.

Does this mean that we shouldn't ever pause? No, again.

In point of fact, Shakespeare did occasionally build pauses into his verse. Every once in a while, we stumble across an abbreviated line, with perhaps only five or six syllables, or one syllable, such as Richard III exclaiming "Ha!" in a line that stands alone. If we investigate what is happening onstage at that moment, we almost always find a good reason for a pause.

Life needs shadows to bring out the highlights. Where all is highlight, everything is a blinding blur. If *every* theatrical moment features a pause that is fraught with endless "meaning," then that meaning cannot be set into any kind of a context and thereby no unique meaning may be recognized or understood.

Take the play that has been rattling around at a healthy pace for a while: the audience gets accustomed to this; they feel themselves buoyed by ongoing words, words, words. And then the words stop.

Whatever happens in that moment, will rivet the audience' attention.

Whatever happens *after* that will get the laugh or the tingles or the gasp or the sigh.

We look to that which is different to understand the meaning of what has led up to it. When pause follows pause, very quickly we stop endeavoring to pry open the actor's brain to figure out what is inside.

A S I D E

I flash forward to the present. Just today I attended a presentation of one of my own Molière scripts. A play that ran less than two hours (including intermission) when I directed it, runs 2:45 now.

It's not a bad performance, by any means.

And yet they are not using the momentum of the lines to engage the audience and haul them, speeding down that relentless track toward the climax.

Here, the average line takes a couple of seconds to get underway.

The lines themselves, when spoken, are clear and understandable. (*Bravo.*)

But then the actors add a panoply of vocalized noises in-between the lines. Somehow, the words that I gave them to work with are not enough, and they need to add: "Mmmn?" "Nnng!" "Eh?" "Heh-heh." "Ah!" "Oooh!" "Grrr!" and even "Yes!"

These are actors who do not trust themselves to be able to deliver the meaning *on the lines themselves*, and so they are putting their energies *around* and *between* the lines. What had been simple, clear and eloquent, was becoming muddled, stretched, and repetitive.

Or… perhaps they do not trust the lines as I wrote them to convey all of the humor of which they are capable.

Caution!

I am not talking about speed or rate!

As much as I might hammer home the point, some actors, when the director insists, "don't pause," actually *imagine* the imperative "talk fast!" This is not by any means what I am suggesting. Slow speech can be even more dramatic or effective than quick speech. Quick speech (which often emerges as maddeningly incomprehensible "blurty speech") can be extremely frustrating, as the performer fails to take that extra instant to close off or clarify those consonants, or make him or herself understood, especially with words which may be slightly unfamiliar to the modern ear.

The proper rate of speech varies by venue!

The size and shape of the performance hall determines how long the sound will travel before hitting a reflective surface, and then bounce off, in a direction which will overlap and interfere with the next sound wave that is emerging from the mouth of an actor. The timing may demand a slight one-hundredth of a second's greater effort toward clarity and definition, to complete a given word before moving on to the next. And an actor who is still struggling with an accent or a characterization, or simply with baroque phrasings such as "incestuous sheets" may not have the discipline, the heightened awareness or the self-control to respond to the resonance of the room.

But just like the "sixth sense" that the actor develops for whether he or she is or is not standing in the light, the actor must cultivate this aural awareness. We sit and listen to a play, and we can immediately sense which actors have this awareness available to them, and which don't. It is the difference between being heard… and not.

Here we find the actor's mind working on many different levels simultaneously. This is living in the moment, while simultaneously observing the moment. The actor is essentially re-writing, re-arranging the score from which he or she performs, even as he or she is performing.

It may be the size of the auditorium, the relative fullness of the seats, the crying baby in the third row, the cougher in the back row, the cell phone, the dropped line, the missing prop, or the overwhelming unanticipated laugh… A certain kind of actor immediately recognizes whatever obstacle separates the audience from full comprehension, and supplies the vocal placement, the extra hundredth of a second between each word, the ad lib, or the suspended moment to restore the audience to the necessary state of awareness, before moving them forward once again.

This is the three-dimensional chess of acting.

Chapter 11

The Triumph of Rhetorical Delivery

The storm is in the words.

In 1983, Lawrence Olivier was to play King Lear on PBS. I was excited by the prospect, I looked forward mostly to the "storm scene:" the most famous scene of my favorite play being done by the man regarded as the greatest actor of our time. How can it get any better than this?

Lear divides his kingdom between three daughters based on their testimony of love. His two, lesser-loved daughters parade their love with exaggerated enthusiasm. The favorite daughter cannot flaunt her love so outrageously, and refuses to play the game. Embarrassed, Lear exiles his good daughter, and divides the kingdom between the others. Before long, one daughter complains of the ruckus of the knights attending the now ex-king, asking that Lear divide the retinue in half. Offended, he goes to stay with the second daughter who, in turn, insists the first was too *generous*. Why does Lear need any knights at all? Furious, with only his "Fool" in tow, Lear stumbles out into the face of a raging storm, and shouts his anger into the teeth of it.

When the scene arrived, I was ready to see just how the speech should "really" be done. Upon the heath, Olivier shouted into the face of a ferocious storm. Sheets of rain poured down, thunder rumbled, lightning crackled, wind howled, and an orchestra trumpeted and timpanied a tempestuous score.

Does anyone see a problem with this?

When *Lear* was originally produced, there was no sheet of metal shaken backstage to sound the thunder.

There was no wind machine spun to send the wind whipping past.

No "rain stick" evoked rain, no practical effect showered actual water, no giant fans blew leaves, and certainly no lightning flared on the backdrop.

Shakespeare probably never imagined that such effects would be possible.

In fact, he wrote those effects OUT of his play.

Because the storm is in the words.

And this version of the play overwhelmed the actor with sound effects and music, intent on creating a storm that was *already there*. Just as the imagination creates "Verona" the moment that the actor says, "Ah, here we are in Verona," so does the imagination of the audience create the storm of King Lear.[15]

---

[15] The modern sound designer seems to see this scene as the great challenge to his or her craft. Only occasionally do we find rumbling thunder relegated to the background, rather than battling the actor for prominence.

The Storm Scene.

Read the following aloud, using the "tricks" from *Hamlet*: use volume (*Rattle the lights*!), over-articulation (*Make ugly faces*!) and saliva. (*Spit*!) Listen for the storm in the words that you are speaking.

Again, we've got to do this out loud. We cannot just read it.

Again, check in. Take ten silent seconds to simply notice where your head, body and spirit are at.

I include the lines of the Fool to give us the context of the scene. Skip over them this time and read just Lear. And, go!

> KING LEAR
> Blow, winds, and crack your cheeks! rage! blow!
> You cataracts and hurricanoes, spout
> Till you have drench'd the steeples, drown'd the cocks!
> You sulphurous and thought-executing fires,
> Vaunt-couriers to oak-cleaving thunderbolts,
> Singe my white head! And thou, all-shaking thunder,
> Smite flat the thick rotundity o' the world!
> Crack nature's moulds, all germens spill at once,
> That make ingrateful man!
>
> FOOL
> O nuncle, court holy-water in a dry house is better than this rain-water out o' door. Good nuncle, in, and ask thy daughters' blessing: here's a night pities neither wise man nor fool.
>
> KING LEAR
> Rumble thy bellyful! Spit, fire! spout, rain!
> Nor rain, wind, thunder, fire, are my daughters:
> I tax not you, you elements, with unkindness;
> I never gave you kingdom, call'd you children,
> You owe me no subscription: then let fall
> Your horrible pleasure: here I stand, your slave,
> A poor, infirm, weak, and despised old man:
> But yet I call you servile ministers,
> That have with two pernicious daughters join'd
> Your high engender'd battles 'gainst a head
> So old and white as this. O! O! 'tis foul!

Excellent! Did you hear the storm? What words gave you the storm?

"Crack your cheeks!"

"Blow!"

"Thought-executing."

"Oak-cleaving."

"Smite flat."

A N EXERCISE

"Spit, fire! Spout, rain!"

[Eventually, I cut them off...] Great, yes, it's all through that, and even more. It wasn't even the literal words that described the storm, such as "winds," "thunderbolts," "thunder," "rain." Certainly these words inform us of the storm's presence, but the singing, searing sense of "smite," "spit," "crack," "cleaving," all give us the feel of the storm. Even "pernicious daughters" is filled with the shower of the storm.[16]

Can you hear the music in it? The rhetorical challenge? The opportunity to create an even bigger and wilder storm, simply through the use of vocal technique? Can you understand why sound effects were completely unnecessary, and may even be counter-productive in this instance?

Let's look again at the nature of "Art and Selection."

- Not only has Shakespeare selected lines that would be believable in Lear's situation…
- Not only are they selected down to the syllable so that stressed and unstressed syllables alternate…
- And not only will the speaking process spark an emotional action in the actor…
- But the very vowels and consonants themselves will stir an awareness of a violent storm *within the listener*. By the end of the speech, they may well be surprised to discover that the actors' hair, the stage floor, and their own clothing, are still dry!

Punctuation and Breath Control

AN EXERCISE

We're going to try a piece of this speech again: the ending.

There is a hierarchy of punctuation, in which the briefest, almost unnoticeable hesitations of the speech are created by the ***commas***. Properly played, the pauses they imply should not give us sufficient time to take a breath, and we want to avoid interrupting the flow to take a breath if possible.

We then graduate to the ***semi-colon***, another very slight catch in the momentum.

And then the ***colon***, which might possibly let us squeeze in a breath.

It is the ***period***, however, along with the ***question mark***, which enable us to take a full stop.

And the ***exclamation point*** implies the longest stop of all.

[16] From advertising, we understand the concept of "subliminal messages," messages that someone sees and receives, but doesn't consciously notice. I propose the word, "subaural" for messages such as these: heard and received, subconsciously, but not quite rising to conscious awareness.

I am proposing that we take the final four lines of this speech, and perform them without interruption. Do not take a breath from "But yet..." until "...tis foul!" (I realize that just at the very end, there is a period and three exclamation points, but indulge me for the moment to play straight on through without a breath.)

Are you ready? Again, rattle the lights, make ugly faces, chew the consonants, spit, and all on one breath. Take in a deep breath and go!

> But yet I call you servile ministers,
> That have with two pernicious daughters join'd
> Your high engender'd battles 'gainst a head
> So old and white as this. O! O! 'tis foul!

Excellent! It wasn't so hard as you had thought it might be, was it? (Though some of you should probably give up smoking.) But now we're going to add to it. We're going to add a line and a half to the beginning, and we'll continue to play through to the end. Don't give up. You always have more air than you think you do.

As always: Support! Rattle! Ugly! Saliva! And just one breath! Ready? Go!

> ... Here I stand, your slave,
> A poor, infirm, weak, and despised old man:
> But yet I call you servile ministers,
> That have with two pernicious daughters join'd
> Your high engender'd battles 'gainst a head
> So old and white as this. O! O! 'tis foul!

Again, excellent. But different, this time, yes? Even though it's just a line-and-a-half that we added! Now, quickly: check in again. What are you feeling?

"Out of breath."

"Angry."

"I feel frustrated."

"I feel a rush."

"I feel exhilarated."

"I feel light-headed."

Yes. That's exactly it. "Light headed." The oxygen is sapped from his brain. The process of speaking is generating the mindset that Lear is going through. Look at just how few stops Shakespeare has given you. In the first half of the speech, before the Fool speaks, he'll stop perhaps every two to three lines. But see how few stops are present in the latter portion. Aside from the exclamation points at the beginning and the end, all he gives you is colons and commas.

Can you begin to sense just how rhetorically capable the actor of Shakespeare's age needed to be? These were not actors as we tend to think of them, so much as they were athletes of speech and performance.

Furthermore, this level of rhetorical complexity demanded an intelligence to support the physical dexterity. In the course of a single sentence that begins with "Nor rain, wind, thunder, fire," and ends with "So old and white as this," we, as King Lear, weave notions of the daughter's ungratefulness together with the fury of the storm, admitting our own helpless submission to the anger of the storm, and yet turning the argument on its head by suggesting that the storm *itself* has entered into a conspiracy with the daughters against a pathetically old man.

Look to the Periods

This is not unique to *King Lear* by any stretch. The most prominent tangles of speech that daunt us from any Shakespearean soliloquy are best approached by first noting the placement of the periods within the speech. This is Shakespeare's most overt signal that the idea, initiated at the beginning of this sentence, often many lines above, has found its conclusion. There is, for instance, an astonishing two-minute speech from *Coriolanus* that is punctuated with only four periods!

A speech such as this cannot be fully grasped on the first read through. Only through a diligent practice of balancing one idea against the next, and against the next – the quadruple negative scattered over several lines of verse that ultimately flips the idea to a positive – do we discover what side of a given idea the speaker has come down upon, or realize that the assumed sincere assertion is an ironic one. It is a laborious, but sometimes thrilling process, as the power of the speech that awaits the full unraveling of the actor's analysis proves worthy of all our efforts.

Mastering the Rhetoric

The actors of that age had available to them the same vocal apparatus that we have today, but they worked it a lot harder and they danced their way through the clauses and crescendos. What would they have used?

Breath control. The very expulsion of the breath from the chest fosters the frame of mind vital to the character's full expression.

Volume. Creating the storm, Lear has to put up one hell of a fight… a mighty struggle, especially when there's not a lot of breath to support it. But the thunder of Lear's voice needs to boom more than the thunder of a sound effect.

Pitch and tone. Major shifts in thought demand changes in pitch, as the several shifts, perhaps best distinguished by the colons in this speech, take us to different places in Lear's argument. Try the speech using the colons as markers to place the voice differently, over-exaggerating the shifts: dropping the tone low or to raising it high.

Lists. Lear has several lists in this speech, and it's easy to get lost in them. A list may grow in intensity near the end, but the essential nature does not change, nor should it take deep thought to jump from one to the other. A few of Lear's lists: "Rumble… Spit… Spout," "Rain, wind, thunder, fire." "Gave you… called you… you owe…" "Poor, infirm, weak and despised," "Old and white."

Lists hammer a point home, suggesting that not only is this true in one instance, but *here*! Look! *Here, too*! It overwhelms the listener with evidence.

Climax. Amid the final throes of that great speech, Lear has set up his final point with a series of shifts and adjustments, not quite sure of whether he even has the right to be angry at the storm. As he discovers the true object of his rage, he stops dancing around his topic, his focus narrows, and he gains in speed and intensity, until "with two pernicious daughters join'd your high engender'd battles 'gainst a head so old and white…" pounds relentlessly. The jaw drops open with every stressed syllable. We can imagine and even feel Lear being battered by the storm.

Space. Finally, the train is pulling into the station, as the steam is running out of Lear's delivery. The oxygen is depleted, the anguish overwhelms him and there is a sense of space in the words. The harshness of the consonants has diminished and Lear, a wounded animal, is left with pure open vowels, words that howl: "Old," "white," "O," "foul!" One can feel the pressure lightening, a surrender growing, and a space that the words (especially one-syllable words) can take, in rhythm and time, as Lear spends his last bit of energy and, perhaps his last bit of sanity. Subsequent scenes find him overtaken by madness.

The most rudimentary reading of this speech would have to employ all of these elements: breath, volume, pitch, tone, lists, climax and space. These are the building blocks of rhetorical device, keeping the audience in tune: listening, following, understanding.

Imagine, if you can, a reading of this speech sprinkled with pauses, as our modern actor attempts to *indicate* emotion *between* the words, rather than using the words themselves! Even as he thunders toward the climax of the speech, I can hear the inner monologue grinding progress to a halt:

> "**But yet I call you …** [*let me think, what phrase is wicked enough for you? Ah!*] **Servile ministers!** [*Take that, why don't you… storm! And you know what else?*] **That have with two** [*you know, as bad as they've been, I just can't quite find the word that captures the extent of… wait!*] **pernicious daughters** [*what is it that they did? Why, of course, they*] **join'd your** [*you know, it's almost as though they conspired about me from high over my…*] **high engendered** [*and they weren't just arguments, no, they were*] **battles 'gainst** [*well, of course they took on all of me, but what really hurt was…*] **a head** [*not just a young head, but*] so old [*and it's not really even the salt and pepper thing anymore, it's really*] **and white** [*look at me; LOOK AT ME, PEOPLE!*] **as this!** [*You think I've been upset before, just listen to*] **O!** [*And if that one didn't get you, listen to this!*] **O! Tis** [*Depraved? Vicious? Unsavory? Unfair? No!*] **Foul!**"

That is, of course, simply an entirely different speech. Imagine this same tone with Hamlet:

> "To... post with such... dexterity to... incestuous... sheets!" (William Shatner, eat your heart out.)

Let's remind ourselves of the climax and single-syllabled denouement of our Hamlet example:

> CLIMAX:
> O, most wicked speed, to post
> With such dexterity to incestuous sheets!
>
> DENOUMENT:
> It is not, nor it cannot come to good.
> But break my heart, for I must hold my tongue.

As much as I talk about the brilliant rhetorical devices in Shakespeare, I can't help but feel that some actors assume they were nothing more than elaborate coincidences, upon which persnickety modern teachers stick arbitrary labels after-the-fact. As if an infinite number of monkeys pounding on an infinite number of typewriters would have come up with the same material.

But here, the rhetorical climax comes screaming out at us, and the space embodied in the words and the phrasing, grinds the monologue to a halt in its denouement. There is an amazing rhetorical vision feeding us all that we need, and we ignore that at our peril.

Chapter 12

Iambic Pentameter, Rhyming and Reality... And Why We Go to the Theatre

You get to be a part of something that is larger than yourself, and in the process, you will master a rhythm that you participate in, but which will also support the entire play, lifting it out of the everyday, and onto a higher plane.

Shakespeare's preferred rhythm was iambic pentameter. When I adapt Molière, I use it, too. Molière actually tended to write in Alexandrines, which are possible in English, though more complicated. Rather than re-invent the wheel, I acknowledge that English-speaking actors (myself included) are trained in iambic pentameter, largely because most actors, at some point, study Shakespeare. With many it becomes a very natural speaking rhythm, and I proceed assuming that these performers have already mastered this art.

I equate an actor's knowledge of iambic pentameter to a musician's knowledge of the measure. A single glance at a measure of music and a musician knows exactly how to play it: how long the notes should be held, the pitch of those notes, the rhythm of the music, etc.

What We Know

Likewise, an actor, looking at a line of iambic pentameter should know:

- A line of iambic pentameter is generally 10 syllables long. The syllables alternate between unstressed and stressed syllables, creating five "feet" of iambs (an unstressed syllable followed by a stressed syllable). Through the course of a ten-syllable line, there will be five stressed syllables.
- Sounding out the rhythm of these lines will give you important clues as to the way that the line should be delivered, and even how some words are intended to be pronounced. Depending on where it falls in the line, an actor may call a woman "MADam", or he may call her "maDAM". The actor may refer to his city as "PARis," or he may call it "parEE." Or, a multi-syllabic word may be contracted or expanded in some ways to fit the pattern. A shoemaker may be called a "COB-ul-LER" or a "COB-lur;" a shameful act may be "IG-no-MIN-ee-US," or it may be "IG-no-MIN-yus." When Gloucester in *Henry VI, Part 3* says "As one who stands upon a promontory," we know that the final word is intended as "PROM-on-TREE" rather than "PROM-on-TOR-ee." Or, when Hamlet cries "With such dexterity to incestuous sheets," an analysis of the line's "scansion" will suggest the pronunciations "dex-TER-ty" and "in-CEST-yus".

- We are not required to deliver the line this way! Personally, I enjoy using all of the syllables of "dexterity" and "incestuous" in hammering home Hamlet's line. And Shakespeare may even have wanted to suggest an emotional disturbance by putting a stutter-step into the rhythm of the line. There are a million other options and discoveries waiting to be made along the way which will give us greater power in the performance, but when we make them from a perspective of awareness, we have graduated from victims to masters of our art.

- Or, as they say, "We need to know what the rules are in order to know when to break them."

In other words, our process of tackling Shakespearean performance takes us from a lack of understanding of rhetorical device as we ride our impulsive emotional understanding of the words as best we can, to a phase in our development in which the structure itself seems to be an imposition. Working within the meter feels restrictive and constraining, hammering particular syllables in a manner that seems divorced from meaning, much the way that staying on-the-beat in a musical performance leaves us feeling like all of the life has been squeezed out of the sweep of emotion, or the playfulness of the music.

But working through this stage, there also arises the occasional moment of "mastery," in which a series of options present themselves to the verse speaker, a point in which options of breath, volume, pitch, space, climax and more, appear to the speaker in an instant, and the fullness of the moment and the knowledge of the piece enable the actor to actually respond to an instantaneous emotional wave that rises and falls in the space of a syllable, without ever losing sight of the "period" waiting at the end of the speech that holds it all together.

What We Suppose

There are things that we know automatically, and may almost always assume. There is more, however, that we might well *suppose* about a given line:

- All things being equal, each successive stress of an individual line should be greater than the one that precedes it. This growing intensity climaxes in the line's final syllable, before dropping back and building again.

- More often than not, all things are *not* equal, as character traits, emotional impulses and stress for logic steer the actor away from this "default" position (which keeps the lines from getting too repetitive or "sing-songy").

- While the playwright may often put some sort of a stop in at the end of this line, quite often s/he does not. *The punctuation* gives you the pauses, *not the line-break*. The first mistake of many young actors is to pause at the end of each line of verse, even though the sentence itself may not end until several syllables into the next line.[17]

[17] To some Shakespearean scholars, this is a radical statement. There are elaborate arguments on behalf of pauses at the ends of iambic lines. Those kinds of pauses are almost instantaneous

- As noted, there is a hierarchy to punctuation and pause. The shortest is the comma, followed by the semi-colon, the colon, the question mark, the period and the exclamation point, largely in that order.
- The way the stresses increase through the course of a five-foot line creates a natural build, giving the final syllable a stronger "punch" than anything before it, even if there is no punctuation at the end of a line. In rhyming verse, this will keep the rhyming word present in the audience's mind, so that they know instinctively which rhyme they are meant to puzzle out.
- Often we will discover an 11-syllable rhyme in iambic pentameter. This is not "cheating," nor is it a mistake. It is a natural phenomenon known as the "feminine ending." The phrase "feminine ending" implies the ending of the line is not as strong as the usual "masculine ending." That eleventh syllable is unstressed, leaving the line "hanging" with a weaker conclusion. Rather than eliminate half of the words of the English language from our vocabulary of possible line-ending words, the feminine ending allows for that single extra syllable, which gives the playwright a larger palate of words from which to draw.
- Further examination will often find this eleven-syllable line partnered in a couplet with another eleven-syllable line. This matters much more in rhymed verse and enables us to pointedly rhyme words such as "creator," "later," "date her," "satyr," "alligator," "Darth Vader," etc.

Rhymes

"But I was told by my teacher that we were supposed to HIDE the rhyme."

If the playwright wanted it hidden, why did he put it there in the first place? As the author, why did I stay up until three in the morning trying to find a rhyming word?

A rhyme is an aural phenomenon.[18] It comes to us invisibly, through the ears. It is meant to be spoken aloud and appreciated for its music.

A "rhyme" by definition lives in its sound. Like everything else, it passes by us at the speed of life, and we should not have the time to contemplate what those words look like on the page. It is certainly a shame that there aren't more words that rhyme with love, but regrettably "move" and "prove" do not, however close they may be in spelling!

Such "rhymes" will "sound wrong" to us in the moment, and demand that we re-arrange our thinking a bit before we visualize the word on the page and bring ourselves to accept the similarity. But if we have taken the time to

---

glitches in the rhythm. Here, I am referring to pauses made as if those lines of verse were each conclusions of a 10-syllable statement, when they are clearly not.

[18] There is some delicious irony to the fact that I cannot describe an "aural phenomenon" and be completely understood unless I am writing the word "aural" on paper, or spelling it out for a live audience, who will otherwise assume that I've said "oral."

send ourselves through this thought process, then we have *abandoned the play*, leaving it behind to grapple with an intellectual conceit which has nothing to do with the action.

"But there are near-rhymes and visual rhymes in Shakespeare!"

Yes, but probably far fewer than we assume. We tend to assume that four hundred years has had no impact on pronunciation, and Shakespeare pronounced his words the way we pronounce them now. Shakespeare was writing during a transitional period in which an entire library, featuring every available published work, would have fit on a single shelf. As such, the actual spellings of many, many words had not solidified (they had no dictionary then) and pronunciation was more flexible. Reading Shakespeare in the original Quarto or Folio is an arduous task, and the spelling is extremely unfamiliar and inconsistent.[19]

(The work of Shakespeare, probably more than any other influence, gave the English language an "anchor," with words that readers would remember, repeat and revere, to hold it in place long enough to take root, standardize, solidify and grow.)

All is not lost. The word "of" *does*, in fact, rhyme with "love," no matter how dissimilar the two look!

The trend toward "hiding the rhyme" comes to us in response to poor execution of rhymed speech. A ponderous, bland, unemotional, uninvolved reading of rhymed verse (which happens to emphasize the rhyme) quickly leaves us disenchanted by its repetitiveness. When the actor is motivated by the character's desire, using speech to achieve those objectives, the rhyme will not distract from, but enhance the melody of the speech.

Popular Entertainment

"But that's so unnatural!"

Yes it is, and thank goodness!

Keeping in mind that the word "art" also serves as the source word for "artifice" and "artificial," let's take a look at the big picture.

What is the most popular form of theatrical entertainment in the United States of America?

"Well... the musical."

Exactly. And just what is natural about the musical?

... (Laughter) ...

---

[19] Shakespeare, himself, never signed his name the same way twice! This has led many to question whether "William Shakespeare" was the *nom de plume* of some other Elizabethan writer, retroactively associated with the actor who had been born in Stratford.

"... nothing?"

Let me ask this way: Just what is unnatural about the musical?

"People sing!"

"The endings are hokey."

"People dance!"

"People sing in groups."

What about that moment in which the lead character falls in love? He realizes it and his chest expands. He almost floats on air for a moment. He's getting ready to burst into song... What's happening in that moment?

"The orchestra is starting up!"

Exactly! I'm having my big moment, and thirty people, ten feet away are anticipating it and providing me the perfect accompaniment. I magically shape my expressive needs with rhythm, melody and rhyme, with the support of 30 musicians in tuxedos and gowns! And then, let's say my special lover enters the scene as I am singing. What happens next?

"She sings too!"

That's right! She has a verse of her own! Which will play on all the same themes! In the same rhythm! With the same melody! What's next?

"They sing together!"

Yes! SHE KNOWS ALL THE WORDS! And she knows the tune! And she can not only sing along, but sing the soprano part against my baritone! Her voice will go up where mine goes down, and the two of us will harmonize! Next?

"You dance?"

That's right! The two of us match each other's movements, step for step, bend for bend, all the way down to pointed toes or flexed feet! In perfect synchronization! Then what happens?

"The chorus comes on!"

The whole freaking town! Each and every one of them! Knowing those same words! Those same steps! Those same bends! And they're all singing in beautiful, spontaneous arrangements, riffing on this same central idiom that they just happened to know that very instant!

And in the course of this, do we ever stop and say, 'Oh, that's so unnatural!' We never say that! But for some reason we use that to criticize any other play we might do! And so, given how false it is, how unnatural, how artificial, why do you suppose musical theatre is so popular?

(...)

Because people *love this crap!* It's why we come to the theatre! We are all looking for that perfect moment! The moment when it all makes sense! The moment when the gods conspire to place the perfect voice in the perfect body with the perfect words and the perfect sound, the perfect set, costumes, and especially that perfect unifying idea which makes sense of it all. We want that moment where we can finally say, "Oh, I have seen perfection, which is so often denied to us down here upon this earth, and if the Lord might take me now, I would be a happy man!"

I have always found the plot of *Doctor Faustus* to be quite persuasive. Faustus is looking for his perfect moment. The moment in which he might say, "Stay, and do not leave. Let me live forever, frozen in this moment." It is the perfect sentiment to be realized in a theatrical work. It is the very reason we go to the theatre.

And we actors fight that all the time.

We question our motivation. We question the logic. We question the probability. We question whether it is all *reeeallly* necessary. We don't understand all that we have to give, and all that the audience gets from it, and we hold back.

"Why do I do this?"

"Why do I say this?"

"Why would I exit, here? Or enter there?"

We are contributing to an experience that is larger than the narrow confines of our minds. We get to be a part of something larger than ourselves, and in the process, we master a rhythm that we participate in, but which also supports the entire play, lifting it out of the everyday, and onto a higher plane. We speak in rhymes, gently tantalizing the audience with new word puzzles, to the point that they sit just a bit more erect, that they lean farther forward, wondering… "there's that word, left lying on the table … like a loaded gun waiting to be fired." What could come next? They hope that they will somehow "get it." They fear that they may have "missed it."

This is the experience to which we contribute.

Every now and again, these same questions and doubts will arise, reaching far beyond word choice, but into your private life. The question may be one of, "How do I play this villain without people seeing me as evil?"

Or, "I'm playing an unmarried pregnant girl. Will people think I'm a slut?"

Or "I've got to say/do some really nasty things on stage! How do I justify that?"

The answer lies in a question. Does the action on stage contribute to something larger than your reasons for resisting? And is that something a statement that is worth making? In each question lies the opportunity to make the theatre about something larger than the concerns of a single individual.

We may choose to release the bonds of resistance for the liberation of a potentially transcendent vision. When the audience senses that it is, in fact, worth it to you to have given over resistance on behalf of something larger, then they look even harder to see just what that something larger might be.

Chapter 13

Finding Chaos Within Order

...a vision of the world that is unified, and controlled, even though each piece of it seems to be reckless and unconstrained.

I watch an early rehearsal of a scene from my version of Molière's *The Bourgeois Gentleman*. The actors have a good sense of character, but aren't quite *there* with the style. The rest of the cast sits in the audience, as we are using this scene as an object lesson in sharing lines.

On the first pass, the actors are concentrating on blocking, and since the scene is somewhat of a chase scene, the activity repeatedly takes them out of their connection with their lines. The cast observing is passive, probably a little apprehensive, wondering what the "judgment" of the guest/author/adaptor is going to be. At the end, my thoughts for them are fairly simple:

> Okay, first of all, for now let's let the blocking go. Just stand by your partners and let's put all of our focus on the words.
>
> Now, as I was listening, we had a signal-to-noise ratio... or in this case, a dialogue-to-silence ratio that was somewhere around four-to-one. For every four seconds of sound, we had about one second of silence, mostly having to do with picking up our cues. So let's try it again, and put all of our concentration into picking up cues.
>
> Of course, if you're waiting on silence to know that it is time for you to speak, then you're already too late, so make sure you inhale as the person with the line prior to yours is speaking! It's like that moment in which you're sitting at the stoplight, and the stoplight changes from red to green. It takes a good second or two for your brain to cue your foot that it's okay to shift from the brake to the accelerator, and another second or two for the car to actually ease its way into motion. That's actually a good thing as far as driving is concerned... it creates a safety buffer so that we don't run into the guy who's racing through the intersection at the last second... but not so good for drama or comedy. We don't want that kind of "safety" on stage.

The actors do it again, and this time, they're much more in synch. Aside from a couple of glitches, they're participating in an iambic pentameter patter that doesn't let up for pauses of silence. A couple of times there's even some exciting overlap in the lines. But something is still not quite right. The audience is certainly more interested this time, but we have not yet proven the validity of this approach. All that I've gotten them to do is to fill the spaces…

Okay, that was great... Our signal-to-silence ratio is now more like 10-to-1! Now this time, I want you to put some passion into it. In the midst of your sharp entrances, jumping on each others' cues, I want you to ***fling*** yourself into the moment. Put all of the emotion that you can into your very brief lines in sudden sharp bursts... and still continue to pick up the cues as each of you stand poised to jump all over any preceding lines. The reason that you are picking up your cues is because you are passionately desperate to get a word in edgewise!

This time, they FLING themselves into the scene. Even without movement, these lines get hurled sharply and passionately from one to the next, but despite their reckless abandon, the glitch moments from the last pass seem to have disappeared!

More importantly, the rest of the cast, who are now seeing the same scene for the third time tonight, are suddenly seeing and hearing the words in a new way, and are convulsing with laughter! And in that moment, it strikes me just what it is that works about this scene:

The four characters have four individual psychological threads that carry each one through this scene, and each contributes in a seemingly reckless, random fashion to the emotional interaction. In that sense, the scene is chaotic, with four people "flinging" their emotional selves in four different directions. Seen individually, the psychological threads make logical sense; seen together, it is a scene bursting apart in four separate directions.

And yet, within the chaos is perfect order. The wild emotional outbursts still manage to fall within the constraints of iambic pentameter, and hit their rhymes, again and again. In spite of the seemingly random idiosyncrasy of four different human beings, each in the midst of their own emotional explosions, the audience is still aware that these four have created a perfect balance… a vision of the world that is unified, and controlled, even though each piece of it seems to be askew and unconstrained. The contrast between those four very different visions of life creates a hilarious juxtaposition, and the laughter does not let up as the scene proceeds. It ends with a round of applause.

Imagine the three approaches to the following scene: once pausing, once picking up the cues, and once again with reckless abandonment, and you may begin to touch on the size of the vision that holds these four characters together.

The Bourgeois Gentleman was one of Molière's prose plays, so the imposition of verse into this scene is my particular invention, though each line, as it stands, is roughly the length of Molière's original. The action of the scene and the rapid exchange of lines as they are depicted here, are his invention.

Bourgeois Gentleman, Act III, Scene 9

LUCILE
Please listen.

CLEONTE
I will not.

NICOLE
Allow me tell ...

COIVELLE
I'm deaf to you.

LUCILE
Cleonte!

CLEONTE
Oh, no.

NICOLE
Covielle!

COIVELLE
No, no.

LUCILLE
Oh, stay!

CLEONTE
I won't.

NICOLE
Just wait.

COVIELLE
I'll not.

LUCILE
A moment --

CLEONTE
No.

NICOLE
A minute --

COVIELLE
Ha!

LUCILE
I've got
To tell --

CLEONTE
We're through.

NICOLE
One word.

COVIELLE
It's over now.
There are some things I simply can't allow.

LUCILE
Well, since you're so absorbed in this disease,
Go on, think what you like; do as you please.

NICOLE
Well, since you're in no mood now to excuse,
Go on, then, take it any way you choose.

CLEONTE (*Turning toward LUCILE.*)
All right then, let's hear why you were so rude.

LUCILE (*Walking away.*)
Not now. I am no longer in the mood.

COVIELLE (*Turning toward NICOLE.*)
All right, why don't you tell the reason for --

NICOLE (*Walking away.*)
No, I don't want to tell you any more.

CLEONTE
Just say ...

LUCILE
No, I'll shut up now.

COVIELLE
Just make clear --

NICOLE
Not one word.

CLEONTE
Please --

LUCILLE

Oh, no.

COVIELLE

I'd like to hear --

NICOLE

Good luck.

CLEONTE

I beg you --

LUCILE

Leave me.

COVIELLE

I implore --

NICOLE

Go on.

CLEONTE

Lucile!

LUCILE

No.

COVIELLE

My Nicole.

NICOLE

Not your.

CLEONTE

For Heaven's sake!

LUCILE

I won't.

COVIELLE

Speak.

NICOLE

Take a hike.

CLEONTE

Just reassure me --

LUCILLE

Nothing of the like.

COVIELLE

Just ease my mind --

NICOLE

I don't believe I will.

CLEONTE

I see. Well, since you will not ease this chill,
And scorn to give the least justification
Or to invest in slightest of persuasion,
Then look your last on he you've trifled of;
I go to end my life of grief and love.

COVIELLE

And where he goes I, too, will now be flowing.

LUCILE

Cleonte!

NICOLE

Covielle!

CLEONTE

Huh?

COVIELLE

What?

LUCILE

Where are you going?

CLEONTE

I told you where.

COVIELLE

We're going to our death.

LUCILE

You go to die, Cleonte?

CLEONTE

To still this breath,
Since that's the cruel wish that you express.

LUCILE

You think I want you dead?

CLEONTE

You do; oh yes.

Chapter 14

Shakespeare Class: Ripping a Page from Your Soul

We see characters offering up their bodies and their souls in Shakespeare on such a regular basis, that we forget that the offer has a very real, very passionate substance behind it.

Once in a while, I get to sit in on a class, and some of my theories suddenly find practical application. And I see where we get off track.

I watch a series of monologues.

And I am reminded of how Shakespeare looks on the page.

It can be an intimidating page. A single character speaking iambic pentameter which streams down one or two pages at a time without interruption. The class is doing monologues, so the first thing that confronts them is the structure of the verse and the enormity of the project.

We go into a Shakespeare monologue already knowing too much.

We go in knowing how long it is.

If it's an audition, for instance, we know we're going to talk for about two minutes, complete our "moment," say thank you and exit.

In the midst of life, we never know how long we are about to talk.

Foreknowledge of how long we are going to talk leads us toward predictability.

In reality, we could get cut off.

We could get struck by lightning.

We could get so pissed off, that we exit to challenge someone to a duel.

We could simply shrug our shoulders and give up.

But surprise! We keep talking! We manage, somehow, to complete a thought! And then, another surprise! We add a second thought to that initial thought that takes us to an entirely different place! A place that perhaps we did not even imagine! And then a third thought surprises us! And each thought may have its individual climax, but somewhere in the course of the speech (and this should not be too much of a surprise, given that we originally chose this speech for its dramatic value) Shakespeare gives us a word, or a phrase, that is dripping with passion.

And we have got to let that word *rip a page from our soul!*

My favorite film actor is actually Al Pacino.

I'm not "a fan," *per se*... I couldn't list more than half of the movies that he's appeared in. It's just that every time I see him work, I am conscious of his boldness, his presence and his evident background in stage work. He is animated. He is vocal. He is "over the top."

And in almost everything I've seen him do, he has a moment that "rips a page from his soul."

There is one example that you are probably familiar with, a popular movie of several years back. Pacino plays the blind former army officer in *Scent of a Woman*, who realizes that the boy who has been sent to look after him has gotten into trouble at his elite private school, which is now looking to get the boy expelled for refusing to rat out a fellow student. He accompanies the boy to a school assembly that is evidently a show trial, in which conviction is inevitable. Pacino's character finally gets up to speak in what we assume will be a pathetic argument against deaf ears.

And then comes the line...

Here's what, in typical screenplay typeface, it probably looked like:

"If I were the man I was five years ago, I'd take a flame-thrower to this place!"

But that's not what it *sounds* like. It *sounds* more like this:

"If I were the man I was five years ago, ***I'd*** take a

FLAME-THROWER ***to***

this place! ***"***

AN EXTENDED ASIDE

Most film actors would have recited this much more subtly. Their biggest dilemma would probably be whether or not to take a pause before the word "flame-thrower," to show just how important the *choice* of words is. Pacino let the entire sentence come roaring out of him. He was not "strategic" in his use of the words. But in the process, his character was "heard"... largely because **he would not let himself *not* be heard**.

Most importantly, he recognized the imagery of the sentence, and reflected that imagery in his delivery. The words came shooting out, much like the roaring flame of a flame-thrower. It was pure Shakespeare.

Looking at our Shakespearean monologues, they seem far removed from the performers, to the point that these characters get put "in a box." They seem to be narrowed versions of what is possible.

- While the actors' own speaking range may swing through a full octave and more, they seem to be limiting the character they are portraying to only two or three notes at their disposal.

- While physically they may be free and liberated and dancing and frisky, their Shakespearean character is burdened with two lead feet and a posture which allows nothing beyond a single, "characteristic" gesture.

The world of possibility narrows and narrows and the audience "gets" everything the actors are expressing about the character in the first moment of the monologue, and have no reason to pay attention any more.

The character has been trapped within a box inside of their minds, and there is nowhere that they can go.

Antony in Julius Caesar

Antony memorializes Caesar in one of the most splendid rhetorical flourishes ever written, all the while insisting that he is a terrible speaker. In fact, he suggests, "I shouldn't be here speaking at all, because I could never inflame your passions in any way but, well, if Brutus were here, Brutus, of course, would have you all *really pissed off!*" (My words, not Shakespeare's.) It is a magnificent rhetorical device, opening the door for Antony to say whatever he wants! Since Antony is beginning to quote the imagined Brutus' speech, he can allow himself to escape the imposition of censorship, by putting the words into someone else's mouth.

I observe the actor performing this monologue, and I miss the circumstances.

Who is he addressing?

"His fellow citizens."

Are the killers of Caesar still on stage?

"No, they are not. Brutus introduced Antony and left."

How free is he to speak his real mind?

"Not free at all. He has agreed to eulogize Caesar, but to hold the assassins blameless, and reports of any seditious speech will immediately rumor their way back to Brutus."

These specific factors give the speech its context and its dramatic tension. Very little needs to be done to actually establish this context. All the actor needs to do is to sense the danger of speaking an inadvertent word... the strategizing behind his deferential pose ("I'm just an ordinary plain speaker, but if Brutus were here…") in order to get these people onto the true path. And once that complex situation is vivid and important in Antony's mind, once the tension of each moment is underlined, we are ready to rip that page from the soul.

After an epic eight minutes of this deferential tap dancing, Antony has thoroughly laid the groundwork and is ready to cut loose with:

But were I Brutus,
And Brutus Antony, there were an Antony
Would ruffle up your spirits, and put a tongue

In every wound of Caesar, that should move
The stones of Rome to rise and mutiny."

Although it might not appear so at first glance, that final line is a page ripped from the soul. Through an outrageously, intricately winding back-door passage, Antony has traced and retraced his way into a safe rhetorical position within which he can now incite the passions of the crowd. And what does he say? He would put "a tongue in every wound of Caesar." That is to say that Caesar's multiple wounds would each scream for revenge, and those cries would be so passionate that not only would the people listening to this oratory take up arms, but the stones! The loyal stones that pave and line the beloved city would rise and mutiny! He is moving *the stones themselves* to action, treason and mutiny! And if the stones themselves are moved, what kind of action does that demand of the live human audience to Antony's speech? How can they possibly remain aloof?

And while Antony may still be tap-dancing through the early parts of this speech, marking time and allowing his audience to see the argument in this special frame he is positioning, narrowing, and tightening around the treason of the conspirators, by the time he gets to "move the stones of Rome to rise and mutiny," he has unleashed a furious beast. His peaceful rhetoric is cut loose with a cry so searing that it cannot be contained or described in 10-point font:

"...a **tongue**
In every ***wound*** of ***Caesar***, that should **MOVE**
The STONES of ROME to RISE AND ***MUTINY!"***

This is one of those lines that gives chills. Shakespeare sets the stage carefully, delicately, dancing with ideas, distracting with rhetoric, and in the blur of that confusion, a clarion call pierces the fog. And those of us in the presence of the actor performing it feel the hairs sticking up on the back of our arms. An extended speech leads to a single line, and the actor's physical and vocal commitment to the moment stirs a *physiological response* in our bodies! Even the present-day audience instinctively, impulsively, cries out with rage!

Leontes in A Winter's Tale

The king has convinced himself that his pregnant wife is having an affair with his best friend, leading him to the unthinkable question of whether the child she carries is even his own. In portrayal, the actor darkens, his face freezes into a grimace, his voice growls and mutters.

He has placed himself inside a box made entirely of his imagining.

How do I know this? I interview him.

I imagine that you probably have a best friend somewhere? Someone you trust ... someone who you might trust with your own life?

"Yeah ... yeah."

Okay, good. And perhaps you have, or have had someone that you've been very deeply in love with, who you care about more than anything?

"Yes, sure."

Okay, and I really don't intend to reach in too far here and do any damage, but I want you, just for the sake of this exercise, to put the two of them together in your mind.

"Okay."

So there they are, together, doing it behind your back.

"Yes."

Now I want you to talk for just a moment about the feeling that comes up on you as you imagine this. What's going on for you?

"Well, it hurts. I mean, how could they do that?"

Yes, yes ...

"I mean, there they are together, and I never imagined ..."

Okay, that's all we need. I just want you to hear what has just happened with your voice.

(*I begin to take on his inflection pattern*.) It's beginning to trail upward with your hurt and the impact that this destructive thought pattern has upon you. I mean, "How could they DO such a thing? This is horrible, dreadful! I can't BELIEVE they would ever betray me in this fashion." Listen to what's happening within you. Where the melody of your own speaking REALLY takes you, and let the character spring from the inspiration of your own natural instincts.

Don't impose obstacles on the character that are entirely of your own imagined creation. Maybe you think that he's older, or maybe you see that he's the king, and you assume, he's got to talk like this, and he's got to bear himself 'regally.' Maybe it's the very job description of 'king' that seems to demand a low baritone. But from the very essence of your own humanity, when you've been cut to the core of your very soul, there is a whimpering, helpless cry that begins to emerge in such a moment.

Leontes says:

> "Inch-thick, knee-deep, o'er head and ears a fork'd one!
> Go play, boy, play; thy mother plays, and I
> Play too, but so disgraced a part whose issue
> Will hiss me to my grave: contempt and clamour
> Will be my knell."

"Inch-thick" in *Hamlet*, at least, refers to a woman's make up as a metaphor for the depth of her falsity: Her make-up, painted onto the skull itself would need to be an inch thick to simulate a face. "Knee-deep, o'er head and ears," further suggest the depths of his wife's falseness, or even the woman in her grave. He may be describing a "fork'd", or lying, or devil's tongue, which is so outrageous that it reaches over those "head and ears." Or perhaps he is even describing the "forked" position of his wife's legs. Whatever the actor does to clarify this to himself, it is uncertain the audience will understand it in exactly the same way, but what is more important is that the actor has a clear vision of this image that is possesses his imagination.

But jump forward to the words "hiss," "grave," "contempt" and "clamour." Shakespeare never uses words like this by accident. We can hear the venomous snake in the "***hiss***." It is a sound anticipated by "***issue***." (If we paused after "issue" at the end of the line, we would never feel the connection between the two.) "Grave" is an open echo in stark opposition to the "hiss." "Contempt" squeezes and contorts the face while CLAMOUR[20] pries it wide open again.

In particular, "hiss" and "clamour" are descriptive of sounds, as is "knell." We cannot deliver them in an offhand manner, as if they were just words drawn from everyday speech. Shakespeare has provided us with the sheet music for a symphony. We need to learn to "read" the music in Shakespeare's verse, or else we are like a pianist plunking a concerto on a single key.

Joan of Arc from Henry VI, Part 1

Joan conjures spirits and asks them their aid in leading the French army to victory. The spirits are largely unresponsive. She offers them a sacrifice: "Take a limb from me." They decline. "Take my life," she offers. Still they are passive. "All right then, take my very soul."

In class, the actress conjures them with an air of mystery. Her voice adopts that spooky tremolo that we know is representative of the mysterious world of witchcraft. It is not horribly exaggerated, or child-like, but it is clearly influenced by what has been handed down to us over years of tales around the campfire.

But from Joan's point of view, there is no spooky mystery. She has her spirits that attend to her, and she simply talks to them. She bargains with them. They respond impulsively, impishly, peevishly. They refuse to do her bidding. She ups the ante, offering up a limb… no? …take my life… no? …well then take my very soul!

Caught up in the manner of delivery, the manufactured tremolo in the voice, the actress is not ready to honestly make this kind of an offer. She offers up a limb, offhand.[21] She puts her body on the table, as if she makes that kind of an offer on a daily basis, and her soul goes almost as easily.

We stop, and we look at the content. What is she *really* offering?

A limb? To be hacked off with violence, with all of the pain and screaming and horror and viscera and blood that will ensue?

---

[20] Shakespeare loves "clamour." (Petruchio in *Taming of the Shrew* recounts "And with the clamour kept her still awake.") It's a word which seems almost quaint to us. But it is battles and armor and guns and weaponry give us "clamour." Think of "noise" times a hundred.

[21] Sorry… couldn't resist.

Her body? Either to be sexually ravaged, or to be destroyed, perhaps in a fiery conflagration?!

And then her soul? In other words, to be damned to hell for all of eternity? Just speaking this last phrase aloud, I get chills down my back! Who could speak these things without a sense of the horror and the consequence?

Joan says:

> "I'll lop a member off and give it you
> In earnest of further benefit ...
> ... My body shall
> Pay recompense if you will grant my suit.
> Cannot my body nor blood-sacrifice
> Entreat you to your wonted furtherance?
> Then take my soul, my body, soul and all,
> Before that England give the French the foil."

Typography cannot capture Shakespeare's music. And Shakespeare never would have thought to copy down a stage direction which he might suggest to the actor directly, or which the actor would readily see, poised within the speech, ready to come screaming out. Otherwise we might never attempt a line like "Then take my soul, my body, soul and all" without twenty-point type and ten exclamation points to follow. In the midst of her desperation, and within the course of that single line, Joan offers her soul, hesitates and changes direction for the slightest instant, offering her body instead, and realizing that there is now no turning back, she renews the pledge of her soul, complete with everything else she has to offer. It is a moment of spiritual and emotional nakedness in the open field of battle.

It seems that we see characters offering up their bodies and their souls in Shakespeare on such a regular basis, that we forget that the offer has a very real, very visceral, horrible, passionate substance behind it.

A performer speaking these words with commitment, and a sense of the fullness of the intent, leaves us gasping, chilled, horrified, riveted.

Hermione from The Winter's Tale

Like Joan, another Shakespearean woman puts her body and her life on the line. A day after giving birth, her husband (Leontes from the scene discussed previously) has accused her publicly of infidelity. He has ripped the newborn baby from her arms, chastised and humiliated her. In shock and horror, the wife pleads, argues, cajoles and finally defies. What has she left to lose? All has been taken from her as the result of her husband's fantastical imagination.

In class, we find the performer rooted to the spot. Feet apart, burdened heavily. Likewise, her voice is burdened, stilted. She has assumed a "tone," a tone that is intended to show us how she feels. I ask what is going on.

Why isn't she moving?

"Well, she's just given birth," comes the answer.

"She's just had her baby, and she's in pain, and she's bleeding and can't move."

THE OBSTACLE: It is the obstacle that the actor is playing.

Up until this point, all of my theatrical instincts and every impulse of my directorial experience suggests activity that demands Hermione walking away and coming back. Throwing up her arms in despair, suggesting, "I give up; you've taken everything from me and I have nothing left, and talking to you is like banging my head against the wall" and then coming back to renew her attack in the confrontation, topping her own arguments again and again. And yet childbirth stops this conversation in its tracks.

But the more I think of it, the more rousing and powerful the monologue plays if the woman plays the objective *in spite of* the pain. Playing the obstacle leaves us in a space of no possibility. Playing the objective, even if it means that the actual amount of possible movement is extremely limited, will send our emotional responses off the charts![22] When every step is a searing pain, then that objective and that desire and passion must be overwhelmingly, amazingly powerful! Especially if that character continues to take one step after another!

Hermione says:

> "Sir, spare your threats...
> ...Now my liege,
> Tell me what blessings I have here alive,
> That I should fear to die? Therefore proceed.
> But yet hear this: mistake me not; no life,
> I prize it not a straw, but for mine honor..."

Following the outrage of "Tell me what blessings I have here alive, That I should fear to die?" the two-word sentence... "Therefore proceed" seems to disappear into the shadows. It is almost legalistic. But in those two simple words, Hermione throws aside any and all recourse to justice, and life itself. Without even an exclamation point to distinguish it, an actor may well breeze through these words as if they were blasé. But they are filled with the weight of a human being challenging death, accepting not only the possibility, but embracing the *likelihood* of death, because something else is more important!

In fact, the horrid acts of these past hours have eradicated any value to this life, and she says "I prize it not a straw." Saying this phrase, the face pinches, the nose flares, the lips tighten. And then, "But for mine honor ..." the face stretches, opens, gapes. The lips close with the beginning of the first three words, and gape open as each vowel escapes. An actor attempting to rush this phrase will lose the echoing fulfillment of what the character truly values.

---

[22] In his famous "tree exercise," Stanislavsky depicts a student in *An Actor Prepares* pretending to be a tree, but finding himself conscious only of the obstacles that a tree, with roots in the ground, might face. It wasn't until he contemplated the immediacy of a tree's objective in the face of fire, that the predicament of the tree stirred passion and life. In spite of ultimately impossible obstacles, our objectives drive us to action.

Well before this, "Sir, spare your threats," ignites this speech. Hermione then unleashis a 15-line tirade itemizing the wrongs done to her before concluding with "Therefore proceed." "Sir, spare your threats" cuts the air with sharp exclamation. It cleaves the empty, confused rhetoric of Leontes from the truthful response to follow. It cries out, "Do what you will!" And the word "threats" alone, is a sharp, sticking thrust in response. It has a *whip* hidden within it. It begs for italics, boldface and exclamation. An actor saying this line casually is again overlooking the musical notation screaming from Shakespeare's margins.

Try this line, at least once, with "Sir, spare your threats" as a howling cry, an anguished interruption, and see how *that* level of anguish gives fire to the remainder of the monologue. See if, in the process of setting the emotional bar way up there at the top, the rest of the monologue does not spill out passionately in pursuit.

Juliet in Romeo and Juliet

Juliet hears the news: "Tybalt is dead, and Romeo is banished." She then proceeds to lament upon the news, weighing the death of Romeo against every possible disaster that she might have preferred to happen. Tybalt's death is nothing in comparison. She might rather that the lives of her Father or Mother be taken, or even that they BOTH might be killed, than to lose Romeo to banishment.

It's a monologue about comparisons: Romeo vs. Tybalt, Mom and Dad's lives vs. Romeo's banishment. Again and again she props up imaginary comparisons, and Romeo being banished wins out every time. Shakespeare builds the comparisons magnificently, but the actress needs to be willing to let that word, "Romeo," rip from the very bowels of her being. Or else the comparisons come up hollow, and the monologue is just a nicely written rhetorical exercise.

Juliet says:

> "'Romeo is banished,' to speak that word,
> Is father, mother, Tybalt, Romeo, Juliet,
> All slain, all dead. 'Romeo is banished!'
> There is no end, no limit, measure, bound
> In that word's death; no words can that woe sound."

Notice all the commas. Each one pauses Juliet's momentum. Her breast heaves forward as her energy is arrested again and again, underlining her helplessness. At last she strings a series of words together, and Shakespeare gives Juliet the open vowels of "no words can that woe sound."

If you have held any doubt about just how conscious Shakespeare may have been about the *physiological effect* that his words have on the performers playing them, and on the audience hearing them, consider a moment the meaning of "No words can that woe sound.'

Shakespeare tips his hand. He is clearly conscious that the words themselves possess a special magic, resonating with emotion. Juliet is desperately seeking words to cry with the agony of her mourning (much as Shakespeare, himself, is seeking to supply them to her), and she finds words that do that, all the while scorning the inadequacy of these same words!

As desperately as Juliet, Shakespeare cared about the words that he chose to express a given moment. And while he certainly had incredible instincts about selecting one word over another, we realize that the choice of one word over another is a conscious effort on Shakespeare's part.

Once we fully accept this, we become responsible for transforming our very vision of what acting is all about. We are now detectives, seeking the forensic evidence of life, bubbling and bursting out from within the sounds.

Enobarbus in Antony & Cleopatra

Given my suggestions so far, one might expect a Shakespeare play to be filled with nothing but characters roaring out, howling, screaming and screeching their horrors and their revenges and their retributions and their fury, all the while offering up severed limbs and horrible death.

We've been working with a slightly misleading sample. What we've seen are speeches selected for performance as monologues. We find characters working out their feelings in their heart of hearts as they climb the rhetorical heights and confront blinding passions. The words that Shakespeare provides touch some primal contact within their souls that releases as a riveting howl of passion.

But here we find Enobarbus.

He describes Cleopatra's ship, the oars, the dock, the grandness of the bow, before proceeding to describe Cleopatra's beauty and the wonder of her retinue, fanning her as willing slaves. It is a monologue filled with wonder and amazement and sweet hunger. And the actor sits there in class and simply speaks the words, and we see the ship, the queen and the retinue.

The actor is using this as an exercise in stillness, and his lack of movement enables us to "see" everything he talks about. Only two notes strike false.

The speech is cinematic in its quality. We see the ship in a long shot, zooming closer and panning across the bow. The "camera" continues around and inside, where it examines the beauty of the Egyptian Queen in her splendor. We find ourselves so close to the Queen in our close-up, that we are then capable of turning outwards and examining what surrounds her, the slaves with their fans, gloriously cooling the famously hot. It is a moment of being inside and looking out, but the actor is still portraying himself on the outside, looking in, and cannot create the two lines of attendants on either side, as those attendants remain "out there" in front of him, and the wonderful "follow shot" is interrupted, complicating our efforts to comprehend. We can hear the words, and understand that he speaks of a glorious retinue, but we cannot feel the sense of it, because it remains at a distance.

Moreover, why is Enobarbus telling us this? They are dazzling words, eloquently spoken, but he still needs a reason. To whom does he speak?

"Caesar's men. His supporters."

And why is he going on like this?

"Well, they're confused. They don't understand why Antony has abandoned them to go off and play with this Egyptian Queen. I explain what they're not seeing."

That's what we've been missing. It's that ongoing feeling of "If you only knew," that drives this monologue from Enobarbus, and takes him from a passive admiration of all-things-Cleopatra, to an active expression of "No, no, just wait until you know, and then you'll change your minds!"

Enobarbus says:

> "The oars were silver,
> Which to the tune of flutes kept stroke, and made
> The water which they beat to follow faster,
> As amorous of their strokes ..."

And:

> "... on each side her
> Stood pretty dimpled boys, like smiling Cupids,
> With divers-color'd fans, whose wind did seem
> To glow the delicate cheeks which they did cool,
> And what they undid did."

The speech is a glorious juxtaposition of cause and effect. The water is not pushed back by the oars, but lovingly follows the oars that stroke it. The wind of the fans cools the cheeks of the queen, and yet makes them glow from the tenderness of their caress. And there in the final line, "And what they undid did," the speaking is a delicate caress of the lips, a tapping of the tongue against the upper palate.

Most modern actors would be too lazy in their speech to separate the two "d" sounds between "undid" and "did". But we need the entire word, "undid" laid out for our consideration, before it is contradicted with its opposite, revealed in the fullness of its juxtaposition.

Mark Antony in Antony & Cleopatra

Observing helplessly from shore, Antony sees his fleet surrender to Caesar's men. He is furious but helpless. In performance, the actor's body belies his voice, and his feet move as if with great weight, plodding and pacing. I suggest that the actor either remain riveted to the spot, or spring into action, but nothing in between.

Antony says:

> "My fleet hath yielded to the foe; and yonder
> They cast their caps up and carouse together
> Like friends long lost. Triple-turn'd whore! Tis thou
> Hast sold me to this novice; and my heart
> Makes only wars on thee. Bid them all fly; ..."

One cannot say "Triple-turn'd whore!" without making the mouth stretch and squeeze and pucker and squinch. By itself, it generates all of the anger and disgust the actor needs, just in the process of speaking. And again, "Bid them all fly" rips that same page from Antony's soul. (After all, he could have said "Bid them all run!" or "Bid them all flee!") "Fly," however, forces Antony's mouth into a wide, gaping cry. Couple that with the image of Antony's soldiers flying, and we have a moment that transcends small realism.

We tend to forget, reading Shakespeare, that these turns of phrase are even metaphors. We see the phrase "Bid them all fly," and we assume that was just the way they talked back then, and we lose the thrill of the moment. Especially when the line ends with a semi-colon, and there is more speech to follow.

Remember: Antony doesn't realize that there is more speech to follow, until after he lets "Bid them all fly" rip from his soul. Only then does he think to say:

> "For when I am revenged upon my charm,
> I have done all. Bid them all fly; begone."

We must forget how the speech ends, and live in the moment that the speech is "singing in" right now. While there may remain some energy, some anger, some bitter fury to this last couplet, there is an unmistakable break to the rhythm and a diminishment of passion. Antony's helplessness has caught up with him. It is only here that this sense of defeat has beaten him down.

Chapter 15

Shakespeare Class II: Essential Transaction, Balance of Power and Acting Choices

Every scene has a purpose, and in the course of it, some transaction will unfold, moving the action of the play forward.

Spending five weeks on an extended guest artist stay, I asked my director if I might do some scene-work with her Shakespeare class.

Choosing three different scenes, I played Prospero (from *The Tempest*) Angelo (*Measure for Measure*) and Iago (*Othello*).

The students divided up evenly, and we trimmed the scenes to counter imbalances of length, and also to keep the focus on the student-actors playing Ariel, Isabella, and Roderigo. Since Ariel might be interpreted as either male or female, all twelve of the students would have two scenes to choose between.

Digging in to work on three scenes simultaneously, I realize that, as different as these scenes are, the beginning phase demanded answers to the same three basic interpretive questions:

- **What is the essential transaction that this scene represents?** In every scene, while moving the action forward, some transaction will unfold. The easiest way to uncover the answer is to compare the beginning of the scene to the end. In the process of fulfilling this essential transaction, the purpose of the scene is fulfilled, whereby the play is driven forward.
- **What is the balance of power in this scene, and how and when does it shift?** All three of our scenes feature a confrontation which results in a change in status of one person over another. Some ultimate victory may be evident (as in *Tempest* and *Othello*), or this victory may yet await a subsequent confrontation (*Measure for Measure*), at which point this preliminary struggle for power will bring about a result. In each case, the relative position of each character alters in key ways. Our preparation, identifying and underlining these transitions will keep the play's action in the forefront, keeping the audience aware of the stakes and the stages of the struggle. It might be as simple as asking: "Do I win or lose this round?"

- **What and where are the acting choices that need to be made?** We can clearly identify options that represent forks in the road that our characters will encounter. Or, these might simply be moments where Shakespeare could effectively be interpreted several ways. We don't need to actually make those choices at this early stage; those will become more evident as we study the language in greater detail, dovetail our interpretations against our fellow actors, and put the work up on its feet.

Once these basic interpretive questions have been resolved, we begin to ask...

- **How might these choices manifest in the arrangement of the stage and blocking of the scene?** As we resolve balance-of-power questions, and study the transactions, some blocking choices will begin to suggest themselves. Much will be determined by our earliest commitments to basic choices as we arrange the stage. Simply putting one actor in a chair (*Measure*) will tip the balance of power, as it forces the standing actor to make the initial approach, further suggesting subservience.

These questions will surface in any scene. And thoroughly answering these questions should give actors a head start, long before engaging a director or scene designer, or independent of such collaborators.

The following three scenes should not be confused with Shakespeare's original text. I trimmed them strictly for the purpose of keeping the guest actor (myself) from entirely dominating the process. Interruptions in the iambic pentameter, and the occasional ellipsis (...) will suggest where some of Shakespeare's original has likely been clipped away.

THE TEMPEST: ACT I, SCENE 2
(PROSPERO/ARIEL)

ENTER ARIEL

ARIEL All hail, great master, grave sir, hail! I come
To answer thy best pleasure; be't to fly,
To swim, to dive into the fire, to ride
On the curl'd clouds. To thy strong bidding, task
Ariel and all his quality.

PROSPERO Hast thou, spirit,
Perform'd to point the tempest that I bade thee?

ARI To every article.
I boarded the King's ship; now on the beak,
Now in the waist, the deck, in every cabin,
I flam'd amazement. Sometime I'ld divide,
And burn in many places; on the topmast,
The yards and boresprit, would I flame distinctly,
Then meet and join. Jove's lightning, the precursors
O' th' dreadful thunder-claps, more momentary
And sight-outrunning were not; the fire and racks
Of sulphurous roaring the most mighty Neptune
Seem to besiege, and make his bold waves tremble,
Yea, his dread trident shake.

PROS My brave spirit!
Who was so firm, so constant, that this coil
Would not infect his reason?

ARI Not a soul
But felt a fever of the mad, and play'd
Some tricks of desperation. All but mariners
Plung'd in the foaming brine, and quit the vessel;
Then all afire with me, the King's son, Ferdinand,
With hair up-staring (then like reeds, not hair),
Was the first man that leapt; cried, "Hell is empty,
And all the devils are here."

PROS Why, that's my spirit!
But was not this nigh shore?

ARI Close by, my master.

PROS But are they, Ariel, safe?

ARI Not a hair perish'd;
On their sustaining garments not a blemish,
But fresher than before; and as thou badst me,
In troops I have dispers'd them 'bout the isle.
The King's son have I landed by himself,
Whom I left cooling of the air with sighs,
In an odd angle of the isle, and sitting,
His arms in this sad knot.

PROS Of the King's ship,

The mariners, say how thou hast dispos'd,
And all the rest o' th' fleet.
ARI Safely in harbor
Is the King's ship, in the deep nook, where once
Thou call'dst me up at midnight to fetch dew
From the still-vex'd Bermoothes, there she's hid;
The mariners all under hatches stowed,
Who, with a charm join'd to their suff'red labor,
I have left asleep; and for the rest o' th' fleet
(Which I dispers'd), they all have met again,
And are upon the Mediterranean float
Bound sadly home for Naples,
Supposing that they saw the King's ship wrack'd
And his great person perish.
PROS Ariel, thy charge
Exactly is perform'd; but there's more work.
What is the time o' th' day?
ARI Past the mid season.
PROS At least two glasses. The time 'twixt six and now
Must by us both be spent most preciously.
ARI Is there more toil? Since thou dost give me pains,
Let me remember the what thou hast promis'd,
Which is not yet perform'd me.
PROS How now? Moody?
What is't thou canst demand?
ARI My liberty.
PROS Before the time be out? No more!
ARI I prithee,
Remember I have done thee worthy service,
Told thee no lies, made thee no mistakings, serv'd
Without grudge or grumblings. Thou did promise
To bate me a full year.
PROS Dost thou forget
From what a torment I did free thee?
ARI No.
PROS Thou dost; and think'st it much to tread the ooze
Of the salt deep,
To run upon the sharp wind of the north,
To do me business in the veins o' th'earth
When it is bak'd with frost.
ARI I do not, sir.
PROS Thou liest, malignant thing! Hast thou forgot
The foul witch Sycorax, who with age and envy
Was grown into a hoop? Hast thou forgot her?
ARI No, sir.
PROS Thou hast. Where was she born?
Speak. Tell me.
ARI Sir, in Argier.
PROS Oh, was she so? I must
Once in a month recount what thou hast been,
Which thou forget'st. This damn'd witch Sycorax,
For mischiefs manifold, and sorceries terrible
To enter human hearing, from Argier
Thou know'st was banish'd; for one thing she did
They would not take her life. Is not this true?
ARI Ay, sir.
PRO This blue-ey'd hag was hither brought with child,
And here was left by th' sailors. Thou my slave,
As thou reports thyself, was then her servant,
And for thou wast a spirit too delicate
To act her earthy and abhorr'd commands,
She did confine thee,
Into a cloven pine, within which rift
Imprison'd, thou didst painfully remain
A dozen years; within which space she died,
And left thee there, where thou didst vent thy groans.
Then was this island
(Save for the son that she did litter here,
A freckled whelp, hag-born,) not honor'd with
A human shape.
ARI Yes – Caliban her son.
PROS He, that Caliban
Whom now I keep in service. Thou best know'st
What torment I did find thee in; thy groans
Did make wolves howl, and penetrate the breasts
Of ever-angry bears. It was a torment
To lay upon the damn'd.
It was mine art,
When I arrived and heard thee, that made gape
The pine, and let thee out.
ARI I thank thee master.
PROS If thou more murmur'st, I will rend an oak
And peg thee in his knotty entrails till
Thou hast howl'd away twelve winters.
ARI Pardon, master,
I will be correspondent to command
And do my spriting gently.
PROS Do so; and after two days
I will discharge thee.
ARI That's my noble master!
What shall I do? Say what? What shall I do?
PROS Go make thyself like a nymph o' th' sea; be
subject
To no sight but thine and mine, invisible
To every eyeball else. Go take this shape
And hither come in't. Go. Hence with diligence!
EXIT ARIEL.

What is the essential transaction that this scene represents?

Ariel enters excited and proud, demonstrating her[23] great efficiency, attention to detail, and dazzling success, while Prospero remains efficient and businesslike. He needs his questions answered and is not concerned with Ariel's moods. Ariel is disappointed, despite the fact that Prospero is clearly pleased with her work, he is

[23] I'll use "her" since three of the four variations of this scene featured a woman as Ariel. It may also help the reader distinguish Ariel from Prospero.

making no reference to the freedom she's been promised. She stands up to him, and he rises to her confrontation, dominating her utterly. She backs down, cowering, and promises obedience. Satisfied, Prospero relents and reveals his plans to set her free. The transaction is one in which Ariel fails in her demand for her freedom, and yet finds it promised to her, but only once she relinquishes the demand. While the beginning of the scene found her excited, the ending finds her thrilled. She has passed through the confrontation to find her liberty waiting at the other end. Prospero has moved from stern taskmaster to generous, if reluctant, benefactor.

What is the balance of power in this scene? How and when does it shift?

While Ariel has energy, Prospero has power. Ariel's considerable powers seem to rest in the control and manipulation of the elements: Earth, Wind, Water and Fire. She can do amazing things, but seemingly not to Prospero. Prospero's power lies dormant until summoned, and Ariel seems to forget the power that Prospero controls. Perhaps due to his usual benevolence, she has underestimated his willingness to assert himself, and thinks that he may well surrender it, now that this business with the King's ship has been executed.

Prospero has clearly not confided to Ariel his plans for the passengers of the ship, or the details of his scheme. He keeps his own counsel, and reveals only the piece that Ariel is responsible to execute at any given time. When Ariel confronts him, he chooses not to reveal more of his plans, but to dredge up the past, and throw Ariel off balance with the horrors of her past life, tormenting her with the fear that her rude assertiveness might face her with even greater horrors than those of her painful past. This peek at Prospero's great power is sufficient to make Ariel quickly crumble and grovel. His previous cold and businesslike attitude kept Ariel from imagining that her master might turn on her with the severity that she formerly endured at the hands of "the foul witch Sycorax." The disavowal of her angry assertiveness creates the space into which Prospero may now step, redeeming her with the promise of a freedom soon-to-come. The scene ends with Prospero barking orders, and Ariel thrilled at the opportunity to obey.

What and where are the acting choices that need to be made?

Ariel is a magical sprite. What does that mean in terms of her movement? She seemingly has special powers over Air, Water, Fire and Earth, but we see little or none of that on-stage. If I were a being with those kinds of powers, how might they manifest themselves in my movement? I might well look to any (or several) of these elements for inspiration. A "watery" Ariel might be like liquid, constantly moving, undulating. A "firey" Ariel might "flame" upwards, with sudden eruptions of energy. An "airy" Ariel might soar, floating, hovering, and only occasionally settling. An "earthy" Ariel might be more grounded, rooted, drinking substance from her "roots."

This last strikes me as the least likely interpretation, particularly given her hatred of the time she spent confined in the tree. She wants, rather, to fly, to undulate, to "flame amazement."

How does Prospero feel about Ariel? They've known each other for years. Most likely they've been constant companions, as she's done his bidding through the years. And yet, she knows little about his plans, and probably knows almost nothing about his history. At times the relationship seems fond, as he calls her "my tricksy spirit," while on other occasions he calls her his "slave." Is there no sense of caring or compassion when it comes to Ariel, or is this "tough love?" Is Ariel nothing more than a tool to him, or is he distracted by the fulfillment of his elaborate scheme, years in the making? Is Ariel a simple puppy where Prospero is concerned? What does that say about the anger that has possessed Prospero ever since his exile? We seem to want to think of Prospero as the "good guy," but has his fixation on revenge possessed and corrupted him?

Blocking choices:

We begin by giving Prospero a mound... a position of dominance upon which he may sit or stand. In class, we stack several of our "acting cubes" atop each other so that Prospero sits three to four feet above the stage level. The power that he commands will be felt from this position, and he needn't actually expend energy to maintain this power.

Meanwhile, as we establish our "rules," Ariel is free to move anywhere, except for Prospero's mound. Her abilities are expressed in her use of the space, which need not even be confined to the stage. She may move into and through the audience, she may dance across the stage itself.

Prospero begins staring off into the distance, over the heads of the audience. Presumably, the sea, the ship and the "tempest" have all been off in this direction, and Prospero is extending his powers to "see" the situation. While Ariel dances delightedly in celebration of her success, Prospero is only secondarily interested in the details. He continues to plan and to organize his thoughts. As he commends her service and prepares the next phase of the work, he rises and leaves the mound, walking downstage. Perhaps his abandonment of this position of power gives Ariel the confidence to confront him, requesting her freedom.

In response Prospero turns into a brick wall, impenetrable, gradually turning his full attention on Ariel, while she withers under his gaze. He circles and stalks as she freezes in her tracks. His voice rises and she responds to each sharply spat word as a new twist in the tree in which she imagines herself entwined. Prospero moves towards and away, attacking the now-rooted Ariel: dominating, twisting and crushing her from a variety of directions, until he finally draws away to assess his own handiwork and Ariel's penitence. Satisfied, he moves back toward his mound, forecasting Ariel's liberty, and releasing her from this brief psychological torment. Forgiven, Ariel springs back to life, dancing and fawning at her master's knee. She springs away, hesitates when he adds further instruction, springs away again, comes back once more, and is finally sent off decisively.

MEASURE FOR MEASURE, Act II, Scene 4 (ISABELLA, ANGELO)

Enter ISABELLA

ANGELO How now, fair maid?

ISABELLA I am come to know your pleasure.

ANG That you might know it, would much better please me
Than to demand what 'tis. Your brother cannot live.

ISAB Even so. Heaven keep your honor.

ANG Yet may he live a little while; and it may be
As long as you or I. Yet he must die.

ISAB Under your sentence?

ANG Yea.

ISAB When, I beseech you? That in his reprieve,

Longer or shorter, he may be so fitted
That his soul sicken not.
ANG Ha? Fie, these filthy vices! It were as good
To pardon him that hath from nature stol'n
A man already made, as to remit
Their saucy sweetness that do coin heaven's image
In stamps that are forbid...
ISAB 'Tis set down so in heaven, but not in earth.
ANG Say you so? Then I shall pose you quickly.
Which had you rather, that the most just law
Now took your brother's life, or, to redeem him,
Give up your body to such sweet uncleanness
As she that he hath stain'd?
ISAB Sir, believe this,
I had rather give my body than my soul.
ANG I talk not of your soul; our compell'd sins
Stand more for number than for accompt.
ISAB How say you?
ANG Answer to this:
I (now the voice of the recorded law)
Pronounce a sentence on your brother's life;
Might there not be a charity in sin
To save this brother's life?
ISAB Please you to do't,
I'll take it as a peril to my soul,
It is no sin at all, but charity.
ANG Pleas'd you to do't at peril of your soul,
Were equal poise of sin and charity.
ISAB That I do beg his life, if it be sin,
Heaven let me bear it! You granting of my suit,
If that be sin, I'll make it my morn-prayer
To have it added to the faults of mine,
And nothing of your answer.
ANG Nay, but hear me,
To be received plain, I'll speak more gross:
Your brother is to die.
ISAB So.
ANG And his offense is so, as it appears,
Accountant to the law upon that pain.
ISAB True.
ANG Admit no other way to save his life,
...That you, his sister,
Finding yourself desir'd of such a person,
Whose credit with the judge, or own great place,
Could fetch your brother from the manacles
Of the all-binding law; and that there were
No earthly mean to save him, but that either
You must lay down the treasures of your body
To this supposed, or else to let him suffer –
What would you do?
ISAB As much for my poor brother as myself:
That is, were I under the terms of death,
Th' impression of keen whips I'd wear as rubies,
And strip myself to death, as to a bed
That longing have been sick for, ere I'ld yield
My body up to shame.
ANG Then must your brother die.
ISAB And 'twere the cheaper way:
Better it were a brother died at once,
Than that a sister, by redeeming him,
Should die for ever.
ANG Were not you then as cruel as the sentence
That you have slander'd so?
ISAB Ignomy in ransom and free pardon
Are of two houses: lawful mercy
Is nothing kin to foul redemption.
ANG We are all frail.
ISAB Else let my brother die,
If not a fedary, but only he,
Owe and succeed thy weakness.
ANG Nay, women are frail too.
ISAB Ay, as the glasses where they view themselves,
Which are as easy broke as they make forms.
Women? Help heaven! Men their creation mar
In profiting by them. Nay, call us ten times frail,
For we are soft as our complexions are,
And credulous to false prints.
ANG I think it well;
And from this testimony of your own sex
...let me be bold.
I do arrest your words. Be that you are,
That is a woman; if you be more, you're none;
If you be one (as you are well express'd
By all external warrants), show it now,
By putting on the destin'd livery.
ISAB I have no tongue but one; gentle my lord,
Let me entreat you speak the former language.
ANG Plainly conceive, I love you.
ISAB My brother did love Juliet,
And you tell me that he shall die for't.
ANG He shall not, Isabel, if you give me love.
ISAB I know your virtue hath a license in't,
Which seems a little fouler than it is,
To pluck on others.
ANG Believe me, on mine honor,
My words express my purpose.
ISAB Ha? Little honor to be much believ'd,
And most pernicious purpose! Seeming, seeming!
I will proclaim thee, Angelo, look for't!
Sign me a present pardon for my brother,
Or with an outstretch'd throat I'll tell the world aloud
What man thou art.
ANG Who will believe thee, Isabel?
My unsoil'd name, th' austereness of my life,
My vouch against you, and my place i' th' state,
Will so your accusation overweigh,
That you shall stifle in your own report,
And smell of calumny. I have begun,
And now I give my sensual race the rein.
Fit thy consent to my sharp appetite,
Lay by all nicety and prolixious blushes
That banish what they sue for. Redeem thy brother
By yielding up thy body to my will,
Or else he must not only die the death,
But thy unkindness shall his death draw out
To ling'ring sufferance. Answer me tomorrow,
Or by the affection that now guides me most,

I'll prove a tyrant to him. As for you,
Say what you can: my false o'erweighs your true.
(*Exit.*)

ISAB To whom should I complain? Did I tell this,
Who would believe me? O perilous mouths,
That bear in them one and the self-same tongue,
Either of condemnation or approof,
Bidding the law make curtsy to their will,
Hooking both right and wrong to th' appetite,
To follow as it draws! I'll to my brother,
Though he hath fall'n by prompture of the blood,
Yet hath he in him such a mind of honor
That had he twenty heads to tender down
On twenty bloody blocks, he'ld yield them up,
Before his sister should her body stoop
To such abhorr'd pollution.
Then, Isabel, live chaste, and, brother, die;
More than our brother is our chastity.
I'll tell him yet of Angelo's request,
And fit his mind for death, for his soul's rest. (*Exit*)

What is the essential transaction that this scene represents?

The scene begins as Isabella, the petitioner, applies to the judge, Angelo, for her brother's pardon. The judge may accept or decline the petition, and immediately declines, but then proceeds to crack the door back open, one sliver at a time. There may be a way to save Claudio, but he will not speak it aloud. Nor is Isabella willing to jump to any conclusions. He is laying hints and suggestions in her path, barely acknowledging the abstract moral argument which Isabella presents in her literal response to his evasive allusions, engaged in his own struggles to hide his steamy desire. Gradually, Angelo's hints gain substance, until Isabella's understanding is unshielded and unavoidable. In the process, Angelo has exposed himself, vulnerable to potential humiliation. Isabella can easily say "no," (which she does), and may now threaten his position with public accusations.

Angelo, caught (figuratively) with his pants down, counters her threats with furious threats of his own. He will cover his actions at all cost, lying and denying any reports of this encounter, and will belabor Claudio's impending death into a long, slow torture unless she swallows her tongue and fulfills Angelo's demand, sacrificing her own body. He exits and Isabella invigorates her resolve, reassuring herself with thoughts of her brother, who, in his outrage over Angelo's horrible bargain, will surely support her decision.

What is the balance of power in this scene? How and when does it shift?

At the outset, Angelo seems to have all of the power, to grant or deny the petition. But his power has been quietly undercut by his lust. This struggle within himself keeps him from taking decisive action towards Claudio. As the scene proceeds, he puts more and more power into the hands of Isabella, while pretending disinterest and control, as if he was chasing some hypothetical bit of logic. Isabella senses that she has some greater influence than she imagined, and dances with the logic of Angelo's reasoning. Eventually, if she has not realized it previously, Angelo's desire for Isabella becomes evident in two unmistakable lines: "Show it now, by putting on the destined livery," and "Plainly conceive, I love you." With this last, Angelo has given the legitimate power formerly backed by the status of his office over into Isabella's hands.

He can no longer speak from a position of righteous authority, and when Isabella rises to seize the power that Angelo has momentarily released, Angelo *roars* back, dropping all pretense of moral standing, and challenging her from a bold, pragmatic, political position. His honored status and his unblemished record will make him the more credible voice in any dispute, as long as he is willing to lie his way out of it. As he reasserts the upper hand, he elevates the stakes: Isabella must sleep with him, not just to win the "carrot" of the release of her brother, but to avoid the "stick" of torture which her brother will endure as a result of her resistance. The truth of Angelo's power is self-evident, and Isabella, unwilling to forfeit herself sexually, sees her last remaining option as winning her brother over to an acceptance of death.

What and where are the acting choices that need to be made?
How has Angelo been impacted by this sudden wash of desire? Has he known love before? Is he lost, without his moorings, and thereby the more desperate as the scene opens? Or is he dealing with it calmly and strategically? What is the strict source of the desire? Is it in Isabella's face? Her body? Her words or her manner? Their shared Puritanical repressiveness? In other words, does the process of the scene, no matter how the conversation unravels between them, inflame his desire that much more? Is Isabella conscious of this? Is she manipulating that desire, either subconsciously or directly? Is she radiating any womanly enticement in her interaction with Angelo?

Or is this a desire that he can resist? Can he feign disinterest? Is it the very process of articulating his desire, which Isabella forces from him which makes his lust take on a life of its own? Does he, in fact, *speak it into existence*?

How does Isabella enter the scene? Is she defeated already? Has she a chip on her shoulder? Is she divided within herself, not even knowing if she has any right to argue on behalf of the sin that her brother has committed? Is it Angelo's insistence as he presses the suggestion of a sexual encounter that gives Isabella the reassurance and the balance that she needs to argue on behalf of her brother?

When does Isabella realize the implications of Angelo's suggestion? Does it strike her like a thunderbolt with "Show it now by putting on the destined livery?" Or does it grow throughout the scene as a budding suspicion? Is her unwillingness to understand Angelo an evasiveness that comes of instinct, or of cunning? Does she see him angling to transform his logic into action, and consciously tangle him in complex logical/moral arguments?

Struck with Isabella's threatened retaliation, just how wounded is Angelo? Do his threats stem from fear and humiliation, or from anger? Is Angelo, in fact, cruel?

Blocking choices:
We begin with Angelo in a chair. Perhaps it is the Duke's abandoned throne or just a seat of judgeship, but it gives him a "presence," which admits petitioners to approach, perhaps to kneel and kiss his ring, were he offered that respect. At the start, Angelo looks away, sorting his thoughts, dreading and hoping. As Isabella enters, he glances towards and looks away again, over the audience, fearful of what Isabella may read in his eyes. Isabella enters a few paces, inquires with her head respectfully lowered. Angelo pronounces his sentence, and Isabella heads slowly but deliberately for the door, before being stopped by Angelo.

As Angelo hints at another possibility, Isabella responds more vigorously, re-entering the room and kneeling at the side of Angelo's seat. She may or may not touch him. (If she does, it will send a shudder through Angelo's body, such is his tension.) Angelo finally meets her eyes, momentarily assuming the camaraderie of a fellow Puritan.

When Isabella does not immediately assume the tone of the pious prude, Angelo finds hope, and wedges his logic into that opening, rising and crossing downstage, looking away over the audience. He cannot meet her eyes, lest she realize his true motive, but all of his concentration remains behind, and over his shoulder. Waiting carefully in place, Isabella dodges a direct response, while Angelo impatiently presses the point, crossing away, and placing the sentencing of Claudio again, out over the heads of the audience, but turning back towards Isabella for the "charity in sin." She reframes that question as a challenge to Angelo, and he dodges away, circling above her.

Isabella remains in place, while Angelo traces narrowing half-circles upstage of her, working his way closer and closer to the point, and continuing to balance the depiction of Claudio and the "all-binding law" downstage, contrasted by the option he has begun to suggest, laid more directly in Isabella's arms.

As Isabella insists that she would not "yield her body up to shame," Angelo swallows his disappointment and returns to his seat of power. They trade lines from this position until Isabella acknowledges that women are, indeed, frail. Seizing on this, Angelo resumes, crossing upstage to Isabella's far side, rounding back towards her on "show it now, by putting on the destin'd livery." Isabella backs away with "Speak the former language," but Angelo steps in, grasping her by the elbows and confessing his love.

Isabella is horrified, pulling back and away from this grasp, but Angelo continues to step forward, bargaining and assuring. Finally Isabella stands her ground and responds. She faces Angelo down and threatens.

Humiliated and exposed, Angelo lashes out. Furiously, he stalks and circles, mocks, and spits his words. He may even grasp and press against her on "And now I give my sensual race the rein." As he realizes the vastness of his own power, he presses his strength one step further. While Isabella has turned away in her horror, Angelo steps up behind her, with his lips scant inches from her ear, tormenting: "Thy unkindness shall his death draw out to ling'ring sufferance." He draws back, straightens himself for a final shrug of defiance, and strides out confidently.

Alone and evicerated, Isabella has nowhere to turn. She talks at, but not to, the audience. She may take faltering steps in one direction or the other, but finds herself stymied in every move she might make. She grasps for the only support she knows: her brother. He will be her rock, her steady refuge from this torment. She begins to inch toward the exit, with growing confidence. Stopping for the final resolution: "Then, Isabella, live chaste, and, brother, die." She exits with what is left of her resolve.

OTHELLO, Act IV, Scene III
RODERIGO, IAGO

(*Enter RODERIGO*)
IAGO How now, Roderigo?
RODERIGO I do not find that thou deal'st justly with me.
IAGO What in the contrary?
ROD Every day thou daff'st me with some device, Iago, and rather, as it seems to me now, keep'st from me all conveniency than suppliest me with the least advantage of hope. I will indeed no longer endure it; nor am I yet persuaded to put up in peace what already I have foolishly suff'red.
IAGO Will you hear me, Roderigo?
ROD Faith, I have heard too much; for your words and performances are no kin together.
IAGO You charge me most unjustly.
ROD With nought but truth. I have wasted myself out of my means. The jewels you have had from me to deliver Desdemona would half have corrupted a votarist. You have told me she hath receiv'd them and return'd me expectations and comforts of sudden respect and acquaintance, but I find none.
IAGO Well, go to; very well.
ROD Very well! Go to! I cannot go to, man, nor 'tis not very well. By this hand, I think it is scurvy and begin to find myself fopp'd in it.
IAGO Very well.
ROD I tell you 'tis not very well. I will make myself known to Desdemona. If she will return me my jewels, I will give over my suit and repent my unlawful solicitation; if not, assure yourself I will seek satisfaction of you.
IAGO You have said now.
ROD Ay; and said nothing but what I protest intendment of doing.
IAGO Why, now I see there's mettle in thee, and even from this instant do build on thee a better opinion than ever before. Give me thy hand, Roderigo. Thou hast taken against me a most just exception; but yet I protest I have dealt most directly in thy affair.
ROD It hath not appear'd.
IAGO I grant indeed it hath not appear'd; and your suspicion is not without wit and judgment. But, Roderigo, if thou hast that in thee indeed, which I have greater reason to believe now than ever (I mean purpose, courage, and valor), this night show it. If thou the next night following enjoy not Desdemona, take me from this world with treachery and devise engines for my life.
ROD Well; what is it? Is it within reason and compass?
IAGO Sir, there is especial commission come from Venice to depute Cassio in Othello's place.
ROD Is that true? Why then Othello and Desdemona return again to Venice.
IAGO O no; he goes into Mauritania and taketh away with him the fair Desdemona, unless his abode be ling'red here by some accident; wherein none can be so determinate as the removing of Cassio.
ROD How do you mean, removing him?
IAGO Why, by making him uncapable of Othello's place; knocking out his brains.
ROD And that you would have me do?
IAGO Ay; if you dare do yourself a profit and a right. He sups to-night with a harlotry, and thither will I go to him – he knows not yet of his honorable fortune. ...If you will watch his going thence (which I will fashion to fall out between twelve and one), you may take him at your pleasure. I will be near to second your attempt, and he shall fall between us. Come, stand not amaz'd at it, but go along with me; I will show you such a necessity in his death that you shall think yourself bound to put it on him. It is now high supper-time, and the night grows to waste. About it.
ROD I will hear further reason for this.
IAGO And you shall be satisfied. (*Exeunt.*)

What is the essential transaction that this scene represents?

Iago is challenged by a series of problems, including difficulties with Cassio, Othello and Roderigo. He has been stringing Roderigo along for an extended period of time, receiving jewels and monies under the pretense that they were being passed along to Desdemona. Despite all evidence to the contrary, Iago has managed to fool Roderigo into the belief that Desdemona has responded to his overtures. Though previously content with Iago's promises of pending dalliances, this time Roderigo finally pushes back. Iago passively allows Roderigo to push, and is about to brush him aside when Roderigo threatens to go to Desdemona personally, and demand the return of his jewels.

Iago diverts Roderigo into a more pressing concern: Othello has been reassigned to Mauritania, and will take Desdemona along with him. With Cassio set to be propped up in his place, the only way to prevent Othello's reassignment and Desdemona's departure, is to kill Cassio. Roderigo insists that he "will hear more of this" and Iago reassures, "And you will be satisfied," perhaps in much the same way he has previously assured him of his eventual success with Desdemona. Thus, Roderigo is transformed from suspicious nemesis to willing patsy, while Iago brilliantly turns the off-balance confrontation into a strategy which will eventually solve all of his pending problems.

What is the balance of power in this scene, and how does it shift?

Roderigo begins the scene expending energy, which gives him the momentary illusion of power. He talks, touches, threatens and intimidates, and Iago lets Roderigo spill his reserve, barely taking notice. As long as Roderigo is only threatening Iago, Roderigo is no threat at all. With the insistence that he will go to Desdemona, Roderigo has grasped power away almost by accident. By this time, however, his anger spent, he has nothing left to press this point. Iago quickly steps in to fill the vacuum, redirecting Roderigo's energy to his advantage.

From Roderigo's point of view, his threatened solution would have destroyed any hope of a relationship with Desdemona. While Iago's alternative strategy is horrible, it will, at least, keep the hope of the love of Desdemona in play. Iago has recovered the real power of the scene, redirecting Roderigo's slight, often ineffectual power, into the support of Iago's own scheme.

What and where are the acting choices that need to be made?

The moment of meeting sets the tone. Has Roderigo been drinking? Has he been pacing? How angry, how physical or desperate is Roderigo? Has his pursuit of Desdemona left him tapped of finances? Is there a bill collector pressing him? Is Roderigo guarding Iago's door, waiting for his return? What kind of "old boy" relationship do Iago and Roderigo have? How do their meetings normally go, and what is the greeting that Iago is accustomed to receiving? Is Iago simply "blowing him off" with "Go to, very well." Or is there more of a threat behind it? ("If you do 'go to,' you will regret that choice." That is to say: "Just try it.")

When does Iago realize that he will actually need to take Roderigo seriously in this encounter? And, more importantly, when does Iago launch the scheme to kill Cassio, using (and eventually killing) Roderigo in the act? Iago may have decided it before the scene even began, but how amazingly devious might it make Iago, if we see him in the process of seeing the obstacle arise, improvising masterfully, instantly turning the situation into a plot of multiple layers of complexity. Can we see the "lightbulb" going off?

The key decision of this scene follows Iago's insistence of "Give me thy hand." Depending upon whatever energies Roderigo has brought to this moment, he may well refuse to take the hand, or he may hesitate, or leave his hand available for Iago to grasp, or he may even offer up his hand readily. The rest of the scene will unravel entirely based upon the actor's choice in this moment, with either mutual conspiracy, or unresolved distrust. Roderigo may be won over, or continue to resist.

The line, "By knocking out his brains," will speak volumes about the relationship between these two. Is Iago condescending? Mocking? Testing? Floating out the "trial balloon?" Coaxing? Teasing? Defying?

"And you shall be satisfied." How does this punctuate Iago's exit? Is this delivered with overwhelming energy? Forcefully? Overly sincere? Brusque? Putting off? Matter of fact? This moment frames the power shift observed in this scene.

Who is, in actuality, the larger character, physically? In a fair fight (in which Iago would be unlikely to engage), which of these two, would win? How much of Iago's victory is intimidation, and how much is pure cleverness?

Blocking choices:

Fresh from consoling Desdemona and ushering her inside, Iago wheels to find Roderigo waiting for him. Roderigo may be sitting, pacing, blocking the way, or drinking. Roderigo steps out to meet Iago before he can reach his own door. Iago stops, allowing Roderigo the space, putting up no defenses. Roderigo moves past him, pacing, doubling back, perhaps jabbing a finger in Iago's chest, or pointing defiantly at the ground. When Iago fails to put up the anticipated defense, Roderigo continues to move, leaving Iago with a clear exit to the door on "Go to; very well."

Roderigo stops Iago, and, receiving no satisfaction, stops him again. One variation of this scene found the actor playing Roderigo drawing a knife on "I will seek satisfaction of you," while another, larger actor went for Iago's throat in this same moment. Either way, the use of physical force or intimidation proves no use on Iago, who does not even bother to defend himself, but chooses instead to distract the dimwitted Roderigo with flattery.

Iago commends Roderigo, offering up his hand, which Roderigo may or may not take. If Roderigo takes the hand, then Iago knows that he has him under his control already. If Roderigo holds out, then Iago has greater work to do, continuing to give flattery to his wary companion. Either way, once Roderigo asks if the plot is "within reason and judgment," he is trapped within Iago's web.

From this point, Iago may move freely, swinging around to Roderigo's far side, placing the "special commission" out over the heads of the audience, where he will also depict the upcoming confrontation with Cassio.

Roderigo is stopped short with Iago's euphemism of "the removing of Cassio," and leans in for clarification. With a slight adjustment, Iago closes the distance to an intimate proximity, driving home the point, "By knocking out his brains." Roderigo draws back, taking it in. He might wish to see Cassio removed by some unnamed, other… but by his own hand?

"Ay; if you dare do yourself a profit and a right." Iago has appealed to Roderigo's courage and valor, the very qualities for which he commended Roderigo only moments before. But before he can think, Iago is in motion again, depicting the scene as it in front of them: There is Cassio, going to meet a whore, a schedule for the execution already set, and a backup plan with Iago seconding the attempt. Iago moves from one side to the other, dizzying and enveloping Roderigo in the process. (In the scene which found Roderigo drawing the knife, Iago, having disarmed him, here, places the knife back in his grasp, entrusting him to commit the deed, and thereby honoring him for his "purpose, courage and valor" with the unspoken message, "We can trust you with knives, now.")

Iago moves toward the door, encouraging Roderigo to come along, and Roderigo holds back for just a moment, demanding further detail and rationale. Iago promises to satisfy him, but offers no hard evidence, just at this moment. He exits, and Roderigo, pausing, follows. In the scene with the drunken Roderigo, he hesitates to reclaim his liquor bottle, before following Iago inside.

Your results will vary ...

Once these questions have been fully explored, we get to dive into the fun part.

Here we get to address the very specific, extremely detailed issues that come up with the particular scenes, the particular words, the characterizations, and the manner in which the transaction, the balance of power, and the acting choices are underlined, and sometimes exploded through the particular words that Shakespeare has provided.

As this exploration is unique with every play, as the questions raised are always different, and as the realizations and discoveries are as particular to my own background and inspiration as yours would be to you, dependent on the complexity and familiarity guiding our relationships with these individual plays, I have created these comments as a separate on-line appendix, available at **www.timmooneyrep.com/aatsol**, so that we might not be distracted from the "through line" of our discussion.

For some of you, this phase may be the heart of the matter, digging into the "meat" of these scenes in ways that reveal the ultimate goal toward which this work drives us. For some, it may take a lifetime of experience to envision this material with such specificity, detail or nuance. If so, continue on to the next chapter, and examine the appendix once you've got another year under your belt… or at some point that you have been cast in a classical play.

Chapter 16

A Date with Tartuffe

We assume that everything is to be found either on the surface of the text or in the dark caverns of our own personal histories, when bubbling there, just underneath literal meaning, lies a delicately layered web of suggestion and implication.

Molière's Tartuffe is a religious impostor and a hypocrite. He wins over the master of the house, Orgon, who offers him his daughter in marriage (even though he has already promised her to another). When Orgon is away, Tartuffe attempts to seduce the wife, Elmire, connives to get Orgon's son disinherited, steals Orgon's private papers, and claims Orgon's home for himself. In short, Orgon's blind devotion to Tartuffe destroys the family.

We're going to work with one of Tartuffe's speeches in which he attempts to seduce Elmire.

In spite of his pretensions to sanctity, Tartuffe is, at base, a sensualist, and his affection for Elmire is only one aspect of his hunger and lust. The very sensuality of speaking certain words aloud may give him pleasure, which can make this a fun exploration of vowels.

EXERCISE: "Mystery Date" (aka "Elimidate")

AN EXERCISE

We take four men from the class, and divide about forty lines of Tartuffe's speech between them. I enlist four female volunteers to whom the men deliver their portions of the speech. The women act as judges. Who is the most moving among the group? Who is the most *seductive*?

The four men form a line, shoulder-to-shoulder, and the four women sit opposite that line. I continue to talk to the class at large, while the actors look over the lines they are assigned.

It's a tough experiment, particularly as the actors are seeing the words for the first time. And yet, the women have no problem choosing the winner. They know who has hit upon the right note to stir their response.

Molière is a complex enough playwright to capture a bad man who may also be very attractive, and even Elmire, while choosing to remain faithful to her husband, may find herself strangely tempted amid this man's spell. Or not… but for today's exercise, we're going to assume that Tartuffe is a compellingly seductive character.

At the end of this scene, I'm going to once again hold my hand over each actor's head, and you all will vote with your applause. And while I'm here, standing with my back to them – so I am not talking about any particular one of them – let me mention that the result of this exercise almost always surprises me. It is, quite often, the dweebiest, most nebbishy looking guy who ends up having a rich reserve of passion, desire and seduction lurking somewhere within. When we audition in isolation, we tend to assume that it's always going to be the hunkiest-looking guy who wins the role, whereas in this scene, you can see other priorities rising to the surface.

Don't worry this time about rattling the lights, making ugly faces or spitting. I'd encourage you to focus on the vowels, and feel them vibrating your ribcage, and melting in and out of the consonants. Some of the most charged moments come from the desire to linger at great length on a vowel, but having to finally close it off into the consonant that concludes the word.

So! Enough time to look it over? Any pronunciation questions?

No? Anyone not sure about the rules?

(Suggestion of "rules" sends up a bright red flag.)

"Um... Are we allowed to move off of this line?"

Your objective is to seduce Elmire.

"Are we allowed to touch...?"

Your objective is to seduce Elmire.

What this exercise may ultimately tell us is a little something about casting and how we come off on stage. What I discover is that those who do least well on this experiment are the ones who feel the need to *add* character, or to maintain a quick pace through the speech.

Any lecture that I may give regarding rhythm or pausing has nothing to do with speed! As long as there is sound emerging from your mouth, there is action. You may choose to spend a full second teasing a vowel out from the back of your throat, the hollow of your chest, or somewhere significantly lower...

So, speak the speech. And work the relationship. Tartuffe has a clear goal, and every word can contribute to its accomplishment. I've provided a break to note when the baton is passed from one actor to the next, but treat it as if it was just one single speech that continues through four actors.

TARTUFFE, Act III, Scene 3 [24]
Let not that preference here incur your bias:
Amid the glow of charms that shine celestial,
I lose my modest hesitation, lest you'll
Discount my love as Christian charity.
My pious stance is mere posterity.
The world may paint me as a soul angelic
While I know that perception as mere relic.
What you've perceived in hot, prolonged gaze,
I manifest in humble, loving praise.
If this seems contradictory position,

Fix blame upon the object of my mission,
For no amount of earnest flagellation,
Could keep my keen desire from graduation.
Your love did spark my holy veneration
While weaker thoughts you drove to penetration.
If you might stoop to give your benediction,
Relieving me of manly predilection,
All day and night, I'd gladly sing your praise,
In thanks to God, for my remaining days.
A side note, with which you might be impressed:

In life's white lies you'll barely need invest.
Some other men, these days, are braggarts brash,
Who quickly turn their triumph into trash.
No sooner is a woman fondly known,
Than it's detailed, exaggerated, grown.
They do destroy the very love professed,
By laughing at the love that they once blessed.
Men like myself, however, breathe discretion,
And leave behind no whiff of an impression.
As my repute I value more than gold,

No tempting echo prompts me to make bold,
Enabling me to offer you, my sweet,
A saintly safety; rapture quite complete…
I know that good which on your soul is written
Would not condemn one so acutely smitten.
You know the reach of human limitation,
And might forgive a moment's violation.
But more than any other, know you this,
No human is immune to dreams of bliss.

[24] Full script available via www.playscripts.com.

Now, let's take the vote. Who won the contest of "Mystery Date?" What did they do to win it? Look at exactly what the contestants did or didn't do.

So often in the theatre, casting has nothing to do with the specifics of our acting choices. We aren't inside the heads of the auditors, so we can't see what they see. We can't quite see how self-evident character is, emerging of its own accord from somewhere deep inside the soul of the actor.

It may simply be that we don't realize that we can use more of our power in an audition setting. Or perhaps, out of discomfort with our own sensuality, we use our acting skills to throw a "character" between ourselves and the audience. The conversation that this exercise opens up will be an important jumping off point.

Look for the depth of meaning and implication in the speech. On how many levels is Tartuffe operating? Where is he daring to step just a little farther over the line? How conscious is he of the several suggestions that he can slide in behind the literal meaning? How prepared is he, at any given moment, to deny the suggestions that drip from the words? How far can he push that envelope? How distinct are the edges of that envelope in Tartuffe's mind at any given moment? How much can he get away with?

One of the problems of modern acting is that we assume that everything is to be found either on the surface of the text or in the dark caverns of our own personal histories, when bubbling there on the page, but just underneath literal meaning, lies a delicately layred web of suggestion and implication.

I started the exercise by lining four Tartuffes up along a line, and sitting four Elmires in four chairs about four feet away. Did the several Tartuffes leave the line, or hold back? Quite often, actors will remain at a distance, assuming that this, like our previous exercise, is more about vocal delivery.

Who told you that you had to stay on that side of the line?

"Well, you put us here."

What did I say that your objective was?

"To seduce Elmire."

So why did you stop yourself?

"So, are you saying that the actor needs to get physically intimate with his acting partner in the course of this monologue?"

No, I'm asking why you stopped yourself. You had the impulse to do something, but it was you who decided that there were rules stopping you. Realize when you do that! Notice where else you see that happening in your acting, or in life! You make decisions entirely against your character's desires because you imagine that some authority has told you that this is the way that it "should" be performed.

But now that you mention it, yes, sudden demonstrative physical intimacy is sometimes the biggest mistake: going for that big physical gesture, like climbing onto, or straddling Elmire's lap, which everybody laughs at in the moment that it happens. And yet it has no context in the course of an ongoing seduction, and leaves you with no place to go. You get the momentary laugh... and then we all feel just a little bit icky and uncomfortable and don't know where to look or what to think.

But the actor who successfully recognizes a borderline of propriety (and defines that borderline by attuning himself to the energy that he feels radiating back at him from his acting partner) and dances carefully across it and then back, and then across it again, pushing the envelope a little further each time, can keep us entranced with his every move, and every sound.

Some of the most sensually electrified encounters feature no touching whatsoever, but find Tartuffe hungrily breathing these lines into Elmire's ear. Proximity creates electricity and electricity can be... well, shocking.

Molière!

This speech tends to be quite an eye-opener. People had no idea that Molière was so modern. So immediate. So subversive. So lascivious.

Molière was the most modern of our classical playwrights. He put the circumstances of the world directly surrounding him to immediate use. Tartuffe was no mythical figure, set in some far away land. He probably lived and circulated among the audience of Molière's plays. The depiction of this character ignited a *firestorm* of controversy! When we produce Molière and limit ourselves to what we assume the past was like, we set ourselves on an ever-narrowing course, limiting our own expressiveness, until our vision of what is "acceptable" in a play by Molière is more constraining than liberating.

Between Molière and ourselves lies the great historical re-write of the Victorian Era. It was a time in which Shakespeare was "Bowdlerized," as his works were cleaned up by a dramatist who knew much better than we did, what was and was not "good for us." (This even included putting a happy ending onto *King Lear!*) With the passing of the Victorian Era, we were left with inaccurate assumptions about the early modern age, and assumptions from that era continue to live with us today. We have a notion that the people of the sixteenth or seventeenth century were somehow cold and formal and bloodless, or that they were somehow less wild, or enthusiastic, or ribald, or passionate… or subversive… than us.

A close reading of *Tartuffe* should put that notion to bed.

Part III

PLAYING FULLY

Chapter 17

They Were Just Like Us

Someone besides myself felt what it was like to be an outsider, to have dangerous opinions, to feel intense, immediate passion, to tell outrageous jokes, to be different, to take a risk, to challenge the odds, to care, passionately.

Why do we do classical theatre? Why is it so popular?

"Because the plays written back then were so good."

Yes, the plays that have *survived* this long are very good. But it is not that "plays were better back then." What we see is simply what has survived. Just like now, there was plenty of crap along with the good stuff. The good gets revived; the crap disappears.

"Because we like to see what life was like back then."

Is that what really motivates you to go to the theatre? Because that sounds more like a reason to go to a museum. People who feel that way may want to visit the Louvre, or the Tower of London, or to study paintings, or read history, or perform in Civil War reenactments, but they will not necessarily be excited about the theatre. In fact, if this is their reason for going, they will probably resent the theatre's intrusion into the realm of their interest.

The theatre is always a live transaction, an exchange between actor and the audience. The audience attends to see an action performed. In the transaction lives the aesthetic experience. Not in the words or the costumes or the settings, but in the way that these words or these characters stir a response within us. In his day, Molière was considered a heretic and a scoundrel. He was excoriated as "a devil not worthy of hanging." When we produce Molière today, do his plays stir this response at all?

No, today they are considered rather quaint, and cute, and clever and nice.

The Great Victorian Re-write still echoes today. It was a time when a table leg was supposed to be covered in order to prevent any lude or lusty thoughts that might be stirred lest that naked table leg reminds us of the naked leg of a woman! If Shakespeare seems more earthy and real to us than Molière does, it is partly because we English speakers have direct access to the texts published during Shakespeare's time, within which Shakespeare's meanings are unavoidable. Molière's works, passing to the English-speaking audience through a translator, only reveals the raw level of humanity that the translator acknowledges.

Also, when we imitate mannerisms, attitudes, behaviors and styles, we only capture the external manifestation of one side of what that transaction once was: the on-stage side of the transaction. Even if we were to capture that side of the transaction perfectly (as a museum might), we inevitably lose the transaction itself, because the audience has changed! Gradually, the work becomes distant from us as the people we observe are more and more *not-us*.

We aggravate this further when we limit our powers of expression to a handful of acceptable gestures, poses, inflections, and attitudes. Our historical study has taught us that these particular behaviors have legitimacy among the acceptable array of activities, and we imitate them almost exclusively. Quickly we begin to view these plays as distant, abstract, unimportant and irrelevant. We remain untouched by them. No wonder some people suppose that the point of watching classical theatre is to learn about history. They don't expect to look up on the stage and see themselves!

In general, there are three reasons for producing classical works:

- They are particularly good plays.
- To study history.
- To facilitate the discovery that *They Were Just Like Us*.

It would be hard to overemphasize the importance of this third reason.

We go to the theatre in the first place, to see *ourselves*. We may go to the movies to see car chases, or technological wizardry, but the impulse of going to see theatre is to gain a deeper understanding of and appreciation for our own humanity.

At the age of fifty, Shirley MacLaine continued to dance, still kicking her leg up higher than her head, executing dazzling, spectacular moves. She noted that, as she performs those moves, every individual within the audience can see themselves, amid their common humanity, dancing in her body. The world becomes a place in which those accomplishments are possible, well into middle age.

When I go to see Shakespeare, Molière, or Chekhov or Shaw, I want to know *myself* better. I want to know that thoughts that I am thinking, in this moment, were known and appreciated years before. I learn that someone besides myself felt what it was like to be an outsider, to have dangerous opinions, to feel intense, immediate passion, to tell outrageous jokes, to be different, to take a risk, to challenge the odds, to care, passionately. Suddenly, I realize that I actually fit in, somewhere in the vast pantheon of human history!

And yet, what does the actor, attempting to perform the work of one of these great playwrights immediately want to know?

How did they stand? How did they sit? How did they talk?

They look to take themselves away from themselves, and into the souls of imaginary people who never existed. No, not even the souls: into the external manifestations of those peoples' activities.

For thousands of years, people have had the same musculature as now, the same bone structure. They made themselves comfortable in the same way. Tight clothing constricted them. Furniture did battle with their posture. They longed to impress the opposite sex with rituals and performance techniques that seem arcane to us today. But the impulse, the desire, was the same.

Although we may need to adopt certain behaviors to capture the moment in time in which they were initially performed, the all-consuming thrust of our action needs to be personal to us, alive and real to *us*. The list of the things we *can* do needs to be longer than the list of what we *can't*. Any limitation that the time period imposes needs to be so incorporated into our existence that we no longer even consider it when we are caught up in the active pursuit of our desire.

We live in the clothes of the character. From one moment to the next we chase our desires, and strategize new tactics with every new wrinkle of the situation we face. Our shoes tell us how we need to stand. We let them, and the knickers, and the tights, and the coat, and the cravat, and the wig (or the corset and the bodice and the dress), do all that work for us. We may incorporate the knowledge of what was supposed to be proper posture at the time, but we must play around the edges of that, sometimes acting in *spite* of this, and eventually must ban the restrictions of such thoughts from our conscious thinking.

In real life we use every ounce of our abilities to pursue what it is that we want. We use every sliver of our wits to twist a phrase, to tell a joke, to conquer our foes, to win the girl (or boy), to challenge the status quo. And when we bring that breadth of life to a character, we enable an audience to discover that "Those people back then were just like us!"

This is the most important discovery an audience may make. They make it, not only in the classical theatre, but in every play that is ever performed, when an idea is expressed in an honest, meaningful way.

An audience, seeing the live performer, is reminded of the passions and the resonance of their own humanity. They are thrilled to know that they are not alone, and that the ideas that they have flirted with have been contemplated before, all around the world. And with this knowledge comes excitement, catharsis and connection to something larger than themselves, and a vision of their lives that is broader and all the more alive.

One of the most profound and touching responses that anyone has ever shared after seeing one of my plays was: "I'm normal!"

They were just like us.

Chapter 18

You Can't Play a Negative

*More often than not, actors are far more articulate about what they are **not** doing.*

We've all heard the old saying, "He wasn't playing to win; he was playing not to lose."

It's usually applied to an athlete who has been thrown onto the defensive, often protecting a lead, usually playing things too "safe."

Usually the result of "playing not to lose" is… to lose.

Stanislavsky has been over all of this ground before, and wrote at length about the importance of objectives to actors. He spent much of his energy encouraging active objectives as opposed to static "state-of-being" objectives. For instance, "I want to be angry" is rarely a person's actual objective. "I want to wring her neck" might be more likely, with anger being a probable side-effect.

But, far worse than state-of-being objectives, actors are far more articulate about what they are *not* doing, or what they are struggling ***to not do***.

What are you doing that for?

"Well, I don't want to be a bitch."

"Well, I don't want to come off like I don't care."

"Well, I don't want to get too big with it."

"Well, I don't want to get too big too soon."

"Well, I want to leave myself somewhere to go."

"Well, I don't want to get too close to him."

"Well, I don't want to just flail my arms without any good reason."

"Well, I don't see why she would do it that way."

"Well, my parents are going to see this show, and ..."

None of these are acceptable reasons to do a thing on stage. They are, in fact, all reasons for *not* doing a thing, and will lead us nowhere but into a safe zone, where nothing is in danger of happening on the stage.

Read that line twice. *"Nothing is in danger of happening on the stage."*

This is a life lesson too, as we cannot play a negative in life, either.

Or, well, we can, but we shouldn't expect anything to come of it.

"I want to avoid what happened with my last boyfriend."

"I don't want to get taken advantage of."

"I am not going to go through that again."

"I don't want to get my hopes up."

"I know better this time."

These are our fears and insecurities talking. And when we give the steering wheel to our fears, we end up never going anywhere.

This is also true of acting. But because acting is filled with choices, the impact is much more evident. Art, by its very nature, is filled with choices, selected from out of all of life. And we can choose safe objectives, or passive actions, or negative goals, or we can choose active, positive, risky actions. Which makes life dangerous, and makes acting dangerous, and makes it all very exciting to watch.

"I want to wring her neck" is one step better than "I want to be angry," which is several steps better than "I don't want to come off looking like a jerk."

But there are the more fundamental voice and body objectives that we are working on every time we get up to act. If I am an old man, getting angry at my son, am I concentrating on "I want to wring his neck?" Or am I thinking, "I want to act like I want to wring his neck?" Or am I thinking, "I want to sound old and feeble?"

In other words, "I want to seem *not*-strong, *not*-young, *not*-vigorous."

Which is the more exciting old man to watch? Certainly it is the one more focused on what he is trying to *do*, rather than the one who is concentrating on trying to *seem* a certain way.

Let's take another example. If I am a young man from the 17th century, falling in love, am I concentrating on "I want to stand in 5th position?" Or am I thinking, "I don't want to come off too modern?" Or am I thinking, "I want to hold my handkerchief very elegantly, and speak in mellifluous tones?" Or am I thinking, "I want to have that beautiful woman, now, now, now!"

Say I am the foppish rival to that young 17th century character. Am I thinking, "I want to seem effeminate and fey?" Or am I thinking, "I want to be as preposterous as I can be?" Or perhaps I am thinking, "I'd sure like to have that woman, too?" Or perhaps some additional agenda, such as, "I'd sure like to marry her and get all her money." (Or, "I'd like to have her brother…" or both.)

I hear all of the complaints already: "But I'm old; I'm not supposed to have the vigor of a 20-year old." Or, "but I'm from the 17th century; I can't come off too modern." Or, "But I'm a fop; aren't I supposed to be effeminate?"

There is a difference between an objective and a given circumstance.

There is a difference between an objective and second nature.

There is a difference between an objective and an obstacle.

If I am the old man, my *objective* is to wring that boy's neck. "Being old" is just the *circumstance* that I am given; it is not an objective that I am playing. It is my *second nature* to move slowly, but it is never my all-consuming objective to move slowly. I am restrained and slowed by my *obstacles*, the creaks in the joints, and the brittleness of the bones, and the thinning of the muscles. I am inhibited, but not stopped. I am still dangerous, if my *objective* is strong enough.

If I am the young man, my *objective* is to have that girl. My *given circumstance* is the seventeenth century setting. I am limited and inhibited by the clothing I am wearing, which I might practically rip the seams out of, even as it forces me into good posture almost as a *second nature*. I may be restrained by the *obstacles* of the expectations of society, or the circumstances of the situation, but my *objective* is no less important or immediate or all-consuming, even if it is only to win a single kiss, or a sidelong glance.

If I am the foppish rival, my *objective* is to get the money *and* the girl while I am at it. Perhaps I am also driven by a love of myself, and my desire to feed my ego, or to demonstrate my superiority in the process. Perhaps winning the girl will give me money and popularity in all kinds of ways that my rival, the hero, finds irrelevant. Perhaps I have lots of added incentives to having the girl, even though my *given circumstances* have me in outlandish clothing, and my *second nature* features light, animated gestures, and my *obstacles* include those secondary motives which I desperately struggle to hide from the girl.

But in none of these cases do I want to "not be too energetic," "not seem too modern" or "not come off too macho" (unless any of these "states-of-being" might threaten to reveal secrets that I am keeping from the girl or her family).

When I performed the Rosalind monologue from *As You Like It*, I struggled for a while, with my efforts to "play a woman." It wasn't until I realized that Rosalind, who is pretending to be a man at this point, gives no energy over to "trying to be woman-like," but is struggling in her efforts "to seem masculine," that I found how to play the scene. However masculine I, the performer, might already seem, it is *not masculine enough* from Rosalind's point of view! She must continually readjust herself, assuming poses, or lowering her voice to seem more masculine than she is. When I make that my point of focus, then the audience identifies with the character's desires, regardless of how "masculine" or "feminine" the actor may seem.

Which brings us to a crucial consideration about casting: The audience will ultimately suspend their disbelief about a self-evident "miscasting" – a woman playing a man, a small person playing a large, a black person playing someone white – as long as we, the performers, are willing to fully take that leap of faith ourselves, and immerse ourselves completely in the passionate concerns and desires that those characters would have in their given circumstances.

Even when the effort of playing the period has been entirely put behind us, audiences occasionally approach and note just how effectively we captured the manner and attitude and physical being of the period. "How very classical!" they note.

"Classical" is a leap that *their* minds make. Audiences embellish their observations of what we do with concepts, stories, motives and metaphors that never quite flicker across our own radar screen in the process of our work. Their minds fill in the pieces that don't quite connect. And, in fact, the better, the more detailed, textured and "true" the work that we do, the more the audience will supply an unbroken thread of reasoning explaining our choices, rationalizations that never once entered our minds, with "choices" that are entirely alien to us.

When people make discoveries and realizations such as this, by the way, never contradict them. It will only stir an absurd argument about the development of your character, or your intent as an artist. Perhaps the only easy response is, "Oh, you caught that? Good. I was hoping that was coming across."

People will also have negative reactions. "Don't do that with your hands! They would never do that!" And in response I could easily put all of my energy into ***not*** doing that with my hands. And the spark of life driving the character would be lost amid the self-consciousness of the actor.

"They" had bodies. Those bodies felt the same desires and discomforts that our bodies do. They may have trained their bodies to function efficiently in certain shoes and underwear, just as we do. Every ten years or so, fashion changes: Jeans, dresses, hemlines, underwear, accessories, shoes... For a while we hear a flurry of complaints about adjusting to the new fashion. A year or so later these conversations go quiet. Do we not still feel the same constrictions? A full range of motion resurfaces after a brief period of adjustment.

Human needs, desires and inclinations reassert themselves into a full range of motion once an obstacle shifts into a state-of-being.

This is the major reason that it is so important to rehearse in clothing, shoes and underclothing that approximates our characters' garb. We need to get beyond being victims to these restrictions in order to take control of our objectives once again.

To get ourselves back on the path of aggressively playing the affirmative objective.

Chapter 19

Objectives and Obstacles

If I then decide that I will never show these characteristics again, I am cutting off my expressiveness at the knees. I am too concerned with what I do not want to show, rather than what my character is fighting to the death to achieve.

Love your obstacles. Embrace their presence. Make them as big and obstructive and imposing as you can, and then fight them like hell. Don't avoid your obstacles to the point that you pretend that they're not there. And don't out-think your obstacles.

Don't decide that your character is too (choose one) pristine, reserved, gracious, wary, reasonable, just, kind, or friendly to put up a fight, or that your character is pretending to be any of these things to the point that the audience can no longer imagine what it is that you want in the first place.

Forget the fact you lose, if you lose. Fight for what you want, desperate to win.

As actors we must love the barriers that the play puts in our way. They give us an emotional life. When Shakespeare writes "To post with such dexterity to incestuous sheets," each of those consonants is an obstacle to the free flow of sound, and fighting our way past the obstacles of those consonants will give us emotion. When the scene designer puts furniture in our way, don't try to convince him or her to clear a path! Unless we absolutely have to make something happen in X number of seconds, the presence of that "obstacle course" will give us an emotional life. If our character has to gather a series of props, by all means, let us start with them scattered all over the stage so that we have to do some work to get them. It will give us interesting blocking, it will set us into motion, and into e-motion.

Imagine a fencer working to score a point on a target… or any two athletic teams in competition. The more furious the defense put up by the opposition, the more the emotion is heightened, the greater heights the performers must rise to, and the greater the excitement at seeing one or the other win.

Any one of us can come up with a million justifications to remain in stasis. We can find or create reasons why our character would never fight that hard for what he or she wants. We might actually convince our fellow actors around us that we are right. Intellectually, these things seem to make sense.

And then the audience comes and sees us perform, and maybe they get the intellectual nature of our character. And maybe they don't. But I would bet that they remain largely *unmoved.*

An audience moves. Between 8pm and 10pm they move from ignorance to understanding, from uncaring to involved, from distant to intimate, from unconcerned to opinionated.

They move because we move, too. Our movement is expressed in the action of the play. A play begins somewhere and ends somewhere else. We should be able to refine the expression of a play's action down to a single sentence, and every element of the play should contribute to (or reveal yet another facet of) that sentence. ("Hamlet struggles to take revenge in the face of unproven suspicions." "Orgon's blind belief in a swindler pretending to piety threatens the household's very existence.") The production should be complex and intriguing and probably elaborate, but even so, the many events of the play are, in some way, unified by a single overall thrust of action.

That action is generated out of the objectives of the characters. In every play, the question is brought up in the minds of the audience: "Will character X get what he or she wants?" That question is almost always posed in the opening scene of every play, and resolved for better or worse in the final scene of every play. This lives as what Stanislavsky called the "superobjective of the character" which, in turn, contributes to the "superobjective of the play."

Any time I see actors being secretive about their objectives, or being all too articulate about why they would never chase after their desire with such power, strength, abandon, or "ugliness," all of my alarm bells go off. I see the heart of the play eroding with every excuse or rationalization.

A Brief Off-Ramp Into Real Life

This is a lesson in life as well. Through a lifetime of experiences, we tend to "get burned," just like a child who has mistakenly placed a hand on a hot stove. Very early in life, we tend to learn not to put a hand on our great obstacle, the hot stove. And so, we stay away.

What if we took this childhood lesson, and stayed away from stoves the rest of our lives? What if we decided that we were very smart, and knew that stoves were evil, and that we would never use them again?

Well, then it would make the objective of "getting something hot to eat" much more complicated. Food would be bland and cold.

We do the same thing in more subtle ways... ways that are actually hidden from us. How many of us can recite an occasion in which we "got burned" in a relationship? What's important about that experience is not the actual "burning," but the particular decisions we made over the "meaning" of that event.

Here are a few likely conclusions we may reach in response to the obstacles facing "successful relationships," some of which may be entirely unconscious:

- "Relationships don't work."
- "People don't care."
- "Men/women are pigs/bitches."
- "People will take advantage of you."
- "You have to hold onto your emotions.

- "Watch out for people who are too attractive, too muscular, too Irish/Black/Jewish/etc."
- "I'm not good enough."
- "Don't get too close."
- "Don't sacrifice your heart."
- "Don't let your feelings show."

If we were to make the same decisions made with the stove, we would avoid relationships altogether, or avoid certain kinds of relationships. The "action" that we would play, would be one of *avoidance of conflict* instead of *pursuit of objectives*. We then proceed to invest in lengthy explanations of exactly why these avoidances are necessary and appropriate. Our rationalizations are epic, and could fill volumes.

And then we wonder why our relationships don't work.

We spend our lives chasing after negatives, investing all of our energy in what we want to NOT happen, rather than what we want to make happen.

We usually succeed in the action into which we *actually* invest our energy.

Since our objective was *to not have* a particular kind of relationship, that is the objective which will succeed again and again. We successfully walk away with nothing, time and again.

Yes, that "stove" may be hot, but if I can value it for something other than the pain it may inflict, and learn to interact productively with the seeming obstacle of heat, I open up a world of possibilities in the realm of food. In relationships, too, I may get burned, but it is only in the heat of those relationships, in the process of taking action, that I might open up possibility in the realm of love and affection.

The On-Ramp Back To The Theatre:

Likewise, with the actor who pursues a negative: He rationalizes a character who wants to *not* get hurt... to *not* get caught... to *not* be mean. He paints himself into a corner, until there is nothing left to *play*.

Or let's say that, beyond my character interpretation, in my career as a performer, I may once have been burned by a critic for being too: mean, haughty, ugly, snotty, exaggerated, gesture-laden, clownish, etc. If I then decide that I will never show these characteristics again, I am cutting my expressiveness off at the knees. I am too concerned with what I want to *not show*, rather than what my character is fighting to the death to achieve.

Choose active, positive objectives, and never give up, in spite of the fact that you may know that you are the bad guy. In spite of the fact that you did, actually, read the end of the play and know that you don't win… and that your objective never succeeds. Until you reach that moment, you aren't allowed to know that you lose!

Until somebody proves to you otherwise, fight with everything you've got.

Chapter 20

Stopping Myself: Hold me back!

"I've got just one request: Talk me out of it!"

I see actors stopping themselves.

The script says that I do not achieve my immediate objective.

I know that I don't actually get away with this.

And so, when I am not stopped…

I stop myself.

This plays out with varying degrees of absurdity.

Perhaps I am an energetic, forceful, powerful character who throws himself into every challenge with his energy up at the level of "10."

But perhaps my opposition puts up only a "5" or an "6."

Technically, it's not enough to stop me in my tracks.

But the script says that it does, in fact stop me.

So, I stop myself.

Even more absurd: My energetic, forceful, powerful self is met by ***no*** opposition. The other actor has not studied any of the lines that are not his!

But I still stop myself.

I may even have a line that absurdly challenges: "For the last time, will you let me by?"

The audience wonders just how it is that I am being stopped, and exactly when all of those previous times had been.

Somewhere, sometime, in the course of our long rehearsal exploration, my fellow actors must learn the consequences of not putting up enough resistance. And the easiest way of doing that (if they are incapable of imagining the amount of resistance necessary) is for me to follow through, achieving my objective.

"Hey! The script says you don't make it through the door!"

"The script suggests that you stop me."

As petty as this may seem, it is a sure-fire way to get fellow actors to give the resistance we need, presenting a legitimate obstacle. (In fact, on our next pass through this scene, we may find our fellow actors giving us a little something extra!) The good news is that such an obstacle will generate the necessary emotional stimulus for which the conflict is screaming out.

Actors tend to avoid conflict and wait for other actors to stop them, rather than playing their objectives, and making their acting partners do the necessary work.

We hear echoes of the Cowardly Lion in *The Wizard of Oz*: "I've got just one request: Talk me out of it!"

Getting away with Murder…[25]

We may reframe this same argument from a different point of view.

When the script says that I do get away with murder, then it is incumbent upon me to figure out just how extravagantly or outrageously I may be able to pull this off.

Too often, when the script says that I get away with murder, I underplay the spectacle of the thing, trying to make this murder as "realistic" as I might.

> Why are you being so quiet?
>
> *"I don't want him to catch me."*
>
> The script *already says* he doesn't catch you. What's theatrically effective about this moment is your bravado, and your willingness to *risk* getting caught against the outrageous odds that otherwise suggest that you *couldn't possibly* get away with this!
>
> What's theatrically effective is just how very, very, very *close* you come to getting caught, and yet, somehow, against all odds, make a narrow escape!

I'm not saying "Don't care about whether you're caught or not." But in the midst of trying to avoid getting caught, draw up a plan of action that will unwittingly bring you right to that edge, time and time again.

The audience will gasp with excitement or squeal with delight.

Any time your initial instinct is to think "But I could never get away with that!" then *that* is probably the exact thing you should *attempt* to get away with. Trust your director to tell you if it doesn't work for the scene.

Why not "get away with murder" in the most absurd, ridiculous, audacious way imaginable?

---

[25] When I say "murder" I do not mean literal murder, but more likely, *outrageous trickery*, a servant taking advantage of a master, a man flirting with a woman (a woman flirting with a man) or a scoundrel running rings around his victim.

Chapter 21

Emotional Inner Life: Playing the Opposite

Emotional states are involuntary, unless they are indulgent.

Another paradox of acting: We actors want the direct opposite of what the character wants.

While we, as actors, want to create the emotion that the characters are experiencing, my character wants to avoid that emotion at all costs.

My character is crying. My character *wants* the tears to dry up and leave him alone so he can get back to life as he had known it. I, as the actor, want the tears to flow freely, so that everyone will believe that I am experiencing the emotion.

My character is depressed. My character *wants* the depression to go away so he can get back to a happy life. I, as the actor, want the depression to take hold and envelop my being so that everyone will feel what my character is going through.

I am not speaking of neurotic characters who secretly love crying and depression and want more of it. Those people are actors within their own lives. But for now we are discussing the less complex human reactions.

"But what about the positive emotions?"

All right, give me an example.

"How about love?"

Excellent, how about love? What do people experience as their ***objective*** when their ***circumstance*** is that they are falling in love? Can any of us remember back that far?

I remember wanting to concentrate and get back to work. There I was, thinking of *her* all day long, when I had a million things to do!

And then there were those occasions where my love was unreciprocated. (Okay, most of the time.) Or even those many, many occasions where I was so certain that any expression of love would go unanswered that I did not even allow myself to indulge in the sentiment. It was not a happy feeling.

Or even when I allowed myself to indulge a little bit in the emotion, it was not a show of joy. I would pop a disc into the player and sing along to sad, sad, sad, miserable love songs. ("Every time we say goodbye, I die a little.") If I liked anything, it was the opportunity to indulge in my misery and to feel justified, self righteous, even triumphant in my right to do so!

Which tells me that when an actor plays "falling in love," and he gets some sort of happy, blissful smile upon his face, he has no real sense of what falling in love is.

Emotional states are involuntary, unless they are indulgent.

I may want to indulge myself in my depression, or my love, to try to amplify the emotion, but in fact, 95% of the time, I am being thrown involuntarily into a state of being over which I have no control, and as such, choose to resist.

In *Much Ado About Nothing*, Beatrice and Benedick have long adored each other, but have hidden that fact successfully over the years through insults and sarcasm. It is only when they discover that the other is supposedly secretly in love with them that they allow themselves to indulge their feelings.

But their, and our, first reaction to an emotion is to fight it.

"I'm sorry, I don't have time to be in love right now; thanks though!"

It is a law of physics

In order to maintain balance, every action is followed by an equal and opposite reaction. When the action is crying, my reaction is to tighten my lip, hold open my eyes, widen my nostrils, stiffen my jaw. Perhaps I paste an awkward smile on my face so that no one will know of my sadness.

When my action is laughter, I raise my hand over my mouth, duck my head, bite down on the insides of my cheeks, contract the muscles of the stomach, lift my eyebrows. I even turn down the sides of my mouth and look out from underneath my eyebrows, as if to hide my laughing eyes underneath them.

When I am upset, or angry, I try to diffuse it with uncomfortable jokes that no one else seems to find funny.

The danger is in playing the emotion directly. I would have to be a pretty simple character to simply smile when I am happy, and cry when I am sad. It is, in fact, the effort that I exert to *counter* that smile, or that cry, that reveals to the world just how powerfully the emotion is acting on me.

And more importantly, it gives me something to play.

If I get sad and cry… if I'm good at conjuring tears… then they come and I play the tears. There isn't much complexity and not much for an audience to follow.

If, however, I am not so good at bringing up the tears, but I spend every last ounce of energy that I have in trying to avoid the tears… trying to *stop* them from coming, then two things happen:

1) The audience has a lot more to follow. Suddenly there is action as an internal struggle rages within me. Rather than an "attitude" that may occupy my face for minutes at a time, an ongoing struggle plays its way across my face as conflicting impulses occupy it for fractions of a second.

2) I fool myself. As I put up the big fight, biting my lip, brushing away the

> tears, tensing my neck, holding back breath that is struggling to expel, and inhaling through my nose, before long the opposite will overwhelm me. I am filling myself with the action of "don't cry," and the crying will rush in upon me, if only to balance my system.

If I'm putting up such strong resistance to an action, my body jumps to the conclusion that the action itself must be incredibly powerful.

Let's look at anger.

Cognitively, I may well know you didn't mean me any harm. The more I work to convince myself of this, the more that the remainder of my being notices the struggle in the convincing. The more the struggle, the less truth to the explanation.

Think of someone who has done you harm. And come up with all of the reasons why you cannot be angry with them. Perhaps they are older, weaker or ignorant. Perhaps they give to charity, or support a family, or do wonderfully creative things in their spare time. I suspect that for every one reason you come up with to not be angry with them, your mind thinks up two more reasons why this reason is irrelevant.

You can't fool your mind, however much you may try.

And your emotions are your emotions are your emotions. However much we struggle against them, there they are. They hear your reasoning, and are always there, waiting, with a "yes, but…" The more you fight them, the more powerful and uncontrollable they become, even if your prevalent action is to deny that they even exist. How many times have we heard someone screaming "I'm not angry!"

We don't like for a force that is out of our control to take hold of us. If we get pushed, our tendency is to push back in the opposite direction. Even if that force is a pleasant one, our initial reaction is to resist. If we can only capture and play that initial reaction of resistance, we capture truth, or what exists as truth, onstage.

One more consideration: When we fight something, we give substance to that something. We make it "true," whether on stage or in life. We tend to resist a headache by tensing up our head, resisting any sudden disturbance to our aching brain. And yet it is the process of releasing the tension surrounding the head, allowing the headache to pound itself out, which will give us real relief.

What you resist persists.

In Driver's Ed we learn to respond to a skid by turning *into* the skid. We lose traction and turn into the direction of the slide, where our wheels can gain traction again and steer us out. It is in the process of steering *opposite* to the skid that we turn our wheels at a 90-degree angle to all of our momentum, which makes the situation worse.

Maintain the fight and you will, as a result, maintain the emotion. By engaging in the fight we give the emotion its reality.

Emotions aren't real.

There is no *thing* that is an emotion.

There is only a process going on within that stirs us in one direction or another. It is, in essence, a conversation that we have with ourselves. A conversation that says, "I must have her, and if I won't have her I will die…" "That's ridiculous, I can do quite well without her, thank you very much!…" "But look! Look at her! If I can't have that…!"

Emotions are constructs of a conversation within ourselves. We can dictate the terms of that conversation. Usually, we play victim to the outcome of that conversation. "I just love him, that's all! There's nothing that I can do about it!"

It is a conversation arguing over the truth of the matter. And as we argue, an essential truth is constructed. That is: that we are experiencing an emotion.

> Antipholus in *The Comedy of Errors* begins his big Act V speech to the king by saying, "My liege, I am advised what I say; neither disturbed by the effect of wine, or heady rash provoked with raging ire…" and then proceeds to seem really disturbed and provoked! In performance, the more that I struggle to hide my ire and my disturbance, the more furiously it spills out from me, and the more outrageously funny the monologue becomes!

How do we lose an emotion? Really lose an emotion? When we actually want to stop having it, or to have something else as our emotion?

We make something else more important.

Emotions occur because we have made something very, very important in our lives. And when it moves, we move. We struggle to resist, or we struggle to get. But put another object in its place, something else to absorb our attention and our being, and emotions surrounding the first thing go away. Maybe not immediately, but eventually, acting in accordance with the more highly valued importance of this other thing, we set the first thing aside and move on.

When we see the conversation in our head as something that we can choose, then we can choose new conversations. Eventually, we mourn the dead, absorb the loss, and start again. Some mourn the loss of a loved one for the rest of their life. That's the conversation they choose. Because they feel it's a conversation they ought to be having. They insist that it is not a choice at all.

Emotions are involuntary.

Actions aimed at fighting or denying emotions define them and give them weight and seeming reality. This is the physical manifestation of an inner conversation. And the more resistance we offer up against the emotion, the longer that emotion will stay with us.

But releasing our resistance, putting another object of greater importance in front of ourselves, initiating a new conversation, changes the emotion.

Some of that is a lesson in acting.

And some of that is a lesson in life.

Chapter 22

Being Ugly

The more important and compelling and heartfelt this objective is, the more gripping your audition piece will be.

Keeping in mind that we tend to focus more on what we don't want in life, than on what we want, here's an actual exchange between myself and a student who was working on our favorite scene from *The Misanthrope*, the one we used for our "Jerry Springer Show" exercise.[26] (The identity has been removed to protect the author; the e-mails have been edited for spelling only.)

Date: Saturday, March 19, 2008 7:05 PM
Subject: Thanks!
Dear Tim,

Thank you so much for the copy of The Misanthrope. It is a different translation than the one I had previously looked at, by Richard Wilbur, but it was very helpful. I am currently using a monologue in it for one of my acting classes. I am playing Arsinoe in her opening speech to Celimene in Act Three, Scene Four. So far as a monologue in the sense that it is an audition piece it has not fared me well. You're most likely extremely busy so I'll try and keep this short. I keep getting told that I'm being too nice and sincere and I should practically contort my face in order to let my character's ugly intention out in the open.

I have always felt that I should resist the temptation to adopt a haughty demeanor and a disapproving tone, looking down my nose at Celimene and heaping disdain for her loose ways. Clearly Arsinoe uses her "piety" both as an explanation of her character and her failure to attract a man and tearing down women who are more successful. There is no question that she is envious, spiteful, malicious. Nobody could possibly disagree. Except perhaps Arsinoe. I feel that for my practical purposes in playing the role, what matters is not what she believes, but what she wants others to believe. Certainly she wants to make it appear, at least that her behavior toward Celimene is reasonable and just, even kind and friendly. My goal, in approaching the text this way, assuming that Celimene would not doubt for a moment, the contrast between what Arsinoe is and what she would like to appear to be would be quite funny,

---

[26] Page 18.

perhaps even touching. I have been told nothing by acting coaches but "Meaner! Snobbier! Haughtier! Not so Pretty!" My question to you is, how would you cast this role? Would the severity of Arsinoe's looks and the "language" of a stylized play be allowed to obscure content? I may be the last person on earth who should play Arsinoe and really need another point of view. I realize this is a lengthy letter and all but a small paragraph would be sufficient. Thanks again for sending me the play.
Sincerely,
[An Actor]

Subject: Re: Thanks!
Date: Sun, 20 Mar 2008 21:18:36 -0600
Dear [Actor],

Thanks for your note. I don't know how much I have to respond with, but perhaps my initial impulse will give you something relevant.

It's impossible for me to tell you whether you are doing too much of this, or too little of that without having seen what you are doing. But as the saying goes, if three people tell you you're dead, you'd better lie down.

Which is not to say that they're right and you're wrong, so much as that when people are trying to tell you something, it's better to try to learn from their observation, taking it purely as an observation, and not necessarily something that is right or wrong.

The crux, for me, always comes back to the strength of the objective, and what I am hearing from you is that you aren't playing it full out, or that you are letting the obstacle, that is, “not wanting to get caught misleading Celimene,” temper your objective too heavily.

Since you are doing this as an audition monologue, people don't have the benefit of seeing the scene in context, to see you work Celimene and hide your intent. Certainly, if Celimene was on stage with you, you would be able to take little moments to let your underlying intent come out, such as any time she had her back turned. Instead, you're putting yourself under Celimene's imaginary scrutiny throughout, and the audience to your audition cannot get the full story in context. Instead, they simply see a saintly woman, which is certainly not what Arsinoe is.

What I hear you saying is what you DON'T want to play in your monologue. I'm really not hearing about what you ARE playing. You need an objective that is going to put you strongly into action. Action being what acting and theatre is all about. And in an audition, I want to see you fighting for something desperately. Because, as the director, I want to know that you will breathe life and excitement and determination and power into every moment that you are on stage, regardless what character I happen to cast you as. I don't need an essay on why this is "all wrong" for your character, mostly because I will fear that when you come to your next character, the one that I am considering you for, you will find a way to make complete commitment to an objective be all wrong for that character too. And then where will I be?

Notice, I'm not telling you to make faces, sneer, be mean, ugly, snotty, haughty, etc. In and of themselves, those would be bad choices, too.

I'm saying that you've got to wade in with both feet and fight to the death to win, and care whether you win or not.

And what is it she wants to win? She hasn't gone to all of this trouble just to seem nice to Celimene. She's got something at stake. What is it? The more important and compelling and heartfelt this objective is, the more gripping your audition piece will be.

Yours truly,
Tim

Dear Tim,

Wow! I didn't expect such a detailed thoughtful response! I am very grateful. You were right about my objective being overshadowed by my obstacle to the point where it wasn't very clear to the audience. I had thought that I would be compromising my objective when all I needed to do was embrace it. I had also forgotten that Molière has a sense of humor and that by letting the comedy of the scene happen I was already adding clarity of intent as well as color. I performed the monologue again in class on Thursday with your wonderful advice in mind and was astonished when my professor applauded and said, "Now that's ugly." I see now what he meant. For the first time I felt like I had come across as ugly without trying. Just by making a commitment to my objective. Thanks again for all of your help. Have a pleasant week.

Sincerely,
[An Actor]

(Professors everywhere are reading this exchange and wishing it was all just this simple.)

Chapter 23

Being Cool

We are living out the lie of what we think somebody probably wants.

I work with undergraduate actors on a scene from *Tartuffe*, and it all floods back.

It is more important to *BE COOL* than to *ACT WELL.*

This may be the second most important lesson in this book, following "Being seen and being heard." It reflects a disease that is almost as pervasive.

In sharing my response with these actors, I note how unimpassioned the performances seem. I express to them the *desire* of the characters. I point out just how their *passion* underlines the thematic motif, and sends the comic by-play *spiraling* through the stratosphere. I express the highs and lows, the roller-coaster changes that the characters roll through in the course of the scene. Two lovers, Valere and Mariane, *desperate* for each others' love, and *convinced* that the other has betrayed them, *fly* and *fall* on a moment-by-moment test, examining each syllable for evidence of their partner's disloyalty! [27]

The actors listen, seem interested, encouraged, amused, cognizant, even delighted.

And then they repeat the same thing that they just did.

The same thing. No noticeable change.

As I speak, they may demonstrate to me that they care. They listen, they nod, they smile, they understand (no one wants to be caught not understanding). They will accept that, yes, that *would be the way* that one would portray that scene.

And then they will repeat exactly what they did before.

Passion takes risk.

Risk makes drama.

And time and time again, I have seen actors much more influenced by peer pressure than they are by the desire to perform well. I was probably one of those actors once myself.

Perhaps they think they are committing to the scene. Maybe they think they are expressing great passions. And perhaps they have simply memorized a single "line reading," and cannot inflect any other way.

---

[27] See Chapter 13 (pp. 76-77) for an example of a very similar scene from *Bourgeois Gentleman.*

But I cannot help but look around them, and see the disease carried equally among their scene partners and classmates. And I realize that *sticking out* in this environment is considered a bad thing. You want, amid the chemistry that balances this particular class, to hit the agreed-upon norm for emotional expression.

In short, you want to look cool.

Because, really, who wants to make a fool out of himself, playing up to the acting teacher? The judges who count are our peers! Those are the people who decide everything that matters: Will I be popular? Will I get lucky? Will I get lucky with the right people? How can my response to a teacher ever supplant that priority?

Somehow, if an actor is to succeed, he or she must be willing to jettison any hope for socio-sexual appeal, and make this moment, on stage, more important.

If we can be true to this, if we can sacrifice our desirability or popularity quotient on the altar of our art, then we may become much more successful much more quickly.

Someday, someone will see us, spilling our guts out on stage for all that we are worth. And he or she or they will decide that they kind of like those guts. And think that we are, come to think of it, rather worth the effort. And we will be much happier with that person or those friends, because they will have accepted and loved us for who we are, even in the throes of our terrifying self-expression.

Otherwise we are living out the lie of what we think somebody probably wants.

Stop being cool.

Chapter 24

Top Ten Bad Body Habits

We "use ourselves" as a starting point, and, mostly as a finishing point.

Just to gather these thoughts in one place for a moment… if I were to make a list of the top 10 things that we, as actors, do physically, that drive me, as a director crazy…

10. We hide behind the furniture, and don't use the vast realm of space that the designer has provided.

9. We try to hide parts of our bodies with which we are uncomfortable.

8. We take the "stage turn" that our High School Theatre Director taught us, which forces us to walk sideways and backwards.

7. Our mouth moves with energy while our feet shuffle and wander (a wandering that continues, even when someone else is speaking).

6. When forced to stand still to deliver a line, our energy comes out in other odd places, like our shoulders or even our fingertips.

5. Our energy for gestures seems to start in the fingertips, and the hands fidget with each other.

4. Our right hand moves exactly parallel to the left hand.

3. We hunch forward, lumber side-to-side, and hide behind our hair, minimizing our availability to the audience.

2. Our hands are in our pockets, or our arms are crossed, reassuring the audience that nothing physical is going to happen on stage, and they can relax, and not pay so much attention.

1. We "use ourselves" as a starting point… and, mostly, as a finishing point.

Chapter 25

Using Ourselves

We need a ticket out of ourselves. Our bodies are being frozen inside the framework of what we assume we can do or not do.

How many of you have performed in a show that was, at some point or another, videotaped?

(All hands go up.)

How many of you watched that videotape and felt really great about your performance? Particularly, how effectively you were able to embody the character physically?

(No hands go up.)

How many times have we seen ourselves performing on video and felt largely disappointed. "I thought I was being so different with this character! I thought it was in my bones, taking me over. But that's just... me... on stage. With my same shoulder slump, my same shuffling walk! I wanted something vivid, but I'm just as drab as ever, and I never really realized just how bland my body was!"

We live our lives in close-up, but the theatre is played out in a long shot.

From the inside, looking out, we feel the character in every breath, every twitch of the eye. From the outside, looking in, the audience sees our silhouette, feels our rhythm, notices our weight, assesses our patterns.

We think that our being has assumed the character, but find that the being that we already are is dominating the message, sending out nine messages about *us* for every one message about *character*.

"Yes, but I'm *using* myself in this character!"

First and foremost you are responsible to a set of messages from a playwright, which need to resonate through your body and find life in your motion. You have refined your *verbal* expression to the point that you have captured the words and the consonants and the vowels as the playwright provided them, and they are getting heard… but now you are distracting from that message with every movement you make. Or, more likely: with every movement you stop yourself from making.

When we "use ourselves" as our single point of reference…

- every gesture, posture, movement or attitude is guilty until proven innocent.

- every time we feel the impulse to do something we ask: "Would ***I*** really do this in this situation?" The answer is usually "no"… even though we were the ones who felt the impulse in the first place!
- we usually mean "ourselves" on a very quiet, contemplative day, the kind of day we have time to notice things like our mood.
- we usually mean we'll be using a tiny fraction of ourselves… the part of which we approve.
- we usually mean that we will eliminate all of the possible behaviors that we have not employed on previous occasions.
- we identify our characters AS ourselves and then we proceed to argue on behalf of our characters' *limitations*, arguing for all of the things that our character WON'T do.
- we are defining ourselves as separate from all of the potential behaviors that we determine to be "not me" and isolating ourselves into the context of an ever-narrowing box.
- we take our own personality and then proceed to *subtract* all of those characteristics that we assume do not apply to the character we are supposed to be playing, thereby losing 90% of the range of expressiveness that a human being naturally has.
- we assume that characters never contradict themselves.

Get out of yourself. Get beyond yourself. Elevate your game.

We need a ticket out of ourselves. Our bodies are being frozen inside the framework of what we assume we can do or cannot do, or what believable movement looks like. We are so focused on what we are not allowed to get away with, given the dictates of so-called realism, that our characters are crushed within a tightening frame of what is or is not acceptable. When we learn period movement, when we adopt the limitations of age, when we adopt particular characteristics, we place all of our concentration on *what we can no longer do*, rather than on what our character is *aching* to do.

We need a different paradigm: "How much can we *get away with*?"

Let us crack open a door to that question by taking ourselves *out* of ourselves. Let us find cracked doors that we may proceed to kick wide open to discover a vision of our character that we did *not* anticipate, and feel the rush of inspiration as a new way of moving washes over us, bringing with it unexpected emotion and insight.

The audience will choose to believe what we act in accordance with, and if we support this action with an internal belief, assumption or assertion, and activity consistent with the notion that this is, indeed, the truth of the matter, the audience will go right along, perhaps being just as surprised as we are at our sudden belief.

No matter how weak or underdeveloped I happen to be, physically, I have the ability to make you, the audience, believe that I am physically dangerous, and could physically intimidate someone much larger than I am. It lives in how I carry myself.

To give the (sexist) corollary, a woman, whatever her condition, can likewise, present herself as more attractive than another woman on stage, no matter how beautiful we perceive that the other woman to actually, physically, be.

Of course it helps that the writer is supporting you, creating a plot where the rest of the world acts in accordance with the belief that you are generating within yourself, as strong opponents run from you, or opposites attract to you.

This works almost as well in real life. When we act in accordance with an invented fiction being true, the rest of the world will come to accept it as so. This is what we call a self-fulfilling prophecy.

Unfortunately, this is also true in the negative. No matter how strong and attractive we are (or how intelligent, witty, important, fun, loveable), when we act in accordance with the opposite being the truth, the world around us will "learn" to believe the opposite about us.

When I plan on "using myself" in this character, I may not be aware of the limitations I have arbitrarily placed, not only on the character, but myself. Who, after all, is to say that this quiet, motionless, physically bland being is, in fact, me? This is the me that I have chosen to reveal to the world. When I rewrite the "prophecy" of my life, the character that my life depicts will change.

My shape or silhouette shows me as a man of action: perhaps erect, perhaps ready to leap at any moment. As a man of confrontation, I lean in. When confident, I stand with legs apart. When afraid, I hunch or cower. If I am annoying, my head leads forward, uncomfortably into the space of another. And thus do we begin the first rough sketches of an alternate human being in space.

AN ASIDE

It often takes both women and men about a decade to accustom to the new physical features developed in adolescence. In reaction, the shoulders curl forward, the hips shift backwards, the actor walks sideways or backs away from things, and stands behind furniture…

When physical changes are accompanied with shame or embarrassment, it may be twenty years (or never!) before these actors are ready to make full use of the body in performance. A performer learning his or her craft does not have an extra decade to develop their natural flexibility and responsiveness.

Be a little brazen.

Try using your entire self – accentuate your hips or your chest in your stance, walk confidently forward and stop treating the furniture as a shield or crutch – and see what happens to your character. It will probably be an extremely uncomfortable process, until this physio-emotional life can lend shape to a character, a character that needn't be confused with you.

…and, perhaps you find that your limited concept of "you" begins to expand and become more inclusive.

Take a character you are working on and isolate the various elements of movement. Make yourself a checklist and, one at a time, check their use of…

- Shape (open or closed?)…
- Space (direct or indirect?)…
- Weight (heavy or light?)…
- Time (quick or sustained?)…
- Flow (free or bound?)…

You will likely find an inspiring choice that would otherwise remain hidden amid otherwise broad strokes of physicality. Perhaps there is a clichéd assumption of your character's physical nature that these explorations can root out from your portrayal… Perhaps you will find yourself fully inhabiting a body that is not your own!

Years of use and misuse disorganize the use of the body. Often, gestures restricted in the belly, chest and shoulders, don't manifest themselves physically until they reach the hands, independent of the body. By the time those gestures reach those hands they tend to be jerky and inelegant: the large muscles at the center of the body inhibit an impulse, that shoots outward and suddenly releases itself in the wrists or fingers.

Or, quite often, the gestures simply do not "speak" through the actor's body at all! The impulse to speak verbally is not connected to the physical desire for expression, and the arms remain immobile at the performer's side, in spite of the desperate passion of the dialogue.

The need for clear, efficient gesture parallels the actor's need to lose the quirks of speech generated by regional dialects or laziness. Speaking with a "standard stage" dialect enables us to shift clearly into other accents or dialects. Think of it as "going to zero." Once we have released the "inhibition" that the habits of life attach, we can more specifically and uninhibitedly re-attach the restrictions and regionalisms particular to the new being that we now inhabit.

And, yes, you *may* well play a character who has your own same physical habits of movement…

…just about as often as you play someone who has your same speech pattern or dialect.

In either case, it is more important to learn to perform well, first. Clear, clean speech enables the actor to move easily into dozens of alternate "voices." An actor with efficient gesture can adapt movement to fit a range of character traits. Improving one's overall abilities opens up the actor to more conscious choices about physical being rather than stumbling into characterization by default, or because we have a vague notion about "using ourselves" in this role.

Chapter 26

Do Not "Rest Assured"

Isolate.

Then amplify.

I find myself in the audience of a college production of a classical play. And all of the problems of adolescent bodies attempting to embody characters beyond themselves come flooding back:

- Everyone stands with arms at their sides. This is so uniform that they must have been coached to do this. It so happens that the entire stage is painted in black and white squares. We assume somebody out there had a concept: "This play is a *chess match*, and these people are all *pawns*!" One character, through the course of his big monologue, takes three steps and stops… three steps and stops… three steps and stops… I'm guessing he's a knight.
- When the actors *do* gesture, the impulse lifts the hand through a bend at the elbow. Upon completion, the hand drops back down to the actor's side, where it sometimes continues to swing uncontrollably for another five seconds or so...
- At times this same elbow-to-fingertip right-arm gesture is precisely mirrored with a simultaneous gesture from the left arm.
- Some actors hold themselves so stiffly that when they do move, the extension of their head and neck sends an oscillation through the spine.
- Two men get into a heated argument, and their noses are three inches apart, but their gestures are slight breaks of the wrist. (I secretly hope that they may reach out and strangle each other.)
- One actor grips hands behind his back, and any tension suggesting he might actually perform some act of violence is thereby relaxed.
- Only one actress stands with her elbows elevated above the bustle of her dress and gestures with her full arm. I find myself believing everything she is doing! In life we have elbows! They give us visual interest as well as a sense of readiness. A man with his elbows (and knees) locked into position is unprepared for anything unexpected that may happen.

The theatre needs to be dangerous sometimes.

Not actual, physical, danger, where the actors run headlong into each other, or fall off the stage, or stab each other. (That's what rehearsals are for!)

But implied danger… tension you can cut with a knife… erratic, impulsive explosiveness with unpredictable characters who are exciting to watch.

Actors hate and avoid this. We desire that every night, and perhaps every moment, should be as predictable as possible… lest we forget where we are, what we're doing, and what our next line is. Or, perhaps fearing that, out of control, we will flail about awkwardly, wildly, uncontrollably.

We counter this by arresting physical impulses as completely as possible. We dig hands into pockets, cross our arms, and grip hands behind our backs. If we must touch each other, it will be in some reinforcing, steadying gesture which will hold the two of us in place for much longer than the initial impulse might ever have demanded. But, having found our moment of dependable interaction in which we are not in danger of doing something erratic or awkward, we cling to that, if only for the sheer predictability of the gesture.

I have flashbacks to a high school production of *The Crucible*, where I auditioned for John Proctor in a climactic scene across from Elizabeth Proctor. The actress and I grasped each other's arms, just below the elbow, staring desperately into each other's eyes (as "two spent swimmers that do cling together and thereby drown their art"). Both of us were cast in other roles.

It is the "predictability" of all of this that is killing your performance.

Get your hands out in front of you: always at the ready to strangle, caress, cling, grope…

Bend your knees a bit, lowering your center of gravity and readying yourself to move left, right, forward or back.

Seek out the impulses that make the tiniest, slightest impact on your body, and amplify them times one hundred!

We do not want tiny, erratic fidgets that happen so quickly and randomly that they simply read as a "blur" to the audience.

But …

- let those fidgets happen in rehearsal, and…
- pick out that one out of every ten or a hundred fidgets that actually ***reveals*** something about the character.
- And then turn up the volume on those.
- Isolate.
- Then amplify.

Chapter 27

Movement: Going Ridiculously Beyond

In rehearsal, anything is possible; every discovery may be valid.

We are working to *get past ourselves* in performance. Sometimes the examples observed in other human beings are too subtle to inform our performance. We latch onto nuances of character: a gesture, a walk, a look, but these are rarely enough to actually "possess" the spirit with a new character. We pick up one point about another person's being, but we leave nine points about *ourselves* in place. As a result, every character we play tends to look the same.

Animal

The closest thing to the movement of a human being, which is not the movement of a human being is, of course, the movement of an animal. In adopting the attitude of an animal, the actor feels new rhythms, weights, and shapes, which, in turn, impact the voice, the interpretation, and the overall mood.

We need to be able to incorporate animal movement freely, even to explore movements *that we would never actually execute in performance*.

Our ongoing struggle is to overcome our area of greatest resistance. We seek that set of muscles or body parts that instinctively ring the alarm of our internal censor who shouts down the new idea with, "Well, I could never do *that*!"

That is the voice that runs interference with a myriad of unpredictable discoveries, waiting just on the other side of our knee-jerk denial.

Find that voice, and do battle with it.

A S I D E

As a director, I am constantly telling actors to go beyond what they would "really" do, "on the night." "Go ridiculously beyond anything you would actually do. Just to find out what's there." I ask them to try on this animal, or that attitude. Sometimes I may find that an actor's gestures are too fluttery, uncontrolled or ungrounded, and as a counteractive measure, I burden them with leg or wrist weights to inhibit their over-active gesturing, to give them greater "gravity."

Or, I have them carry long sticks or swords in rehearsal, giving them the feel of the breadth and consequence of each individual gesture.

"Just indulge me for this one moment, and make the change so over-the-top so that I have to say 'No! That's too much! Come back!'" Inevitably, this direction does not encourage the actor to go "too far." I generally end up getting precisely the performance I was looking for.

Are directors repeatedly asking you "give me more…"? Do they

> ever actually say, "Oh, no, that's too much!" Actors are notoriously subtle. Directors are trying dozens of ways to draw them out, to enable them to play something big, with full confidence. If your director is begging you for some size, learn to go beyond. When you get as many notes about "pulling back" as you do about "going further", then you are a successful performer. Directors love having someone that they have to pull back.

Study an animal. Notice how the animal moves. Adopt that movement fully. A bird, for instance, moves suddenly. She hops more than she walks or runs. Her head turns sharply. Meanwhile, a spider hunches and shuttles. A squirrel runs and draws herself up short. A cat stretches and indulges. A dog jumps and runs; he climbs gleefully upon his master.

Go to the zoo. Look at actual animals and let them remind you of your character. Practice that animal's movement independent of the scene. Jump. Run. Explore the performance space. Be. And then let "the animal" work through the scene. Gradually replace purely animal movement with human movement that is *informed* by the *style* of that animal. The process of integrating that outside stimuli will give you new rhythms, shapes, patterns, and attitudes. Putting Character and Animal together will produce new, unexpected ideas; ideas about interpretation as well as ideas about movement.

Find an "anchor," a subtle reminder, or connection to this inspiration which may bring these discoveries flooding back at you. There may be a gesture, a facial quirk, or even a rhythm to the breath that will enable you to "touch" that animal without breaking out of the "reality" of your character. Just the process of breathing like the animal can bring the character back to life. Suddenly the character is making choices that you, the actor, would never have anticipated.

EXPOSITION

As a young actor, I was performing a character that was very close to me. The character was actually *also* a young actor, worried about his job, worried about backstage gossip, playing chess with a fellow actor who was much more experienced in the theatre. I envied the man's comfort in his job, and I resented his buoyant attitude.[28]

I was having trouble "getting" the character. I memorized lines and blocking, but they felt repetitive. The character felt sorry for himself, and I hated how whiny and self-pitying I was starting to sound.

We did an exercise in animal movement. The other actor became a puppy, with lots of bouncy energy.

I became a spider.

At first, this worked on an intellectual level. The spider would hunch over, with legs and arms akimbo, a helpful posture when pondering the chessboard. It grew very difficult when I had to get up from the

[28] The play was *Actors* by Conrad Bromberg.

board and perform the blocking of the scene, still hunched over. It took a serious mounted effort along with a furious leap of faith to push through the resistance of the uncomfortable part, eventually accepting the fact that much of what I was doing was going to end up "on the cutting room floor." It wasn't something that would literally work on stage.

In rehearsal, anything is possible; every discovery may be valid.

Something "lit up" inside the performance. Once I let go of the "wrongness" of the exploration, new things came to me. A new level of resentment washed over the character. He was limited in his movement, shuttling around the stage while the other character was so free. He was fighting a handicap of his own creation, and he resented having created it, and his inability to break out of it. His speech took on a new rhythm. Rather than whining or moaning his words, he spat them out. He jumped from one topic to another, taking new, unexpected directions without preparation, much as a spider will divert from one direction to another at the slightest impulse. He was *unpredictable*.

The character had actually been ***too close*** to me. Where I had assumed: "Well, I'll just use myself in this play," I had been narrowing and limiting my options. I was dependent on using only those things that I might see myself doing, speaking in a voice that I would have used in my private conversations, exhibiting attitudes that I already had in my personal repertoire. I had no access to a theatrical reality for this character, nor any variation in my performance.

I had enclosed myself inside a box, "The Box of Me." I was confined by the things that I assumed the character would do or say. Or, more to the point, there was a great chunk of my own attitude or expressiveness which I had to leave out from this characterization. If you imagine two slightly overlapping circles, with one circle being the character and the other being myself, the only place that I could express anything was that area where the two circles overlap! It left me with only a sliver of the expressiveness of a full human being.

The scene ended and the director, stage manager and the other actor applauded. My breakthrough came from going outside of myself and coming back in.

Psychological Gesture

Michael Chekhov, nephew, to playwright Anton Chekhov, developed an acting approach known as "Psychological Gesture,"[29] designed to get the actor beyond his or her limitations.

Take your character as you understand him or her to be, and create an honest, impulsive gesture that holds some relevance to what you feel is at the character's innermost core. Perhaps an honest character might be refusing a bribe with palms of hands facing outwards. A sneaky character might divert someone's attention while hiding a hand behind his back. For this initial moment, it's all right, and in fact, preferable, if this gesture is subtle.

- Now, one step at a time, take this gesture and *blow it up*. Make it larger.
- Take a gesture that is in the fingers or the hand, and add the rest of the arm.
- Put the shoulders into it.
- Let the head move with the gesture.
- Draw your movement downwards, into your chest, stomach, pelvis, legs and feet.

Make the whole body contribute to the gesture, and make it work in such a way that you are moving ***beyond a reasonable expression of human life***. You are moving the way that no other being would move.

- Exaggerate even further.
- Practice it to the point that you can assume that gesture at any moment and hit the same, exact position.
- And then walk around as your character expressing him/herself through the gesture.
- Do the scene or play "informed" with this gesture. Let that gesture live and breathe underneath the character.

You will almost certainly never actually use the actual, fully-realized gesture at all. (If you do, it probably wasn't exaggerated enough to begin with!) But the audience will feel its presence.

Metaphorical Inspiration

We start life with a beautifully organized body and gradually we inhibit it with one restriction after another, eventually blocking the flow of energy that wants to respond to stimuli. By taking on metaphorical inspirations for movement we can get beyond our instinctive blocks, and open up moods and mannerisms which would otherwise be entirely foreign.

---

[29] Chekhov, Michael, "To The Actor," Harper & Row, New York, 1953.

Chapter 28

Movement: What Do I Do with my Hands?

We suddenly see our physical being as a ***choice****, in a way that we don't usually, otherwise.*

When it comes down to it, the age-old movement question is...

"What do I do with my hands?"

This is part of the paradox of working as an actor. It is the paradox of knowing and not knowing. Knowing that, as a performer, you are supposed to express yourself, but knowing that such overtly external expression is not what is on the mind of your character.

Your character is not wondering what to do with his or her hands.

Your character ***is not wondering*** what to do with his or her hands.

He or she is wondering what to do about her or his *situation*. People spend much of their lives "up to their ass in alligators," as they say. They do not think about what their hands are doing… usually. Of course, in real life we do every once in a while stop to think, "Just what are my hands doing? And how does that make me look to all of those people who are watching me?"

In real life, we find ourselves in a position of being observed. We find ourselves giving a lecture or a presentation, or just trying to make a good impression on someone new, and our minds travel outwards from our bodies, turn back around to observe ourselves, and make judgments (usually, very harsh judgments) about what the rest of the world thinks about what our bodies are doing. And these judgments will, in turn, impact what choices we are making with our bodies.

In fact, we suddenly see our physical being as a *choice*, in a way that we don't usually, otherwise.

FLASHBACK

I was a high school student, suddenly cast in my first leading role.[30] Apparently my hands became overactive because the director did everything she could to control them. When I was not gesturing wildly, I was digging my hands into my pockets, clasping my hands behind my back, or crossing my arms.

Crossing your arms is a terrific way of *cutting off all of your energy*. If you want to kill the potential of a scene, just cross your arms. The audience will relax, knowing that you will not take any action at any time whatsoever. ("Nothing to see here," says the

[30] Morris in *The Heiress* by Ruth and Augustus Goetz.

ubiquitous cop at the traffic accident.)

Eventually the director (who must have been at her wits' end) coached me into gripping the seams of my pants when the impulse to move my hands got to be too much. I believe I spent half of the play like this. At least.

Fortunately, this was back before things got videotaped, or the embarrassing memory of that performance might well have kept me offstage forever. The impulse to move my hands was deflected into my forearms, and from there into my shoulders. There was my torso, writhing with every physical impulse, the hands oddly anchored by the thighs, while the shoulders shook and undulated. How bizarre it must have seemed!

Whatever my *character* was thinking in those several scenes, I am sure that one of them was not "What am I doing with my hands?"

Peeking at Objective Reality

Stanislavski warns against looking too often into a mirror while preparing a role, as a mirror places our attention on the external aspects of the character. Without the mirror we stay on the inside, looking out.

And yet, we may benefit from seeing what, precisely, the audience is seeing. The trick is to do this while keeping our "inner critic" in check. It is a life's work to learn to look at oneself in a nurturing, encouraging way, to learn to see oneself and say, "Wow, that's really looking great. Now I see some other options that I didn't realize were available..."

Because, once we look at ourselves and say, "Boy whatever it is that I am doing really stinks; I need to do *not that*," once again we will find ourselves attempting to act a negative, which is *impossible*. Yes, we may well succeed in acting "not that," but in the process we will find our way to actually doing less and less.

So the trick is to do. To articulate. To let the impulses of the character "read" in the body of the performer.

To do this, we need a responsive instrument: a body in control of its own use of shape, space, weight, time, and flow[31]; movement that is inspired internally, and released unchecked. In many ways this means working without a model: not trying to look like anybody. Yes, there may be actors who we look up to, but imitating their external reality will not bring a full, textured character to us.

We need to exploit the long list of potential inspiration at our disposal:

- Metaphor (things that are like this character, but which are *not* this character)

---

[31] See p. 136.

- Animal
- Centers of energy (Head-centered? Chest, Stomach, Pelvic ...?)[32]
- Ease
- Full, confident gesture
- Articulation of every joint and muscle of the body
- Big, bold expression carrying us beyond the literal reality of bland, minimal impulse.
- Stretching, yoga, dance, exercise...

It is, in short, a life's work, and the paradox of acting: knowing and not knowing; being aware while creating the illusion of not-aware... will always keep us from complete fulfillment or satisfaction.

And yet, enough experience and exploration can provide us with a vocabulary of movement that is broad and expansive. In time, others will recognize and respond to the ease and effectiveness with which we use our bodies, even though we ourselves may find ourselves living on the inside of the dog suit, wondering just why no one sees what is going on with our internal process.[33]

---

[32] An understanding of the centers of energy, along with a terrific overview vividly describing how bodies develop the way that they do is effectively explored in *Bodymind* by Ken Dychtwald, Tarcher Putnam, 1986. (*Recommended for college-level readers and above.)*

[33] Trust, for the moment, that the "dog suit" reference will make more sense, later, but if you feel like jumping ahead to "How Actors See the World"... there's nothing I can do to stop you.

Part IV

PLAYING WITH DISCIPLINE

Chapter 29

Isolation

The problem with most performances is that our senses are treated to too much information, not too little.

The theatre doesn't have a zoom feature. The theatre doesn't have a sound editor. The attention of an audience will, in fact, zoom, and will, in fact, edit, but it is the actor who makes that possible.

The way the actor does this is through isolation.

This may be as simple as the old-school imperative of not walking and talking at the same time. Fortunately, things that are "old-school" at least happen to be backed by some schooling.

It is far more complex than that, however.

Isolation of Sound

I attended opening night of one of my Molière adaptations. I was, of course, familiar with the text. The scene designer had created an innovative set, with very specific, artsy pieces giving the *impression* of the environment without making the attempt to realistically depict the environment.

It was performed on an old proscenium stage, and the scenery gave way to an unshielded wing-space area to the sides and to fly-space above. The auditorium, complete with balcony, could hold over a thousand people, although there were only, perhaps, two hundred in attendance that night.

Is the problem evident by now?

The problem with most performances is that our senses are treated to too much information, not too little.

In this instance, with only fragments of scenery in back of the actors (and no walls surrounding them), the actors' voices were unfocused. A good actor, and a good director, should virtually "see" the sound waves that voices create. One look at the space, and five seconds of listening should tell the artists that their voices are rising up into the huge cavern above their heads. Voices are trailing off into the wings, and the sound is roaming around upstage, eventually to be absorbed by the curtain. The lack of scenery is depriving us of the usual "bandshell" which would otherwise focus the voice and thrust it forward.

Too much information:

The voice bounces back down out of the loft, back out from the wings, and forward off of the back wall of the stage. This "bounced" voice may be a tenth, or even a half of a second behind the live voice that is now emerging from the actor's mouth. The actor is forming a consonant, while the echo is carrying a vowel. Two or more separate sounds are assaulting the ears of the audience at the same time. If the actor is talking rapidly, or blurting or slurring his words, sounds from two or three entirely different words may be finding the ears of the audience at the same moment!

In reality, it may be a dozen separate sounds: There is the original voice coming directly from the actor's mouth to the audience's ears. There is the reflected voice that bounces down from the fly-space, and across from the wing-space, which may then radiate out toward the audience, or may bounce against the floor, or the opposite wing before emerging "South". There are tiny sound waves also bouncing off of every set piece on stage. The auditorium, itself, has a ceiling, walls, a balcony and many of the old auditoria were not fitted with acoustical tiles. (Often, the best place for an audience to sit is below the balcony, which at least cuts off the echo from above.)

Compound this problem with actors who turn their backs on the audience, or allow themselves to be upstaged, delivering the line away from the audience. Beyond the fact that the audience cannot see the actors' faces (we "hear" as much by seeing the words being shaped as we do by actually hearing), the odds that the words will be understood by the audience decline to a tiny fraction!

The performers and the director, disturbed by the fact that the audience just doesn't seem to appreciate the jokes (which they're not hearing), start to do more physical stuff. They leer and prance. They stoop over to exaggerate the cleavage jokes. They pause and nudge and grin and wince and mug. And the audience bursts with grateful laughter at a joke they can understand!

The implied message to the audience is this: we know that this stuff isn't really funny, but we know how to make it funny!

As much as I enjoy cleavage jokes, even ***I*** begin to question: but just why should *that* be funny *here*? Isn't there a different joke being told in the text at this particular moment?

The implied message becomes "I can be funny in *spite* of the play," and once we begin to do anything in spite of the play, then we're really not working *with* the play.

First, we stop upstaging ourselves

We can save ourselves at least 50% of the effort and strain that we might expend in talking louder (and straining our voices) by facing our mouths downstage to begin with. Yes, it may be unnatural. Yes, we do not always face "South" in real life. But a) this is not real life, and b) the audience will be grateful.

Observe the shape of the open mouth. It is a stage, with the lower row of teeth as footlights, and the upper row of teeth as a teaser. The lips themselves form the proscenium and the mouth creates its own effective bandshell, perfectly designed for the projection of sound. If we take that natural "stage" and align it with the shape of the stage upon which we stand, then we reinforce the personal with the architectural. The two "bandshells" will work in coordination with each other. We get the maximum result for our hard work.

The simple act of turning profile or upstage, in and of itself, will diminish the audibility of our voices 75 to 90%. We all know of the difference in the quality of sound between a train whistle approaching and receding. Very quickly it will drop in pitch and volume. (The "Doppler Effect.") That is the effective impact of turning toward the wings as we are speaking. Unless we compensate with a significant rise in volume, the audience's ears cannot adjust quickly enough. We will have made ourselves impossible to hear.

Even Better

Stand forward of the proscenium line when possible. Yes, the scene designer gave us lots of fun toys to play on. It's a fun jungle gym and we want to use it. Use it when not speaking. Or else we need to be ready to shout over our shoulders.

It's not a question of being louder. The audience would gratefully receive all of the information we want to impart, if they could only get that information divorced of all of the "noise" that the creaky old auditorium throws in our way.

Actors don't believe that they are not being heard. After all, they are shouting! How can the audience not be hearing every word? Place an audio recorder in the last row of seats. And then play it back. You will be shocked.

Actors, while they are on stage, cannot simultaneously be in the audience *not* hearing themselves. And again, they've been repeating these lines for six weeks. They know what their lines are. They've heard them a million times. If their mouths are moving, they must be being heard!

Forward of the proscenium line, the voice goes directly to the ears of the audience with only a tiny fraction of the interference that it encounters from upstage, amid the cavern of the space.

How we got here

Six weeks ago we all started speaking what was, for all rights and purposes, a foreign language. ("Shakespearean?" "Shakesperanto?") We, the recently-cast sat around a table and read the play out loud. We looked at the script while reading these foreign words, and laughed as if it were not a foreign language at all, but the most natural speech in the world. But there those foreign words were, living comfortably on the lips, at the first reading and at every subsequent rehearsal. We spoke the lines, and our fellow "foreign language students" laughed aloud, night in and night out. We worked out timing, played with blocking, with stage business, schtick, bits, lazzi, butt-grabbing, crotch-kicking, sausage-swinging, apple-cart tumbling, pratfalls, dives, ducks, clinches, kisses, prances and poses.

And by the time six weeks of this have passed, we have forgotten that this language was ever unfamiliar to anyone. And an audience filled with people-who-have-never-heard-these-words walks in through that door.

In point of fact, we were probably being heard reasonably well all the way up to a week prior to opening, when we were rehearsing the show in a classroom or a studio somewhere. When the time came to load the set in to the performing space, just across the street, or in another end of the building, we were so accustomed to being heard that we forgot to keep listening!

In the rehearsal room, the voice only has to fill up perhaps 8,000 cubic feet of space. Now a venue with 80,000 cubic feet yawns before us, and in the meantime, we have forgotten that those people out there don't already know the words! At no point during our entire process did we ever express these words in front of people who did not have access to the script from the first read-through, on forward.

During the second intermission of that particular show (the one with the artsy set), I observed a high percentage of the audience slipping quietly out the door. They had given the actors Act One and Act Two to swing at that ball. They weren't going to give them that third pitch.

Isolation of Movement

"Too much information" applies to movement, too. If I am moving during my very important line, then the audience simply won't register it. If I was watching a movie, I wouldn't expect to hear witty, nuanced, urbane dialogue during a car chase.

Here is the classic formula, and I include it just in case you haven't stumbled across it elsewhere:

- If you want to emphasize the line, execute the movement first, and then say the line.
- If you want to emphasize the movement, say the line first, and then execute the movement.

Let's say I am in the middle of a confrontation. My acting partner is across the stage. My line is, "What are you going to do about it, punk?"

- If I walk up to him, and then say "What are you going to do about it, punk?" then the audience will hold its breath waiting to hear what I am going to *say*.
- If I say "What are you going to do about it, punk?" and then cross the stage to square off against him, the audience will hold its collective breath, waiting to see what I am going to *do*.
- If I talk as I walk, no one will hold any breath whatsoever.
- If my fellow actor walks as I talk, no one will know where to look.
- If three other actors in the background hold an animated conversation in pantomime at the same time, then any five audience members may focus on *five different actors* on stage.

And gradually, we find that a story is not being told, not because there is not enough information to tell the story, but because too much information is deflating and disabling our ability to shape the story.

Art is about selection. And selection implies saying "no" to some choices while saying "yes" to others. The responsibility is incumbent upon the actors and the director to select what they want the audience to receive. If five different audience members feel like they have five different choices about what they are going to follow, then the story isn't being told at all. Or it is being told in such a manner that any collective retelling of the play's story will resemble the tale of the blind men and the elephant.

Add to this any random event that may penetrate the environment – a low whistle that is audible any time the wind blows outside, an animal or a child on stage, a train that passes outside every fifteen minutes, an actor who has been given free rein to ad lib every now and then – and the audience will spend as much energy attending to (or bracing against) the random event as they do following the story.

The Zoom Feature

If you want an audience to zoom in on a speech, or a moment, or an action… do nothing.

Do nothing.

If I stand before the audience, motionless, speaking my words, and nothing else is going on onstage, then they will quickly zoom in. My mouth and eyes will be isolated against everything else that is happening. Suddenly, the tiniest movements that I make will have meaning, and I can convey a wealth of information with almost nothing at all. The eyes and ears of the public do the zooming, and the less I do, the tighter they focus. It doesn't matter if I'm swallowed up by that 80,000 cubic foot space. Their eyes will find the single cubic foot of space that matters.

At the end of the scene, as the lights go to a quick blackout, they will see the after-image of the actor burned into their retina. That is how intently they have been focusing.

Chapter 30

The Paradox of Knowing and Not Knowing

You, the audience, are going to have the sort of evening that you choose to have, whether I like it or not.

You know what you are doing with your hands. Your character does not.

You know what is going to happen to you next. Your character does not.

You know what the audience laughed at last night. Your character does not.

There is little point in trying to "fool yourself" into thinking that you, the actor, do not know these things. You will develop the habit of playing just a little bit stupider or more superficial than your character really is.

It is far more productive to bring yourself to the state of *not caring* what your hands are doing or what the audience might laugh at, or how the next moment might go over.

The audience is going to laugh at what they are going to laugh at, and you have no way of getting inside their heads to know just how much they are, in fact, enjoying themselves, and just how the collective mood of the audience is physically manifesting itself in smiles, smirks, giggles, chuckles and laughter.

An audience is a complex socio-political animal, and every such gathering is as unique as a snowflake. The chemistry of an audience that contains one man out on a first date with a woman he has never met before, can change the interplay among the entire audience. Or the chemistry generated by a worker seeing the play with his boss. Or a church activity group seeing the play *en masse*. If a single, grandstanding member decides to walk out of the show, then the rest of the group will worry whether they will seem to be "Bad Christians" if they stay behind! Or if they are seen enjoying themselves too much!

Furthermore, an audience may well be laughing warmly, but the size of the auditorium may swallow up their collective voices, as though they were not laughing at all. The exuberant mood in the house may simply seem flat from our vantage point.

We are struck by how little control we have over the entire matter.

Control is an illusion.

Contribution is real.

As a performer, I can contribute to you, as an audience, having a fabulous evening. I can contribute to an elevated, lightened or impassioned mood.

But you, the audience, are going to have the sort of evening that you choose to have, whether I like it or not.

Other people will also contribute to that effect. If 99% of the audience is in the mood for a rip-roaring good time, their contribution, in addition to mine, will probably win the remaining 1% over. But maybe out in the audience we have members of the walking wounded: somebody who just got dumped, or somebody who has been up since 5 a.m. The sooner we, as performers, set aside the illusion of control, the sooner we can get on with the business of contributing, generously, to the lives of the audience.

I place my focus on what I *can* control. I challenge my body to define distinctions. I distinguish this moment from the next as the story of the play gets told, one moment at a time. Or I break one moment into five separate events as I give the audience a more detailed story than they ever thought they might absorb.

Dance with the audience. Use exaggerated, bold gestures, and then refine those gestures with slight, miniscule adjustments. We have much to work with: Shape, Space, Weight, Time and Flow[34] and the manner in which each of these elements of movement impact every muscle and bone in your body.

This is our performance vocabulary. We may expand our vocabulary, and then draw on it the same way that we draw on the vocabulary that lives in our verbal conversation: without thinking!

When we think about what words we think we ought to be choosing, we inevitably stammer and stumble and stutter. When our attention is on the *content* that we want to communicate, what we care about passionately, the words find their way to our mouth.

We must NOT know, even when we know.

Likewise with movement.

Outside of rehearsal, expand the body. Explore animals, dance, centers of gravity, centers/"chakras" of energy, psychological gestures and character quirks.

Inside of rehearsal, work your objective.

Let the two come together in the dance of character.

Define distinctions.

---

[34] If you have difficulty remembering these qualities of movement, simply combine their first letters to imagine a ship: the "SS WTF!"

Chapter 31

Memorization: Why

It's amazing how many brilliant performers also happen to be hard workers.

The only reason I have ever had to fire a performer is for lack of memorization.

And yet, we don't see much on memorization in the textbooks.

It is the obsession of practically every actor that I know. If they are not complaining about their own inability to memorize, they are complaining about their fellow actors' inabilities to memorize. Virtually every show we work on has an actor who is bad or, at best, very late with memorization.

Every show!

Some of this is surely laziness. Some of it is preoccupation. And some of it is lack of effective memorization technique.

I repeat this lecture in virtually every show that I direct, and it only really works on people who are predisposed to listen, to care, or to memorize their lines anyway. It's one of those things that sound inarguably self-evident, but most actors are secretly glad that those "other" actors are hearing it, never thinking that they may be the problem.

But in the hope that reading this will bring yet one actor to commit more fully...

Budget Rehearsal

We choose a number of hours out of the air. It will be a different number for every person and every role, so it doesn't matter what number we choose, but let's choose "forty" for now. It represents the length of the work-week, so a lot of people understand it as a measurement of time and labor.

Let us say that it will take us forty hours of memorization work to prepare for The Play. Inevitably, if we are going to appear on stage with all of our lines memorized (for some people, still considered "an option") we will need to spend an average of forty hours memorizing the words we are going to be speaking.

With the investment of these forty hours between now and opening night an absolute necessity, what budget of the bulk of our work is going to best support us in our successful performance?

- Early?
- Spread throughout the process?
- Just before opening night?

For many of us, the answer is obviously "C".

But consider the advantages of "A".

We sit down with our script, before the first read-through. We highlight our lines. We study them for meaning, and look up the big words. We read them repeatedly, understand them better, getting to know our characters. In the process, we eliminate hundreds or thousands of interpretive choices which self-evidently do not fit the script that we now know intimately.

As rehearsals get underway, we work quickly and deliberately, securing the memorization of scenes as they come up on the schedule, getting the play under our belts as the director "blocks" us into a scene. After that, we may refresh ourselves on blocking, but otherwise we're ready to put the script aside.

Our performances soar in that middle phase of rehearsals. For the more intense, in-depth rehearsals toward the middle and latter parts of the schedule, we are "available." We have our hands available. We have our eyes available. We have our energy and intensity available. We are ready to hear ideas... brainstorming, criticism, direction. We can explore facets of our character, if only because in order to memorize our lines, we've already had to contemplate the pros and cons of most of the issues that rehearsal will bring to the surface. Our questions for the director cut to the heart of the issue. We look good, the show looks good, and the director is thinking about how he or she would like to use us in their next project.

Let us contrast that with "C," keeping in mind that both actors will ultimately spend *the same forty hours* on memorization.

The "C" actor looks at rehearsal time as a great opportunity to tackle memorization. Alas, when he gets to rehearsal, he finds that his companionship is in demand by someone else in the cast who also happens to be a smoker, and the two of them spend off-stage time standing somewhere out back by the loading dock, puffing and chatting. During the read-through he stumbles in a fog, assisted in the pronunciation of several key words. During blocking, he still struggles with words, and captures little of his blocking on paper. For the moment, he is happy to move wherever the director positions him, because he hasn't studied the script enough to form an opinion on the matter. (But at least he's *flexible!*)

When he does finally assimilate the blocking (sometime during tech week), he realizes that this isn't really a very comfortable place for him to stand, so he stands somewhere else, disrupting everyone who has to relate to him. Other actors perform as if they're getting the response that they need in order to carry out their own actions, and they walk away hoping that he will get it "by the night." As the night approaches, panic sets in, and the actor starts memorization in earnest. But now the memorization work is tainted by panic, and it becomes extremely difficult to actually store words in one's head when every other thought is *"HOW am I going to remember all this stuff!?"*

Even though he may actually spend the same forty hours on the memorization process, our actor squandered not only the opportunity to grow in the role, but also the good will of the cast and the director, as well as his ability to learn the lines accurately.

Because panic memorization is bad memorization. He stammers and fakes his way, jumping multiple pages in the script, and he'll have nightmare performances as a result. He even attempts to hide bits of script amid props and costume pieces: newspapers, books, hats, cuffs, table tops...

The only way that someone would not want to memorize immediately is if they simply don't believe that rehearsal might actually make them better. And with years of resistance to learning, then perhaps they are right. Perhaps no matter what, they simply would find a way to not get better. They think that the "magic" of theatre is the fact that they are "magically" talented, and no amount of rehearsal or work can make them better anyway. So as long as sometime before opening night they get this whole line-thing out of the way, the magic will come, they will haul out their bag of tricks: inflections, vocal tones, gestures and silly faces... and *then* they will be brilliant.

It's amazing how many "brilliant" performers also happen to be hard workers.

Chapter 32

Memorization: How

Our attention span is the most valuable commodity we have.

Now that we've established that none of YOU out there will be "C" actors, how do you "A" actors go about preparing?

Number One: Repetition

I would be willing to bet that everyone reading this (at least the Americans among us) knows the Pledge of Allegiance. Furthermore, I would also be willing to bet that we might well stumble or hesitate in our attempt to *write down* the Pledge of Allegiance from memory (without moving our lips)!

Once we have something actually memorized, our mouth knows it better than our brain does! Our mouths remember the neurological sense of shaping the words, one after another after another. If we take our mouths through that pattern, again and again and again, they will start to anticipate what is next. Have you ever worked your way through a monologue and, even though something distracted you, continued to recite the monologue? It's like saying grace at the dinner table. The mouth remembers. There are always incidents on stage that are waiting to shake us from our confidence in the moment, unless the scene has been assimilated beyond the realm of conscious thought, into the realm of neurological habit.

When that cell phone goes off in the audience, when the woman falls asleep in the second row, when we hear that crash backstage, we will still always have a sense of where we are in the play, because our bodies know the show better than we do. Five minutes later, our conscious minds come back to the scene, having dealt with, adapted to or dismissed whatever went wrong, and we wonder just how we got to this point. It is like driving home when we've got something else on our mind. We largely don't remember starting the car, taking lefts and rights, waiting at stop lights, or pulling into the driveway, but suddenly we find ourselves standing at the front door with keys in our hands.

It is a nearly mindless process of repetition, moving our mouth through the same muscle patterns time and time again. Even when I can't remember what word comes next, if I turn off my brain, my mouth will form the shape of the word. Nine times out of ten, it will be the right word. One time out of ten, it will be a very similar-sounding word.

Number Two: Refocus

The act of reading and the act of memorizing are two different things. We may be able to memorize a series of lines by reading them over and over again, but it will take longer than it would if we refocused our attention off of the page.

Reading is a passive activity, like hearing. We read without engaging the brain.

And when the brain is not engaged, it is probably only picking up scattered information, like lint. The fabric of the material remains unabsorbed.

Stop reading.

Look at the page and absorb words. Then look up. We can look anywhere, but if we look at something relatively uncluttered, like a blank wall, it will help. "See" the image that the words bring forward. Imagine the activity described. *Then* say the words aloud. Even if we have only had to commit these words to memory for the two seconds that it takes to look up and speak them aloud, the brain will have made a slight movement toward absorbing the words. We have become an active participant in the process of memorization, which enables us to memorize three-to-four times faster than passive methods.[35]

Number Three: Realignment

Mindless repetition of the same passage of lines over and over again will probably yield little result. When you are struggling with a page, and cannot seem to bang it into your head, by all means, go on to the next one! Your brain is putting up resistance to those words in this particular space and time. Meanwhile, another thirty-nine pages await our attention. There are also the dozen pages already memorized that could use some review. We need to go where we feel our minds working productively.

A good night's sleep will reveal that we did, at least, retain words and phrases from that unlucky page number thirteen, and are ready for more. Perhaps we have eight lines on that page, but line number five is an intimidating paragraph. We start on it, but virtually "bounce" off of it, as though it were a wall.

That paragraph itself is made up of six sentences. Work sentence number one and *stop*. Do that three times. Repeat until that piece is secure.

- Then add sentence number two.
- Do one and two together a few times. Got those?
- Add number three.
- Four. Five. Six.

Are they starting to slip away?

- Grab hold of sentence number six. Repeat three times.
- Then back up to sentence number five.
- Then five and six together.
- Four, five and six.
- Three, four, five and six.
- One, two, three, four, five and six.

---

[35] Have I mentioned that all statistics cited in this book are entirely invented?

Is it starting to slip again?

- Work through three and four together.
- Add two and five to either end.
- Add one and six to the rest.

We have now worked through a speech forwards, backwards and sideways! By now we've got it. It may slip away, but a little refresher will bring it back.

Our attention span is the most valuable commodity we have. Once we lose that, our work is futile. Keep engaged by doing the monologue, the page, the scene or the play in every variation imaginable. As our attention span slips, we change our approach! By continuing to attempt to bang a thought into our heads the same way, the voice that screams "I'll never get this!" quickly outshouts the part of the mind doing the work.

Number Four: Relationship

There are times when the words may seem arbitrary. Why these words in this order rather than this *other order*? Why repeat these things?

This is no time for budding playwrights. We resist the actual words when we struggle, and look for ways to make the words at fault. The biggest trouble usually comes when we bang up against a list. It is up to us to connect that list in some way, to make item number one lead directly into item number two and so on. It's a series of "cues."

Let's take an example:

"Just a single little, stupid, meaningless, pissant criteria."

This is a list in a line from a play[36]. There are five adjectives to the word "criteria." The performer must say all five in this particular order. First try ***Repetition***. Say the line several times. It may stick by itself. Your mouth may really enjoy saying these words, and you may work on it on a day in which you have enough attentiveness to address the task with awareness and enthusiasm. Assuming that the line has yet to "take," then let's "***Refocus***."

Look up at a blank wall, and actually "see" the criteria, whatever it is. Perhaps it is a written sentence that describes the criteria. [In the case of this play, the powers-that-be have transformed the previously benign Social Security Number into a basis for socio-political discrimination.] "See" it alone (single); see it tiny (little); see it being written by an idiot (stupid); see it affecting no one (meaningless); see it petty and annoying (pissant). And then say the whole sentence without looking at the page.

---

[36] Okay, it's another of *my* plays: *Criteria*, my One-Man Comic Sci-Fi Thriller. I was working on memorizing it while I was writing this chapter. I'm happy to say that years after memorizing it, I still have (at least) this line down word-for-word.

Got it? No? ***Realign*** by working your way through beginning to end, and then end to beginning. ***Relate*** meaningless to pissant, associate stupid to meaningless. And so on. You should have it by now.

No? Still not yet? Then remember this: "SLSMP." Remember that the alphabetical progression from L to M to P is diverted by an S at the beginning, and another S after the L.

We can almost always find that a seemingly random combination of letters will suggest unexpected connections. In this, I notice that all of these initials could actually stand for sizes: Small, Large, Small, Medium, Petite! Essentially, three Small t-shirts with a Large and a Medium t-shirt separating them.

By now we have memorized the line. If for any reason we don't have it by now, we go away and come back, ready to see it more clearly later. We can do this for lines or lists of any length. We can choose incredibly arbitrary methods which will make the words stick. But don't waste the director's time and the cast's time to argue about the word choices! Who cares if the line would be easier for you if the two "S's" were at the end, maintaining the alphabetical order? They're not.

(This is no magic bullet. If you are reading this chapter looking for a way to avoid that forty-hour commitment, you're out of luck. Budget the time. Do the work.)

This method will put the entire play within our grasp. No matter how many lines we have to learn. No matter how complex the lines. The human brain is limitless in its capacity. It can always make room for more.

Budget Rehearsal. Repeat. Refocus. Realign. Relate. Five R's, preceded by a B. (BRRRRR.) Probably pretty important ones to remember. Get them down *cold.* Rite them down.

Chapter 33

Memorization: A Major Project

"Noise" will always be present in some manner. Learning to retain the dialogue independent of the noise is the final, major challenge.

The human brain is limitless. It is only in our conversations about the *limits* of our brains that we create an impasse. We speak and create our own limitations. People who quickly inform me what lousy memorizers they are perpetuate that reality for themselves.

I once thought that a 13,000-word one-person play was an impossible task. I have since added a one-person play of 10,000 words, a play of 8,000 words… another play of 8,000 words and one 18,000 word-play to my repertory… And I don't think I'm done yet.

To answer the first, inevitable question: No, I don't find myself performing lines from the wrong show. The brain doesn't work that way.

A S I D E

This almost never happens to an actor who works in repertory. In performance, the emotional context, the costume, the physical posture and the attitude have all (hopefully) been tied to the very specific words that the moment demands.

The more likely occurrence is that the actor is reminded of similar-sounding lines from the *same* play, jumping several pages in the process.

One actor who had played Ebeneezer Scrooge in differing adaptations of *A Christmas Carol* in back-to-back years reported occasional drift back into the "old" version of the script (given that the lines were near-identical).

Amid my very first performance of *Lot o' Shakespeare*[37], I discovered that two of my Shakespearean monologues began with the phrase, "My liege…" and while I was supposed to be performing *Henry IV, Part 1*, I had, in fact, launched into *Comedy of Errors*.

The Plan

Working on show number two, I started six months in advance of the first public performance. (I generally find that it is only after actually performing a one-person show for about six months that I feel I have begun to master the role.) I want this not only memorized, but firmed up to the point that nothing can throw me. I want every moment filled. Watching videos of my first one-person show, it is evident that during the early performances, there were many unfilled moments where my brain was

---

[37] One-man play #5.

asking me, "what's next?" With no scene partner, each transition must be filled. The solo performer carries the burden of continuous focus and movement.

Since I have written this play, I continue to rewrite as I memorize. The plan is to keep the play to sixty minutes, which means cutting at least five minutes from the script. (The presence of the audience always adds time, and so the objective is to get the rehearsal timing down below 55 minutes.)

I record my lines into an ear prompter/dictaphone and practice speaking the words as I hear them, which gives me the kinetic experience of forming the words. And yet, amid rewrites, no tape is useful for more than about a week, as perhaps 5% of the play has been reworked by then. After that, the fear is that I may begin to imprint the wrong words into my speech pattern.

Beginning

I dig in on the project, taking on a page a day. This script is twenty small-print pages, with roughly 500 words on each, so this phase of the work will take twenty days. At first, I attempt to trace back to review the first few pages as I add new stuff, but my schedule balks, so I concentrate on the single daily page. With about an hour of work each day, I find that a given page has been largely absorbed.

In this phase, I find myself curiously overcome with sleepiness, almost to the point of narcolepsy. Perhaps it's the sheer boredom of cramming raw material into my brain. Perhaps it's the brain's way of resisting. It may be a psychological block, as the unconscious mind reasserts its own unwillingness to take on such a huge project. ("Good God, man! It can't be done!")

If I allow myself to contemplate the vastness of the work in this phase, I feel tinges of despair, but no one ever memorized an entire play at once! One word, one phrase, or one sentence at a time is how the brain absorbs. That one sentence gets linked inextricably to other sentences, and that paragraph to other paragraphs, and that page to other pages, but success at this point demands *blinding myself to the rest of the project*. I reassert my ability to take on this tiny piece, here and now.

With a day spent on each page, by the twentieth day I have forgotten significant portions of what went before. ("I've lost it all!") But memory is a subtle force, and I cannot know how much is actually stored away so far. More than anything, it is the "noise" within my head that blocks memory.

But I Had it All Memorized at Home!

Every actor has spoken this aloud at some point. Usually with shock and surprise.

At home, the four walls are not sitting in judgment. When we get to rehearsal, and lines are due, the people are suddenly looking at us with expectation in their eyes. Our awareness of that assumed judgment will divert us from the stream of thought that takes our characters through all of those particular words.

It is impossible to think of what we are supposed to remember when we are busy asking "Why can't I remember?" We must feed ourselves character thoughts, not actor thoughts. If nothing else, this phase of memorizing prepares us for that imagined performance-judgment of the audience, critics, friends and family that will stimulate that same death-spiral of self-consciousness on opening night.

Note what happens when new people are added to the environment! That feeling will return opening night, at a time when the blank stare will not be a viable option!

Phase Two

I move back to the middle pages of my one-man play.

I assign myself *two* pages a day over the course of the next *ten* days. I'm not ready for two full pages from start to finish, but I can at least re-memorize two pages individually. Pages 11 and 12 get a little more secure. There are lots of glitches where the phrases simply aren't "tied down" yet, but I can, at least, muddle through.

Once I've worked forwards to page twenty again, I go back to pages nine and ten, then seven and eight, etcetera, until I have worked my way through the play once more, this time *sideways*. It's not smooth, it's not pretty, but it is improving. Words where I formerly tripped have been absorbed. Phrasings which seemed awkward become part of my natural expression.

Phases Three, Four, Five

Working on a twenty-page play, the script can be broken up in many different ways. A two-mile jog carries me through four pages, reciting as I run.

I repeat those four pages six times and spend these next ***five*** days with ***four*** pages a day. And I follow that with ***five*** daily pages over the course of ***four*** days.

I am cutting up the play every which way I can cut it. Overlapping chunks of memorization force me to connect the play through what would otherwise be arbitrary mental breaks. Larger and larger chunks give the confidence I will need when I finally toss the book aside and test the material in front of a live audience (most likely, a single person).

Phase Six

The process of adding observers to the mix conditions my brain in an entirely new way. They add "noise," and such noise will always be present in some manner. Learning to retain the dialogue *independent of the noise* is the final, major challenge.

A TEST

Working on a scene on my morning commute, I feel like I've got the words. But will I lose them as soon as I get in front of an audience?

I turn on the car radio and all of my lines disappear. I can't remember more than a sentence or two before getting caught up in the song or the announcer's message or the news blaring. Clearly I don't have the lines secured yet.

I turn the radio down to a level of "1," so that I can only barely discern whether there is a song playing or a DJ announcing. This time, I can manage remembering with only slight stumbles.

I turn the radio up to "2," and do the scene again. I may be able to identify a given song, or know whether the DJ is reading the news or promoting a product, but I can still make it through the scene.

Turning the radio up to "3," the scene goes shaky on me. I can now make out particular words from the broadcast, and as my mind notes the topic of the conversation, it lets go of the scene. (I repeat the scene at "3" once or twice, until I have learned to "box out" the invasive radio.)

The radio then goes up to "4." I recite the scene with no problems.

I continue to increase the volume as the radio works its way up to "10." By the time I reach ten, only a traffic accident, or getting pulled over by the police will shake the lines from my head. I own them now, and have disciplined my thinking against distractions.

Passive vs. Active Memorization

When we listen to words on an audio recorder, speaking them in coordination with the playback, we condition our physical being to shape those words in quick succession, but do not actually memorize. Mouthing the words without engaging the brain does not train us to produce the words on our own.

Often, we are magnetically drawn to look at the script, even when we are relatively certain of the words. Why waste time when the text is right here?

Wait! Resist the temptation to peek. Looking at the script only informs us *during that moment that we happen to look!* When we find our way back to this point, the words will have remained out of our grasp.

But when we take whatever time it takes for the next word to resurface, we are engaged in active memorization. *Even if it takes a full minute* we have used some thought process to connect the lines. An abbreviated version of that thought process will flash more quickly through our minds the next time we work through these same words. The odds of remembering this line the next time around are ten times better than if we had given up and checked the page.[38]

ASIDE

I do twenty-five sit-ups, counting them in French. Between "one" (*un*) and "twenty-five" (*vingt-cinq*) I struggle with four or five numbers which are uncertain to me. I keep meaning to check a reference book, but don't get around to it. The next day, I do my sit-ups again and remember a number or two that I'd forgotten the day before. The day after that, I remember all 25 numbers.

Which brings me to this very simple, but all-important conclusion:

"Repetition"* trumps *"Study."

---

[38] See footnotes #2 and #35.

It is the conversations that run our thinking which say how good or bad we are at memorizing. When we change the conversation we change our memory. Rather than "Why can't I get this?" look at all that has already been gotten.

Phase Seven

I recommend no fewer than three daily repetitions to improve the work.

- The first time through the material reminds me of where I'd left off last. I always remember less of it than in yesterday's final repetition. I have seemingly taken a step backwards.
- The second time enables me to try something new, introducing unpredictable interpretations.
- The third time lets me assimilate the first and second readings, firming up changes. I explore this further through readings four and five.

By the sixth repetition, if I get that far, I have probably arrived at a point of diminishing returns. I do something else for a while and come back later. This is not a sprint, but a marathon. I am digging deeply, placing information in the long-term vault, securing it where the introduction of observers and judgment cannot shake me.

Commit to a plan and work on that plan every day

Don't exhaust yourself with guilt about failure and forgetting, and don't bore your fellow actors with apologies or excuses. The best apology is to come back better tomorrow. Excuses only make the rest of the cast and production staff feel guilty for having expected anything out of you in the first place!

And if you have been blessed with a leading role; don't complain about how many lines you have to learn! Your fellow actors would love the opportunity to share that complaint. Rather, show that you deserve the faith your director has placed in you by being the *first* one to toss the script aside! Respect the honor you have been given by lifting the entire rehearsal process onto a new plane. Inspire others by example.

Chapter 34

Wasting Time

We have no idea just how much there is to do.

If there are ten people necessary for rehearsal to happen, and one of them arrives ten minutes late, then that one person is responsible for having wasted 100 minutes of rehearsal time.

I find myself invited to sit in on a rehearsal being run by an old friend. We arrive moments in advance of the scheduled starting time (6pm), and perhaps a single actor is present.

She spends 25 minutes setting up the stage and getting the stage lights on, during which time all but one of the actors arrives.

Perhaps by 6:30, rehearsal is underway.

I love my friend. And her actors love her, too. It's clear that she's the best director that they have seen in a lifetime of performing in their remote rural town. They would clearly do anything for her.

Aside from arriving on time.

The next morning, I volunteer to do my acting workshop for her class. It is an 8am class.

At 8am, there is one student waiting in class. We spend about 20 minutes trying to figure out how to turn the lights on in the theatre. By 8:20, I have dragged the 5 class members out of the green room and into the theatre, stage lights or no. The class was scheduled to go until 9:15, and I now have fifty-five minutes to cover my two-plus hours of material.

And I have no way to tell them just how much information they just cheated themselves out of.

People dawdle because they don't think there's that much to do.

People don't think there's that much to do because they believe that the act of performance somehow generates a magic moment, and that they either have "it" or they don't. And no amount of rehearsal will help them have any more or less "it" than they currently have.

When we arrive late, set up late, chit chat at length, and only eventually get around to the first actor speaking his or her first line, then the people around us get the message that there's really not all that much to work on. To them, rehearsal may mean nothing more than learning their lines at home and coming to the theatre to find out where to stand.

It is a community theatre mentality. After four years of disciplined undergrad theatre work, one year of community theatre destroyed all of my habits of punctuality. One day, I was startled to look up and discover that I was leaving home to go to rehearsal ten minutes after rehearsal had been scheduled to start, knowing that the theatre was 20 minutes away! And what really bothered me was *how little that I found I was bothered by this!*

People were not there to work, they were there to hang out. And when you are hanging out, of course you must be fashionably late.

The rehearsal itself becomes a series of empty rituals, punching a clock for 100 hours or so in advance of opening night. No wonder we come up with elaborate warm-up exercises and theatre games to occupy us. We have no idea just how much there is to do!

You, the actor, are not the victim here. Those half-dozen actors are caught in a downward spiral with their director. She sets the example of arriving at the very last second, with no hope of starting on time, and then they proceed to get away with arriving later. If they arrived on time, helping to get those lights turned on, their performances would be better.

Any individual who is late to rehearsal makes every other performer late.

1,000 Minutes

Someone is paying for your time. Check your contract. In the professional world, you are often liable for late arrival, sometimes to the tune of hundreds of dollars!

I have even seen an actor arrive late for a performance… ***ten minutes after the curtain was supposed to go up!***

An actor arriving ten minutes late for a performance has not only wasted 100 minutes of the time of his or her fellow performers, but (assuming an audience of 100 people) 1000 minutes of the audience's time.[39]

An audience loans us their time on the gracious assumption that we will do something with it. We squander that time, either by self-indulgent lateness or self-indulgent pausing, at our peril, and at the peril of the producing organization, who will need to convince future audiences to entrust them with their time.

The late-arriving actor always has an excuse. And proceeds to be late again the next night, and the next night after that. Wretched, humble, passionate, craven, shamefaced apologies that are not backed up by a change in behavior… are empty and meaningless.

---

[39] The Dad in me cannot help but fantasize about the "time-out chair" for actors, in which they sit in a corner for 100-1000 minutes, thinking about what it is that they have done.

Chapter 35

Preparing

Nervousness is a luxury of a body that has too much energy available to it.

"How do you deal with stage fright?" is a question that comes up now and then. Suddenly, I realize I've never really seen this in a textbook, although it is clearly part of the actor's everyday experience, and we all develop methods of dealing with it.

I don't mean that stage fright is tangible or inevitable. It's a story that takes hold of our thinking, that grows in the telling. The more credit that we give stage fright for being able to disarm and inhibit us, the more that stage fright will, in fact, be capable of disarming and inhibiting us. It becomes its own self-fulfilling prophecy.

This is not the cliché, dumb-struck, wild panic which the movies or the television shows like to depict. Over many years I have not seen such a phenomenon from anyone older than twelve. I *have* seen people forget their lines, and find that the more that they try to remember them the more they chase them from their brain.

But the stage fright with which I am most familiar is that which comes with a racing heartbeat, shallowness of breath and dry mouth. When these symptoms are accompanied by a fixated fear-of-performance, then the two factors, physical and psychological, impress more fear upon each other in a downward spiral.

The physical symptoms are intricately related, and impact each other like dominoes. When we breathe shallowly, with the air reaching only an inch or two below our clavicle, we increase our heartbeat, which has to struggle to oxygenate the blood. As we continue to breathe in this quick sort of dog-pant, the mouth dries up, and our articulatory mechanism is impaired. The palms will often sweat as well.

And since these things happen in close proximity to our fears, we will often focus all of our efforts at controlling our fears. Alas, the very effort of attempting to control fears is simply a reminder to the system that it *has something to be afraid of*, and the process backfires. We take repeated turns down that still-descending spiral.

Our thinking tends to focus on the wrong things: special people who are coming to the show tonight (the playwright, a director we're auditioning for or, worst: our parents), a moment, or a high note of the play that has been giving us problems, a line that we blew last night, or some wrongness to the costume, or the mood, ruining the whole thing for us before we even start.

These are actor issues, and not character issues. What's best to focus on is what the character desires, and to take actions that he or she would engage in to prepare for the events of the evening. Bring the focus inward and take care of little things: that hair that is out of place, the shirt which will not tuck properly, the argument that our character finds him or herself trapped in. We can work on the character's concerns for a little bit, and allow them to swallow us for a while. (This is the place for Stanislavsky's "circles of attention.")[40]

When our concentration exercises take us into physical activity, then the thoughts will follow. We can only control what we think up to a certain point. The brain will always work its way back. As soon as you tell yourself "don't think about 'elephant,'" then 'elephant' is the one thing with which you will concern yourself. More important, and more within our control, are the things that we can do physically to prepare for our entrance.

Once we're at the theatre, discovering that we're overcome with nervousness, then it's almost too late. Our best option at this stage is to focus on the breath, forcing it to slow down. Exhale all the air in the lungs. And then wait. Wait several seconds. We can wait to take in air a lot longer than we think that we can. And then let the natural expansion of the lungs draw in air.

Don't stop there. Blow the air back out and wait again. Once more, take in air filling the ribcage and expanding the stomach. Continue, extending the time, longer and longer. We are giving the mouth time to moisten with a little bit of saliva. We are encouraging the pulse to slow, and rather than gasping for breath, we are teaching the body to make the most of the breath that it gets. Now, when we start to think "character thoughts" again, we won't be ripped so quickly out of them.

Back up.

Start early in the day

Exercise! Whatever it is that we do to work out the body, do it early on the day of the show. It doesn't hurt to be running through the lines at the same time.

A large portion of our day is consumed with getting ready for the show, which really means treating this role we are playing with the same seriousness and effort that we would give to something which was our full-time job. (When we start treating it as if it *was*, then the date in which it actually *is* will arrive more quickly.)

I used to go jogging on the days that I was doing my show (when my knee was in better shape). I would jog and speak my lines to myself at the same time. Mentally, I would trace my way through a pattern which I traced many, many times before, just touching base once more with all of the words that I will have to speak, before doing them in the spotlight. This is a "neuro-muscular trace."

I ran slowly enough that I would not run myself out of the breath that I needed to speak the lines. When I first started, I could only recite perhaps a third of the play while I was running, and had to finish the remainder of the play separately. Over time, my legs got stronger, my weight decreased, and I could make it through the entire play within the course of a five or six mile run.

The key function of the running was *exhausting myself*. If all of my excess energy is gone, then all I have left is enough energy to do the show. I may yet have another six to eight hours before show time, and am always amazed at how quickly my body recovers from vigorous exercise.

---

[40] See pages 8-10.

Nervousness is the luxury of a body that has too much energy available to it. The quick shallow breathing and the fluttering heartbeat are symptoms of energy that is racing beyond the amount that we need. The process of working out and using up energy familiarizes us with all that the body is capable of. It gives us confidence in our own abilities, as well as our knowledge of the lines (if we work on those at the same time). It gives us the measure of our abilities, enabling us to focus better later, taking on challenges that live on the distant edges of our ability. As we expand our stamina, those challenges fall more easily within the range of our capabilities. Perhaps as we are approaching the final moments of our toughest performance, we may continue to reach greater challenges of physical and vocal expression, allowing a spontaneous impulse to release, and won't give in to the seductive desire to recite by rote.

With this intense preparation, it is unlikely that we will need any of our emergency breathing exercises before going onstage. We continue to breathe deeply and easily throughout the day, without the extra energy that gives us "the jitters."

We can also change what we *call* our fear

When we report that we are "afraid" or "nervous," then we empower those feelings. Rather than say, "I'm really nervous," try saying "I'm really excited." The physical manifestation of the two feelings, nervousness and excitement, (shortness of breath, sweaty palms, increased heart rate, dry mouth...) is identical! The body does not distinguish between the two feelings, but the head does. When we assign the word "nervous" to these feelings, rather than "excited," we set ourselves on the path to something negative. "Nervous" usually has an uncomfortable, disturbing consequence. "Exciting" might catapult us into an amazing result!

TRUE STORY

I was preparing to perform a new re-write of what was then my new one-man musical[41] in front of a large crowd. I was readying the show for a Midnight performance on a Friday night. When I arrived at the conference on Wednesday night, I discovered that seeing "midnight" on the schedule had thrown me off. I was going to be performing the show at midnight on *Thursday!* (that is, the performance itself would technically be on Friday morning, rather than late Friday night) Yipes!

I had twenty-four hours to prepare my big premiere, whereas I'd thought I had forty-eight!

I had a two-day to-do list: shop for several yet-unpurchased props, get a haircut, distribute flyers, and run through the show several times. I set myself into motion, and placed a call to a friend back home with the sudden news.

---

[41] *Karaoke Knights, a One-Man Rock Opera.*

I was just about to say, "I'm going to have a really stressful twenty-four hours..." when I realized the kind of experience I was projecting for myself. I caught myself mid-sentence and said instead:

"I am going to have a really amazing twenty-four hours."

With those words, the cloud lifted. The fears went away. I had turned the story of the coming day into an entirely different narrative. I have no doubt that, had I not caught myself in the process of speaking aloud, I would indeed have had a very stressful twenty-four hours, with dubious results. As it turned out, I accomplished all that I set out to do the next day, and even had a solid tech rehearsal and a strong run-through. The show was a hit, with a standing ovation, and I had an extra day afterwards to relax and bask in the success of the show.

And I wonder whether it is our love of drama, or perhaps our desire for sympathy that leads us to parade and promote the conflict and the stress rather than the thrills, joy, excitement and the pending conquest.

Resist the temptation...

...to have that last bit of caffeine, whether from coffee or a can of soda, with less than a couple hours before show time. If your usual routine is two cups of coffee in the morning, and a can of pop in the afternoon, stop there! Assume that in the heat of the moment, you will have enough energy to keep awake and attentive, and that is all you can reasonably expect from caffeine. Choose something that is going to be good nutritionally; I will sometimes have a cup of tea... the kind that is supposed to soothe the throat (It doesn't matter if it actually does; the fact that I *believe* it does is enough!).

One of the benefits of working in the theatre is that *if* you are really plying your craft effectively, you should be in terrific shape. You'll be eating healthy things, working out, quitting smoking, and adding years to your life. If nothing else, the very process of doing work that we love and believe in, keeps us young.

The natural inclination of my character to win the audience's love and confidence has probably done more toward improving my dental hygiene than anything else. I find that I floss my teeth on show days much more often than on off-days.

Part V

OUT-WITTING YOURSELF

Chapter 36

The Hamlet Moan and Greek Tragedy

Stop beating them to the pain!

Michael Shurtleff said, brilliantly:[42] "*The Three Sisters* is not a play about three women who never get to Moscow, but about three women who fight like hell to get there."

Do the three sisters ever get to Moscow? No.

But *they* don't know that.

Another great modern acting disease: Knowing the ending.

Seemingly, the longer the play has been in circulation, the more inevitable the ending appears to the actors, and the less they actually *do* to circumvent that ultimate conclusion.

This generation of Actors has evolved into a generation of Fate Bemoaners.

The audience doesn't know, like you do.

No matter how famous the play, unless they came to see the show just last night, they don't know how it's going to end, largely because they don't know what YOU are going to do with it.

We actors come to these plays knowing that they are going to end badly, and we measure the quality and emotional fullness or resonance of our performance by our ability to suffer, from beginning to end.

The characters, themselves, don't even know that this play that they're caught up in happens to be a tragedy! Stop beating them to the pain!

I await the first entrance of Hamlet, and listen to him open his mouth and moan.

He proceeds to moan through the course of the evening.

He may as well be dead from the moment that the lights come up.

He's not adding new interjections; he's simply turning most of his vowels into melancholy diphthongs almost to the point of adding syllables to the lines.

The actor has chosen a note. And it is that note that the actor plays. Something like "Oooaaaauhhh!" with a rising intonation. A tone that we might expect from Marley's Ghost, or a man with a toothache.

Hamlet is one of the most complex characters ever written. His famous indecisiveness comes not from a feeling of helplessness or self-pity. When you

---

[42] In *Audition, Everything an Actor Needs to Know to Get the Part*, Bantam Books, New York, NY, 1978.

drown him in self-pity, you strip him of action! He actually has a terrific sense of humor! *Hamlet* can often be very funny play!

When we drown him in self-pity, bemoaning his fate, we take away the many moment-by-moment decisions being made by perhaps the most complex character of all time.

When plays begin, characters face a maze that twists away before them. There are a multitude of directions to take at any moment, and a gazillion responses the character might enact amid the process of navigating the maze.

But when we put that "Hamlet Moan" into the throat of our character, then the ending is inevitable from the moment that the lights come up. All of the decisions for this incredibly active and indecisive and tormented character are already made.

When we put that Hamlet Moan into our character's throat, we bulldoze our way through the maze, and the play becomes one slow parade toward an inevitable ending.

Perhaps we are thrown by Hamlet's famous indecisiveness. His ambivalence.

An ambivalent, indecisive character is not an *indifferent* character: in stasis, frozen, unmoving.

An ambivalent, indecisive character is one who makes *all choices, equally*… He moves all directions at the same time, and thereby goes nowhere.

No one knows that they are caught up in a tragedy, even as the tragedy begins to swallow them whole.

The moment that our characters learn that they are in a tragedy, the play stops being a tragedy. That's like standing in place while steamroller rolls over us.

That's not tragic. That's pathetic. We are placing pathos where tragedy belongs.

The Greeks

If this applies to *The Three Sisters* and to *Hamlet*, it applies even more to Greek Tragedy.

Again, the farther we are from the tragedy, the more predetermined it seems to be, and the less effectual we are in fighting for success.

The Greeks were convinced that The Gods played an active hand in shaping the action. How can we fight against what The Gods have, in their eternal wisdom, determined?

We might as well simply lie down and play dead.

I go to see a performance of *The Trojan Women.* They are so far from Greek vision of courage and nobility and righteous action in the face of the cruel fates, that this production might well be titled *Those Whiny Trojan Divas!*

The Chorus

In the modern day, we know what a chorus is about. When we turn to the Greeks, we lose our way.

The Greek theatre was a single step removed from a Chorus that would collectively recite the entire epic poem from start to finish. It wasn't until Thespis in the 6th century B.C. stepped out from the Chorus to play a character, that individuals even existed in a play. Up until then the performance sprang from the collective (which sounds suspiciously like Communism)!

Plays started as epic poems, to be recited aloud. They were recitations of an aesthetically pleasing idea, or perhaps a supplication to the Gods, much as the modern Catholic mass, in which masses of people will recite familiar words all as a group. The congregation expresses responsibility as a community by speaking aloud their beliefs, their understandings and their commitments.

Having one individual stand alone, outside of that Chorus, was the exception, and not the rule. This was a radical development.

I suspect that modern directors have such difficulty getting actors to accept chorus roles that they reconceive the chorus to convince their actors that, "Oh, no! Each chorus member is going to be an individual in this play! Your part is absolutely crucial to the plot!"

And then they go about giving these individuals names, and personal histories, and inner monologues, and special moments, all of their own…

Most modern productions diminish the impact of the chorus by allowing each actor to speak in a slightly different, individual, rhythm. If this was how we approached the chorus of a musical, would any modern choral director stand for it?

Architecture is Destiny

Imagine yourself standing at one end of a football field, with an enormous stadium surrounding you. Imagine speaking to that huge stadium when it is filled with people, each body absorbing sound, each person making their own odd noise. You have no microphone. Technology does not exist.

Place ten friends at your side, each of you speaking the same text at the same moment. You have rehearsed your speaking to the point that each consonant and each vowel is articulated simultaneously. Certainly there are variations in pitch and tone, but when the audience is sitting five hundred feet away, surrounded by thousands of other bodies, the text can be better understood with the power of ten or more voices driving it.

A true chorus is comprised of members who willingly give up their individual identities with the understanding that the whole is, indeed, greater than its parts.

The chorus was not a stylistic choice. They were a necessity that became the style.

Architecture dictates convention and style.

In the 1940s, the Andrews Sisters would stand behind a single microphone, all scrunched together. We now think of that as their style. We parody it and pay homage to that style all the time.

If the Andrews sisters had three separate body microphones, what would their style have been?

Given the necessity of having a chorus, how did plays evolve in expressing the vision of those playwrights?

The necessary content of plays became more about communities and groups. And about the impact of a given action on society as a whole.

Break one actor away from that group, and let Thespis take on bits of dialogue alone, and suddenly the text becomes hard to hear and to understand. That actor had better have an amazing voice.

Theatres grew smaller.

For the most part, the chorus tells us what is going to happen, and then we watch it unfold. Often they will give perspective, analyzing the ongoing action from the perspective of Man's relationship to the Gods.

Setting a single man alone, in opposition to the chorus, was a radical notion, both philosophically and practically. Words might be lost, which would necessitate that themes be repeated, amplified by the Chorus, representing the community, on stage.

Amid an epic poem, it makes sense—in much the same way as it might make sense in Church—for us to recite and respond. The leader enacts a portion of the ritual, and the chorus (or the congregation) participates and responds.

Do we have a need for that today?

Must we have a chorus to be true to a Greek play?

Consider Dr. Morgan's initial question: "Why did the playwright break the great silence of the universe?" It is the essence of that answer to which we have responsibility: the statement about humanity. Let us distinguish between *convention* and *vision*. The playwright's vision made a statement about man and his relationship to his fellow man and to the gods. No dead playwright is peeking back from the afterlife hoping that we'll use the chorus the same way that he did!

If that imagined dead playwright is watching he or she is more likely looking to see whether their voice can still reach from beyond the grave to attack social injustice, pompous self-righteousness, repression or misplaced priorities. Does society still understand his or her vision for man in his relationship to the Gods? Can the action of this play still move them?

The Greek playwright was handed the chorus, in much the same way that Shakespeare was handed the Globe. It influenced every scene, but often was successful in spite of it.

Each time we stage a Greek play, let us ask, "why?" Why was the chorus there to begin with? Can that function be fulfilled by a single person? Are we inserting a chorus to satisfy the historians and the theorists? Is our petition for tenure likely to be threatened if we re-think the whole chorus thing?

Masks

I often challenge actors on their desire to work masks into plays. If our first fundamental responsibility is "being seen," then this seems to fly in the face of that concern. The actors almost invariably make the following point:

"You know a mask just enables me to 'stretch' so much further as an actor. When I don't have my face to express myself through, it all goes back into my body, and I become much more expressive in my torso. It's evocative, and takes me to places with the character that I never might have discovered otherwise."

But why not make great strides with the mask *in rehearsal*, and allow those great strides to imprint themselves upon your posture? And then remember what the mask inspired, and then give the audience the benefit of your face in *addition* to this wonderfully expressive body? And then proceed to do great work with your face, too? Why not allow the character inhabiting your body, who has become so expressive, to inspire your face to develop into a mask of its own?

"Paper bullets of the brain"[43]

Here is my favorite analogy for creating, or re-creating theatre once envisioned for another place and time, and particularly, for another language:

Let's say you are firing a gun.

In the moment of the firing, you are probably not considering the caliber of the weapon most prominently.

In a situation that might inspire you with the need to fire a gun, your most likely consideration would be on the *impact* that you want that weapon to make.

Likewise, the playwright, in writing his or her play, is most probably focused on the impact that he or she wants the play to have.

While the words themselves are effective *tools* for creating that impact, the author, ultimately, thinks of these words as means to an end.

When it comes time to present a play in a different language, in a different place or time, it is not always the recreation of the identical word or a piece of staging that had such an impact when the play was first produced, that will generate that same impact today.

Think of two different languages as if they were two different guns. One gun is a .45, and another gun is a .22. Obviously, they will need two different caliber bullets

[43] Benedick, *Much Ado About Nothing*, II, 3.

in order to function effectively, just as the authors will need two different sets of words to fulfill the original intent.

But also, in the process of switching from one gun to another, the person firing the weapon will probably need to alter their strategy and method in order to have the same, or a similar impact.

A .45 will create a hole roughly double the size of a .22. Which means that this new gun may need to fire twice to get a similar impact. Or perhaps three times, depending on the relative location of the wound.

Likewise, as we move from French to English, for instance, Alexandrine Hexameter may not be as effective a weapon as Iambic Pentameter is. The syntax of any given sentence may read much more clumsily or awkwardly in English than it did in French. And plays-on-words which have double meanings in French will have no such double meanings in English, and entirely new wordplay must be conceived, once again, with the original impact in mind.

The history books are brimming with reports of the relative impact that these plays had: *Tartuffe* was banned from production for five years, while Molière was branded "a devil not worthy of hanging." The slamming door of *A Doll's House* was "the door slam heard round the world," ushering in an era of women's' liberation. Plays have led to debates, arguments, fist fights and riots.

These various impacts may well have been beyond the scope of what the playwright initially intended; after all, Molière never actually wanted his play banned; what he wanted was to make people think, to shake them out of their complacency, by exposing the hypocrite in their midst.

And quite often, Molière's plays manage to do just that. But the occasion is very rare when we approach the furor that greeted his searing and hilarious attack on hypocrisy in the 1660s.

We have switched from what was a .45, to a .22…

But we only fire once.

It is incumbent on us to ask whether the impact that the playwright might have initially intended would demand that we take that second shot.

Or shoot from a different angle.

Or throw a knife.

Chapter 37

Getting Bad News

*Reach for whatever makes you emotional **now**.*

I have played out the scene of learning of my own imminent death of pancreatic cancer about a hundred and fifty times.

Note: I do not have pancreatic cancer. I intend never to have it.

But I have, in the line of my work, had to play out that scene again and again.

For two successive years, the assignment of "giving bad news" was part of the final exam at a nearby med school, and I played the role of the patient to these doctors-in-training as many as twelve times a day! (I was, what is known as, a "standardized patient.")

If there were ever a sweatshop for actors, this is it: Playing the same painful scene, repeatedly, to an audience of one. The doctor comes in. I hear the news. I pester the doctor for further clarification. I extract from him or her a date, a survival expectancy, and the bomb explodes inside of me: the realization that my days now come with a number attached.

We really don't want to play this scene out twelve times a day! It's not psychologically healthy to play at full tilt, with the stakes as high as the situation necessitates. With each repetition, little pockets of emptiness etch their way inside, scales of sadness or depression start to attach themselves to our thinking. Deep in our subconscious a sense of the very terminality of our existence begins to take over. Little frivolities gradually lose their appeal. And who knows exactly how effectively the psychosomatic suggestion may recreate the symptoms of the disease?

And so, while we may play out some of these scenes with full emotional impact, with tears and angst and pathos, if we know what's good for us, we really need to…

A) counteract these feelings with messages of light and happiness and love in between each scene, and…

B) avoid the emotions themselves in the course of the scene.

This pertains to every actor at some point. If we act long enough, eventually we will find ourselves in a role in which the true emotional expression of that action on a repeated basis will bleed over into everyday life.

So we are left with the question of creating the appearance of the emotion, without abusing our own psyches, much as stage combat will create the illusion of a disabling blow, without the actor enduring that blow, night in and night out.

I begin to experiment. The doctor has no idea what I am really going through. He or she sees my reaction and connects their own dots. They know the news that they have delivered. They see me shudder, go blank, tune out, and struggle with the news. They assume that what they are seeing is the impact of a horrible discovery, too terrible to confront.

Here is the secret:

Reach for whatever makes you emotional *now.*

Whatever is on your mind now will make an impact on you.

We could, I suppose, recall memories of a lost pet, a lost love, personal abandonment, or the dark anticipation of a painful and brief future.

We could think about those things left undone, those relationships unfulfilled, the son without his father, the parents without their son.

And, indeed, we cannot help but flash on these from time to time. They are unavoidable. They give us context. But they are scattered, and perhaps distant or remote by the time we approach the 100th performance.

But turn to what makes you tick *now.*

Perhaps it is the fresh memory of an intimate encounter. Perhaps it is a fantasy playing around the edges of your consciousness. Perhaps it is the embarrassment of a personal *faux pas*. The anger of an indignity. The frustration of a foiled attempt. The passion of a resentment toward your acting partner (in this case, the doctor). These are emotions from all over the emotional playbook, none of which is stamped with "*Death and the Void.*"

And yet, there is something in this that has the power to make us respond. Grab for that, whatever it is. Bring it to the surface. Let it play out.

You may actually be squirming with pleasure! Shuddering with embarrassment! Fuming with anger! Thrilled with excitement! Gasping with passion!

The audience does not know that. The med-student does not know that. He or she only knows the context. And they see a human being moved… impacted in a sudden and uncontrollable way.

At one point, one young med student, intending to tell me of the need to send me for a "biopsy," used the word "autopsy" by mistake.

I laughed. Certainly an inappropriate response. But the student didn't even blink. Who gets to say what is inappropriate in the moment of great pain or shock? The impulse of the moment has its own logic, and its own uncontrollable life. Unaware of his own mistake, the student assumed that I was caught up in some much more complex emotion than he understood, and redoubled his efforts to calm me down.

The audience has no other context to assess but what they see.

There are those who may be horrified that I am advising "faking it."

And yet, is not summoning up our honest emotional reservoir in service of a knowingly false emotional state just as phony, if not more phony, than using an entirely real situation to stir an honest emotional reaction?

What does the audience see? Something has happened. We are moved. And they marvel at the power of an actor to respond with such *idiosyncratic* honesty.

There comes a point at which acting is just a job. And we can't commit one hundred percent of our heart and soul to the job every minute that we are on. But we can give the audience the benefit of what we honestly have available in that moment.

Storm at Sea

John Barrymore, a rather famous drunk and an amazing actor (though the latter was not the result of the former), played an extremely successful *Hamlet* on Broadway for over a hundred performances between 1922 and 1925.

On opening night, he was still recovering from an alcoholic bender the night before, and felt himself overcome with nausea at the onset of one of Hamlet's famous soliloquies. Sidling over to the draperies that framed the stage, he ducked out for a moment to (as he phrased it) "play storm at sea," before returning to the stage to start the soliloquy.

For any other actor, this might have been a career-ending maneuver.

The next day, at least one of the reviews raved about the heart-stopping emotion of that particular moment, celebrating the bold choice, during which Barrymore was so overcome with emotion that he *"actually left the stage!"*

The moral is not to booze it up prior to a performance.

The moral is that we do not know what may be going through the various heads of the audience while we are caught up in the emotional hurly-burly of the moment. Whatever strikes us ***in the now*** will probably strike the audience as an honest emotional expression, whether or not the source of that emotion is "appropriate" to the character or the moment.

Humans are reason-making-machines. And when we, as an audience, see something happen, we provide a reason, even if the reason that we create lives entirely independent of what actually happened.

Chapter 38

Obsessions

Life's little disturbances will creep in on actors, who will always find something to obsess over.

I define an obsession as the inability to consciously direct one's thoughts away from a given topic.

There are actors who have retired from the stage for fear of an obsession which may come upon them while they are performing.

This is not stage fright. Stage fright, as we have discussed, is usually manifested in a form of panic onset, with shortness of breath, dry mouth, profuse sweating. It may be the result of an obsession, but it is not the obsession.

Performers, perhaps more than anyone (brain surgeons and nuclear technicians excepted), need the ability to control and guide their own brain. When thoughts go wandering down unexpected paths at the wrong moment they interrupt our ability to perform.

TRUE STORY

An actor in his early 70's is in rehearsal for a very large role in a two-person play. It is the fall, and during the summer he runs his own summer theatre, a quaint little place in the hills. Devastatingly, during the past summer, the place burned down. Today, he is revisited by the trauma of that incident. He sees the flames, remembers the beautiful work he had put into the place, the decorations in the lobby, the upholstering of the seats. Perhaps he is haunted with the fear of what might have happened if an audience or a loved one had been inside at the time.

Today he cannot remember his lines. He starts, gets one or two lines into the scene, wavers, falters and fails. His acting partner is patient, but she cannot get through to him. The most obvious cues, questions which demand a simple yes or no answer cannot stimulate a correct response.

From the outside, he seems distracted, absent, unfocused, as though he wore thick glasses and was trying to find his way around without them.

The staff is getting nervous. We take breaks to refocus. The actor has a cup of coffee, jokes with his acting partner, shakes out the cobwebs. But when we return to the scene, so does the obsession.

I've had experience with older actors who have struggled with their lines. I wonder if this is a cognitive loss that comes with age. I speak with the director about an understudy. The director is calm. No, he insists, the actor will be all right. Yes, we may consider an understudy in the future, but not today. We knock off early.

The next day, the actor is back at rehearsal, performing perfectly. There is no sign of yesterday's fog. A good night's sleep and some review of the lines were all the actor needed. The incident that had upset rehearsal the day before never resurfaces.

Another example…

TRUE STORY

An actress tells of the last play she performed in, years before, which left her with a fear of going back on stage. She teaches now, and something inside her feels phony, telling students how to act when she will not get back on stage herself.

Years before, amid the run of a play, her director confronted her, minutes before she went on, upset about her performance the night before. He berates, insults and lashes out. "My parents are in the audience tonight; please try to act better than the shit you did last night."

On stage, she cannot remember a single word. Nor does she feel like anything that she does might serve the play. In her mind, now, her performance has turned to "shit," and everywhere her mind turns, that word screams at her more loudly. Her fellow actors see the blank look on her face. She exits early and returns with a book in her hand, finishing out the play, and never returns to the stage.

She describes her condition as "stage fright," but what she has is a conscious and deliberate "fear-of-going-on-stage." Unlike stage fright, this is a rational, reasonable fear. Following the actual experience of a mishap on stage, she deliberately avoids being placed in that position of vulnerability.

The easy response is that she simply needs to "get back on the horse," and to a degree that is true. Her past experience will lead her to take greater precautions in memorization, so that no amount of disturbance can drive the lines from her mind. A couple of successes will also erase that director's insult as the final arbiter of her abilities.

She has, however, turned into a director who is ferociously protective of her actors prior to a show. She will not give notes, and will not let anyone approach or disturb them as they prepare. I am sure she is a terrific director to work for, although I am also sure that life's little disturbances will creep in on her actors, who will always find something to obsess over, protected or not.

While these are two of the most dramatic examples, we encounter obsessions in more subtle forms all of the time. Any emotional experience: an argument with a loved one, a break up, a rejection from a job, a bit of rudeness in passing, a simple misunderstanding, a cell phone and more are waiting to derail any one of us from our intended train of thought.

One day, I made my entrance at the top of a 90-minute one-man play, and only then discovered that this performance would be sign-language-interpreted for the hearing impaired! The delicate series of cues and interactions which led me through these then-freshly memorized words would now be underlined and accentuated by arms and hands signaling less than ten feet away, between myself and the audience that I was addressing. Even thinking about the process of signing (or wondering how the interpreter could ever possibly keep up), threatened to throw me off of the internal maze that was the pattern of my thoughts.

It so happens that this external distraction forced me to focus that much more intensely, and the performance came off with no evident mistakes.

When events like this spring upon me (in more performances than not), I actually do *not* want to be in touch with my deepest emotional self. I rely instead on my great investment in rehearsal. A series of rituals lead me into the character. Physical activities remind me of who I am playing and what I have to do. An intricate score of action and activity carries me along. Sometimes, generous and alert fellow performers will see the blank look upon my face and get me back on track. And, sometimes, amid my one-person play, the blankness will arrive, and the only one who can save me is me. After perhaps ten seconds of garbled nonsense, I grasp a line from moments later in the play, latch onto that and ride it to the rescue. In every instance that I can ever recall, the panic of the moment seemed worse to me than it ever did to the audience who, should I mention it after the show, may well have no idea what I am talking about.

And while I may want to let them know that I can, indeed, do the show better than what they saw, it's better to let them enjoy their ignorance. Suggesting that tonight's play was less than it could be only leaves them feeling cheated.

Don't apologize. Move boldly forward.

Chapter 39

Ritual and the Inner Creative Mood

As long as we believe it, it is true for us. And as long as it is true for us, it is effectively true.

Actors are the most ritualized people I know.[44]

When we speak of ritual and the theatre in the same breath, it is often to contemplate the Act of the Performance as an acting-out of some eternal spiritual impulse, a plea to the gods or somesuch.

My observation is much shallower than that.

Actors make rituals out of everything that they do leading up to their first entrance, and on through the intermission. The ritual may obsess them all day long. It will include…

- Things that they can and cannot eat.
- Things that they must and must not say.
- Things that they must or must not do.
- Places that they have to go, or stay away from.
- A mantra that they repeat.
- A totem that they must or must not touch.
- A song they must hear.
- A passage they must read.
- A prayer they must say.
- An exercise they must perform.
- Jokes that they must tell, songs that they must sing, makeup that they must put on, drinking that they must or must not do, sex that they must or must not have.
- On and on and on.

Actors perform one of the very few live arts, and while (like the musician or the dancer) they are very dependent on skill, actors are more dependent on the "inner creative mood."

The old observation that "no two performances are alike" is truer of acting than any other art form. From a detached perspective, we may note differences between audiences: their general demographic, the time of day, the day of the week… but actors always look at the success or failure of a given night and try to figure out just what went wrong (or right) with *themselves*, looking inside for the answers.

---

[44] Reportedly, baseball players are very similar.

Associations will be made between successful performances and those activities that were engaged in prior to the successful execution of that performance, and thereby a ritual is born.

These activities vary widely. While exercise and nutrition have a definable, demonstrable, self-evident impact, jokes and totems may not. Actors perform these rituals without even knowing why they do them. They drift to what gives them comfort in the face of that which gives them fear. If telling the same joke for the thirty-fifth time sets the mind at ease, then they will repeat it, perhaps even wondering just why they feel so compelled to do so.

Mantras

One of the most popular rituals of performance is that of repeating a phrase, a series of phrases, or a "mantra." Groups that form amid a religious community, will often gather for prayer before a performance. Other times, actors focus their psychological makeup by keeping their thoughts trained on effective ideas.

As "action" was called, Jack Lemmon used to say quietly, "It's magic time!"

I have several mantras and positive reinforcements... self-talk that I give myself to put myself into a position of confidence and character:

- "They love me already. They simply want to know that I love them, too."
- "I own this place."
- "They have never seen anything like this before, and they probably never will again."
- "I have never had an audience like this before, and I never will again."
- "There is no one who can stop me."
- "I am going to screw with their heads."
- "I am going to do a five-star show."
- "I am dancing on air."
- "I am a sexy, joyful, courageous and limitless man."
- "I am the possibility of enthusiasm, beauty and affection."

Try one of these out for yourself. Adapt it to your purposes or make up some of your own. Repeat them thirty times before going onstage. Find what prepares you for your best performance, and be ready to change over to a new one when the first choice becomes rote. Allow that mantra to lend sparkle to your performance in the middle of the show, whenever you find yourself lulled into complacency.

Some actors, myself included, will speak the lines of the play from beginning to end on the day of the performance. (I prefer doing this three times, as long as my voice is holding out.) This keeps the lines in the forefront of awareness, and enables me to react more spontaneously to other potential disturbances and discoveries made "in the moment." Whenever I can get access, I sneak into the theatre early and mark through the blocking on stage, or at home in my living room, when I cannot.

The most evidently practical ritual is the "fight call," in which the actors who have anything dangerous to perform will run the routine at half or three-quarters speed, simply to get the action "into their bones." (Fight calls are responsible for saving lives, so let's not confuse them with our more empty compulsions.)

There are the endless backstage jokes. The actor asks, "Hey, do we have any reservations tonight?" No matter how many times this has been asked, we must respond. "Yes, we have lots of reservations… but we're going to do the show anyway!"

There was the actor in the make-up room, who (to milk further cheap laughs from a series of cheap jokes in the show about sleeping with a woman whose toenails were too sharp), would shave his ankles and put bandages on them. Every night, inevitably, as we observed him perform this ritual, he would sigh with the same faux-resigned attitude: "I have no pride."

There are, of course, well-publicized backstage prohibitions:

Saying "Good luck" to someone is thought to bring bad luck. There are many theories about this, though I prefer to think it was begun by a performer who was told "good luck" and who promptly went off and broke his leg. Which may, thereby, have led to that great fake-out of fate: saying "break a leg."[45]

You are not to whistle backstage in the theatre. (I think one actress actually reported me to her union representative when I did this.)

You cannot speak aloud the title of the play *Macbeth*, or quote from the play. It must be referred to as "The Scottish Play," and any quoting thereof must be followed by some variation of going outside, spinning around in a circle three times and spitting. Or saying a line from *Hamlet*: "Angels and ministers of grace defend us!"

The stories of problems that arise around the "cursed" play, *Macbeth* are legion. Most actors can tell you at least one. The only production with which I have been directly involved saw the director fired in the first week of rehearsal. A second director was hired, and his wife left him. The actor playing the role of Macbeth fell amid a rehearsal, getting a particularly nasty gash in his back. (*Coincidence?*)

There are further *Macbeth* stories of outdoor productions, where clouds gather and thunder rumbles the moment they start to perform, only to subside every time they pause the show.

Of course, people may get fired, divorced, rained on, and at some point, die in any given play. But because it sometimes happens during *Macbeth*, we have a

[45] Perhaps the least fun (and most likely) of the theories is the suggestion that the successful performer would have to stoop or crouch to pick up money thrown by the audience, thereby "breaking" the straight line of the leg.

special bookmark in our minds that reinforces our interpretation of the bad fortune.

Which brings us to the essential point

A ritual has very little to do with what actually does or does not happen on stage. A ritual has almost everything to do with what we BELIEVE will happen on stage. Will rubbing the head of a red-headed child immediately prior to making my entrance actually make me a better performer?

It will if I believe that it will.

Every scientist will tell you that the process of observing cannot help but influence the thing being observed. A ritual is not accidental or random, but is taken with conscious knowledge. The intended result may be conscious or subconscious, but our intent is *to improve that thing which we plan to do next.*

We have lines and actions that we have memorized, which we must remember in succession. I may need to retain sixty to ninety minutes of material, one thing following the next.

Ask an actor to repeat a particular line from a show he or she just performed. They will probably struggle for the wording. Even if they just successfully recited that piece amid thousands more words just performed in quick succession, they will struggle with this single line.

Each line is the product of all that went before it. And what went before it may not even be a series of lines. It may be a look, a movement, a take to the audience. An actor accustomed to performing in a particular environment will have problems in a new venue. Part of what had been memorized was the environment, the relationship to the audience, the echo of the voice, the "feel" of the setting.

The first time I performed *Molière than Thou* "on the road," I lost my lines when I looked up to see that the far wall of the auditorium was nowhere near where I remembered it being! Even though that far wall of the auditorium was of absolutely no significance to the play!

We memorize a string of events and words that trace back to well before we take our first step onstage. It is linked to the things we do at the make-up table, the objects that we touch, the words that we reassure ourselves with, the food that we eat, the relationships we engage in, and so on. When we break this string we threaten the inner creative state. Once a show has closed, actors generally despair of remembering those particular lines again. Those lines were the product of that costume, that set, that make-up, those relationships.

Were we to throw that same actor into a performance of the very same play as produced by a different company, the very night following the closing of the play, we would be astonished to discover just how little the actor remembers!

The actor sees him or herself as the victim of the internal creative mood. It is something that he or she may coax and nudge. It exists as a series of doors that must be opened, so that "the muse" can enter. One cannot *drag* the muse into the room lest the work become somehow "forced." One *seduces* the muse, hoping that she will visit. One makes decisions for her: what kind of food she likes her actors to have, what jokes they should tell, what activities they should execute. When she is satisfied that her path is cleared, she may choose to appear. Is it any surprise that actors are superstitious?

This isn't "the truth" (as though there were some abstract entity out there called "the truth" which would judge whether the muse had or had not made her appearance). But as long as we believe it, it is true for us. And as long as it is true for us, it is effectively true.

Therefore, if there is anything that is under our conscious control it is what we choose to make True For Us.

If we can consciously make something True-For-Us, there may be a benefit to making what is true-for-us into that which is also Healthy-For-Us. That is to say, having that one cigarette or cocktail before going onstage is not a good choice to manufacture into truth. Taking a vitamin, flossing our teeth, exercising… these are better choices. Replace bad rituals with good ones and we may discover that, the more we perform, the more our lives are improving, rather than the reverse.

Chapter 40

Second Night Syndrome

The learning is my immediate downfall... because I then proceed to play to my learning.

Here is how theatre goes:

A) **Final dress rehearsal**: Disasters left and right. No one is paying attention, the show seems boring, the jokes seem lame.

B) **Opening night**: Close to perfect. The show is dazzling, the audience loves it, the damn thing clicks!

C) **Second performance**: What happened to the incredible show? The audience is bored, the jokes aren't working, the play falls on deaf ears!

The rest of the run continues an oscillating process between B and C: brilliance and blandness. One or two nights will be "on," we will assume that all of the problems are resolved.

And then the show will crash and burn and we will realize that the whole thing is a piece of crap, built on an illusion to begin with!

We find ourselves back at the beginning. Everyone who acts knows this pattern. Many instinctively know why.

We are caught again in the paradox of knowing and not knowing. With the final dress rehearsal, we actually know the play too well, but not well enough. We know what we are supposed to be doing. We know the words. But the show that was so hilarious or powerful the very first time we read it has by now gone stale. We know all of the twists and turns that the plot is going to take, and we cannot be surprised by them. The director has spent the last week occupied with lighting, costume, scenery and prop issues, and has stopped giving full attention to the acting. Our resource for where we are going and what needs to happen has ducked out on us.

The next night, that resource is replaced by the audience. And for the first *and only time*, we have no idea what is going to happen!

The first audience is impenetrable, unknowable. And finally, we "hear" the show again. We realize the exact moment that the meaningful bit of exposition falls in place as we sense the light bulbs lighting up over the heads of all of the audience, sometimes accompanied by gasps, murmurs or laughter. We are reminded of the play as it lived six weeks before. With nothing to rely on but my audience and echoes of the director's voice, I focus on the task at hand: speaking the words, navigating each moment, pursuing the objective, being the character.

The audience then proceeds to tell me:

- This bit is funny.

- This bit is serious.
- This is wild.
- This is subdued.
- This is outrageous.
- This is tragic.

I learn from them.

And one night's learning becomes my subsequent downfall.

Because I then proceed to *play* to my *learning*.

My character doesn't know what is going to happen next. He is surprised when something happens to him. He is listening for the next thing, and the next thing. The power of that surprise, like the sharpness of the rise or descent in the roller coaster, is what captivates the audience.

The next night, we arrive knowing what will happen next. We have "read our reviews," and we perform to the strengths of those responses, rather than the demands of each moment. This is an unavoidable human reality.

Performing three times a week over the course of eight weeks, or eight times a week over the course of three weeks, the thing seems to level out quite a bit. We know where we are going, and we are sure of how we are going to get there. The mystery of the audience has been effectively penetrated. We even have methods for predicting the audience. If they laugh at this line, they are subtle and intelligent. If they laugh at this line, they are raucous and enthusiastic. The questions are not about what may happen next (or if we will even get through the thing!), but about what score we will ring up. Will this ongoing joke get a laugh every time? Will the curtain call get them out of their seats? I may get more efficient in performing the play, and more capable in producing the results on stage, but the immediacy and intensity of the audience's reaction seems to diminish.

We take a break, with two weeks between performances, and get some distance, not thinking about the show at all and then remount the play in a new theatre or at a festival. We have unexpectedly recreated the circumstances of the first time. Once again, we don't remember just what is "supposed" to happen from one instant to the next. We're uncertain about our ability to even get through the thing without faltering. This uncertainty finds its way into the performance and actually improves what we do. The rises seem sharper, the declines more sudden.

It is the difference between getting ***there*** and ***getting*** there. The journey makes the play, not the destination. In fact, there really is no "there" to get to. The audience did not pay to see the climax of the play, but to follow the journey, piecing together the elements that contribute to an eventual resolution. They want to work their way through the whys and wherefores. They want to draw together the threads of these lives, now entangled with their own.

Any given phrase or word might impact our audience. Any given line might strike them as the most important thing said all night long. We actors want to say, "No, listen to this! *This* is the important part!" And we build our performance to focus on "this" rather than "that." But the audience will go its own way. References to a lover, a child, a parent, a disease, an event, will take people in their own direction, waking them up to their own lives. That direction, added to a million other possible influences will add up to one all-encompassing event, providing "meaning" where meaning did not formerly exist. They leave the theatre as a collective of people who have been through a common experience... each having arrived, wandering their own path.

We need to stumble upon the thing as if it were the first time. Our controlling self runs the show from the brain, but our enacting selves take orders from elsewhere. We dance along the delicate balance of the controller and the enactor, giving and taking, grasping and releasing, steering and drifting. We repeat what we have done a million times before, all the while trying to forget the fact that we have ever done it once.

That is the predicament of being an actor. A dance with which we are blessed and to which we are condemned.

Or...

Unless you happen to be one of those actors who are blessed with a facility for not caring.

Most of us care so much that we will put up with all the obnoxious treatment that a theatre might give in order to participate. In order to get better. In order to *win* this time. We do it for the joy of being there. For the pleasure of self-expression. To be seen and heard. And the people who are simply there to punch a clock, to get in and get out… often diminish the joy we take in the doing. We feel bad for trying to do it better. We feel uncool for caring so much. We are trying new things, praying for good reviews, bigger audiences, new breakthroughs or discoveries. We want to walk the tightrope, execute the dive, vault the obstacle in the public eye, and nail our landing with a "10.00".

Some are quite content to check in with an above average "7," perhaps nudging towards an "8" and clock out at the end of the night without giving a second thought to what might be waiting on the other side of that "8."

It takes a ton of energy to generate the original creative impulse, dislodging it from its anchor point of inertia. It floats, delicately, looking for a place to land, where it will be received, honored, nurtured, appreciated, and effective.

It takes an ounce of cynicism to kill it.

Chapter 41

How Actors See the World

A good actor not only believes in him or herself onstage, but also understands the specific level of belief that is relevant to the project at hand.

This is a true story, told with as little detail as possible in hopes that the real people involved do not recognize themselves and sue my butt.

As a university faculty member I was requested, on occasion, to adjudicate a performance for festival competition. The term adjudicate has, of late, fallen on hard times, smacking of judgment and finality. We now refer to them as "responses."

But back in the day, they were adjudications, and I went to Iowa to see a production of *Peter Pan* that was, to this adjudicator's thinking, of less than superior quality.

We (they sent us out in pairs, then) instinctively sense that there are issues, particularly when the director is making far too much of our presence. A battery of ready excuses is presented, suggesting that sickness, politics, misfortune, conspiracy or some other forces have taken action against the production, limiting the success of the result. (All of which may be, and probably are, true.) The director is certain, however, that trained adjudicators will see beyond the adversity to the quality of the initial vision. Somewhere in the background of this conversation linger issues of *tenure* as the director seeks something on paper to bear witness to the quality of his work, while the school is contemplating, perhaps, the opposite accumulation of evidence.

This night was not to support the argument on the director's behalf. Which is not to say that the director was a bad director or a bad person. But tonight's show was not so great.

When a play is not executed well, the adjudicator/respondent becomes more suggestive than direct. We make very few sweeping statements about the-quality-thing, and discuss more specifically the "choices" which might have been made in a more opportune manner.

As the evening, and our response, drew on, it was difficult to limit the many "choices" we enumerated, so that, however delicately we may have couched our criticism, and however wittily we may have tap-danced around serious issues, the impression was ultimately left that the play did seem to lack in that ever-elusive category of *quality*.

The next responsibility of the adjudicator is to get out of town without doing any more damage than absolutely necessary.

But on this occasion there were people who wanted to chat, and we lingered.

Evidently everyone was walking on eggshells that night, and I cannot say for certain that the quality issue was not exacerbated by a difficult cast, or the trap of some nasty inter-departmental politics. I simply suggest that the director's demeanor did not start me thinking with confidence about *helmsmanship*.

I was approached by one of the thirty or forty cast members, one that I assume, has gone on to bigger and better things in the many years since this conversation.

> *"I was just wondering if you could tell – you must have been able to tell – that there was one actor on that stage tonight who had lost all the joy of performing?"*
>
> Um... I'm sorry?
>
> *"You must have seen – I mean, how could you not have seen – that there was one actor on stage who simply didn't enjoy performing anymore."*
>
> Well, there were, like, thirty-five people in the cast.

[Thirty-five people on a monster of a stage, which swallowed them up like ants on a hill.]

> *"Yes, but certainly you noticed that there was someone who just wasn't enjoying himself up there."*
>
> Do you mean... you?
>
> *"Yes, I mean, how could you not tell? I was completely bored and put off. I just don't even actually know if I want to be a performer anymore."*

[I looked at him more intently. Some memory of our post-show discussion (in which this actor had been an active participant) clicked in the back of my head.]

> You played... *the dog.*
>
> *"Exactly. Yes. I was the dog. You could tell. Couldn't you?"*
>
> You were wearing... *a dog suit.*
>
> *"That's right! That was me. So. You saw."*
>
> Um... the suit kind of covered you up from head to toe. There wasn't any part of you that was actually showing.
>
> *"Yes, but certainly you could tell in the general... listlessness of my character, that all the excitement was gone."*
>
> You know, given the fact that the suit pretty much covered you up... and most of your 'lines' were, like, barks and growls, I have to say that I wasn't really reading that much into it. I mean, beyond a certain requisite level of... of friskiness, which, I must say, you performed beautifully, the general... *malaise* that you seem to be describing didn't quite *come across the footlights*.

Need I explain how difficult the actor found this to believe, and how earnestly he told me of the sadness of his disenchantment with the theatre?

Nor did I have any difficulty imagining the struggles in rehearsal, as the dog questioned at length the details of its motivation.

This is the way that actors think. It is all about them. The audience must be so committed to the details of this actor's particular, individual performance that they are, in fact, reading the actor's mind! Even beyond distances of a hundred feet, amid a crowd of a cast of thirty-five, and through the intervening, obstructing veil of a dog suit!

If you are not an actor, you may not get what's so funny about this. If you are, you are laughing with recognition of a significant percentage of the people you have worked with.

But this also points up the impossibility of an actor truly knowing how he comes across, or sensing the "big picture" of what the play is all about. To that actor, the play was about him. The inconvenient presence of Peter, or Wendy, or Captain Hook, the bands of pirates or lost boys, simply took away from the story of the dog… who was now disenchanted with the art of acting.

A good actor not only believes in him or herself onstage, but also understands the specific level of belief that is relevant to the project at hand. The rules are different for children's plays than they are for adult plays. They are different between musicals and dramas, between dramas and comedies, between farces and fantasies, and between lavish pageants and psychological explorations, and when you treat a fantasy as weightily as you would treat Chekhov, for instance, you are expending a lot of unnecessary, and probably counter-productive energy.

Mark Twain said "Never try to teach a pig to sing. It wastes your time and annoys the pig."

We actors are at the center of our own special universe. Some actors embrace that notion, and are occasionally more successful for the fact of being unable to comprehend the crude mechanics that shape the audience's point of view. But they are usually not very pleasant people to work with.

Chapter 42

Bluffing

"Yes, I am tough enough, pretty enough, bold enough, clever enough, resourceful enough, talented enough, exciting enough to be this person, hold this space on the stage, wear this costume, kiss this girl/kiss this boy, speak these words."

What we believe to be probably true and get the world around us to act in accordance with as well is, ostensibly, true.

What we act in accordance with being true, and get the world around us to accept as being true, is, ostensibly, true.

This sounds like some kind of heresy, and it probably is, but it's also the foundation for art: Bluffing.

Painter X and Picasso may be indistinguishable in style, execution or content. But the *bluff* that is "Picasso" (the image, not the man), is worth several million more, per painting, than Painter X. Picasso created a vision of the universe and stayed true to his vision. The world came around.

Gladiators!

Let's say I direct a play. And I decide that Play X is about "Man's Inhumanity To Man." And in support of that "truth" I come up with the concept of *gladiators*. I set the play in the round. I decide on a toga theme in the costumes, while the oppressors of the conflict are decked in fur to symbolize the lions in the arena. The blocking features stalking, animal-like movements. There is an unexplained layer of dirt on the stage floor, and a wooden barrier between the actors below and the audience above. For every theatrical element: lights, props, voice, music… there is a corresponding analogy that fits my theatrical "truth."

Now while I may have just described a (purposely) lame concept, I'm not intending to suggest that this is, of necessity, a bad play, nor that anyone is especially delusional in thinking that this is going to work. What is significant is the process of bluffing that is crucial to the work of any artist or, for that matter, to everyday life.

Once I have convinced myself of the essential truth… that my concept will support the action of the play and reveal greater truth behind the work in the process, I must then convince others of this same truth. Unless I can convince others of this truth, or at least of a temporary acceptance of this truth in the spirit of seeing where this notion may lead us, my concept will go nowhere. It will be "false."

I have to convince a producer. Whether it is a single individual putting up money, a board of directors responsible for the work of a non-profit theatre, an artistic director, a faculty, or somesuch, there is some person or persons who either give the go ahead, suggesting that this concept is worth the time, the money, the space and the manpower to be invested, or else withhold that endorsement.

And so I explain my point of view. It floats there in the space between us. They look for my smile. Am I joking? Am I testing them? Are there notes for some other version of the play tucked away somewhere, which I will haul out to present as the "real" concept?

"You don't really mean to suggest that..." comes the reply.

"Actually, yes, I do," I reply, coolly. "In these days of dropping bombs on helpless, underdeveloped nations, choking routes of food supply, limiting access to water, targeting and attacking ethnicities, we are no better than the Romans persecuting the Christians. By setting Play X in the Coliseum, I intend to underline the inherent sadism in Man's treatment of Man..." And so on.

It is not relevant whether anything that I say is "true," so much as that I am willing to act in accordance with it *being* true. Of course, if I have misjudged the political sensibilities of my board of directors, I may find that my "truth" has banged up against theirs and they will start seeking a new director. But, assuming that it hasn't, the play moves on. I have one endorsement, ostensibly the most important, behind me, but that simply sets the framework for a series of bluffs yet to come.

There is the scene designer who was looking forward to doing something more abstract and artsy. He was looking for a stark, poetic *Waiting-for-Godot*-type setting on which the action would play out. That's what the script seemed to call for.

There is the costume designer who had been looking for an opportunity to finally set a play in the eighteenth century. Her resume is heavy on the modern stuff or the Shakespearean era stuff. Her need to fill a niche in her portfolio created a readiness to a particular kind of truth. Working her around to a vision of my truth will take some doing.

While I, as the director, am the nominal authority for this production, what happens when the scene designer and costume designer may each have twenty more years of seniority in the department? (Organization charts are rarely reflective of actual power or influence.)

I am not making many friends in the process of standing for my particular truth. And the acceptance of the truth that I am proposing is getting a tenuous "buy-in" at best. But I seem to have a point, and I seem to have an answer to all of their questions and, perhaps most importantly, there doesn't seem to be some alternate truth that I am interested in. And gradually *my* truth becomes *our* truth.

Probably more difficult than any of these conversations, I must convince a group of actors that this "truth" is worth spending six weeks of their lives in telling.

- That in the process of wearing togas and loincloths, strutting and stalking their hour upon the stage, they will not look like idiots.
- That they are not killing their hopes of a theatre career in the process.
- That they will be *celebrated* as bold, innovative, exciting and risky.

I have a hard time believing it myself. I step back and look at the incredibly shaky house of cards that is the foundation for our play, and know that all it will take is a single person shouting "The Emperor has no clothes!" to betray our truth, to undermine the process and dash us from the heights of passion and vision to the depths of foolishness and ridicule. But I will not be the first person to call my bluff. It will be someone else, and when that person calls it, I wonder if I will have mustered the support of the entire team of actors, designers and producers, to stand behind my vision and empower it to prevail.

Somehow, we have made it through the process. We have built costumes, sets, characterizations, sounds, props, lobby decorations, programs, all in keeping with the essential truth that man's inhumanity to man, as realized in a Roman arena, is a valid artistic playing field for the action of Play X to play out upon.

Which means continuing to bluff the feature writers, the reviewers, the audience and the public at large. Something that began as an instinct had to be developed, defined, enlarged upon, elaborated, enriched, and, sometimes… *bullshitted* into a reasonable facsimile of the truth.

It is not important that this is the truth.

It is important that we all act in accordance with it being the truth.

Because there, at some point, the public will be given the chance to see the thing as a bold, visionary work of genius. Or… crap.

The well-trod concepts that are out there are pretty stale. "I see this play as a circus." "A chess match." "A tennis match." "A prize fight." Name your simile. While you're at it, please, come up with something new. Or come up with something so old that we are charmed by its simplicity.

Because whatever it is then becomes what it is.

And we have to bluff our way through, all the way to the end. And it has to work, not only for the director, but for the producers, designers, actors, the press and the audience. And when it does indeed work, it becomes "the truth."

But what does all this have to do with acting?

If I act like a person who has talent… If I bluff my way through the notion that my emotional life is important, I gradually become that important, emotional, passionate, risky, exciting actor. And just who is to say no?

Of course, it takes work to construct this bluff: First I have to convince a director who is going to cast me. At any moment during the audition I might well sabotage myself.

Actors do this all the time!

We break character. We say, "I'm sorry, that sucked." We apologize. We wink. We even demonstrate by exaggeration just how distant we are personally from this role, almost to the point of rolling our eyes, muttering under our breath, and shaking our heads with every line!

We are afraid we might get caught, not knowing how inadequate that we are. Or aspiring to something we all know we can't be. It is more important to us that we demonstrate that we know better, than that you shoot us down yourself, and scorn us for our scandalous pretense.

We actors must bluff. We must let it all hang out there, before the audience, the director, the fellow actors. Every ounce of our being must defy others to take us seriously. Whatever voices may be screaming in our heads (and they scream pretty loudly), we must counter them with, "Yes, I am tough enough, pretty enough, bold enough, clever enough, resourceful enough, talented enough, exciting enough to be this person, hold this space on the stage, wear this costume, kiss this girl/kiss this boy, speak these words."

Even while our inner being is screaming that we are totally incapable of conjuring the emotional life of the character... When our little monitor is telling us that we should have tears in such a moment, "but where are the tears?!" In every moment of challenge, we must act in accordance with a simple formula:

If it were true, how would I act?

If those tears were flowing, well then certainly my eyes would get puffy, my nose would flare, I would start to sniffle, my hand would reach up to brush the tears away, and, in fact, my entire being would probably struggle against those tears. And this brings us back to our paradox of acting:

While we, as actors are usually fighting to create an emotional state, emotional states are involuntary, and we, as characters are usually fighting to escape them.

I layer my performance with bluffs. Someone this passionate would probably stand like this, feel energy from this part of the body, walk with this kind of a crouch, growl with this kind of a voice, jump onto his lines with this kind of an abruptness, hide these given facts, smile with this kind of a... and so on. The list is endless, and the more bluffs that we surround ourselves with, or bury ourselves under, the more likely we will be successful in our portrayal.

And, eventually, we stop calling them bluffs, and they stop seeming to be bluffs to us. Since, for all practical purposes, from 8pm to 10pm, we do everything that person does, and everyone else in the play treats us as if these qualities belong to us, then in that time and in that place, we *are* that person, and that is what is true about us. ***And the burden of proof lies with anyone suggesting that somehow this is not!***

And, while we're in the process of drawing this line, let us extend it one meter further.

This theory also holds true in so-called "real" life. Whether it's about my nature as a person or my concept of the world, the "truth" is what I act in accordance with.

I am wary of any politician tossing the word "truth" around like he or she have somehow got the handle on the only truth that exists. It is comforting, somehow to think that we might well have that handle in our grasp. But it is in fact, simply our vision of the truth, with which we act in accordance.

Change your action, change your truth.

Part VI

PUTTING IT TOGETHER

Chapter 43

"Oh, What A Falling Off Was There!" Comedy vs. Tragedy

Characters evolve in tragedy. Characters flip in comedy.

What is the "secret" to comedy?

The many answers to this all seem to get more obscure and esoteric. The answer seems evident to me, and I'm sure my particular answer will fail to take into account one of the great metaphysical explanations.

Here's an answer we hear often, that seems to approach the truth. It was one of Woody Allen's characters who said:

"Comedy is tragedy plus time."

That is to say that what seems to be tragic to us in this moment becomes comic when looked upon from a later date… the distance of a year, say, or a century. When we look back from our place of un-involvement, or un-commitment, we find that there is humor where we didn't expect to discover it.

While this may explain how the same events can strike us in either a tragic or a comic vein, it doesn't really explain why the action that we are watching right here, "in the now" may seem either comic or tragic.

We see *Old Yeller* and (*Spoiler alert!*) we cry every time that they have to shoot the dog. And yet, we see the dog getting abused in *Something About Mary* and we howl with laughter. Or, we see the cover of *National Lampoon* that says "Buy this magazine or we'll shoot this dog," and it's hilarious.

Some suggest it isn't the time, but the distance: "Comedy is tragedy plus distance." An audience feels safely distanced from the emotional repercussions of the moment whereby they know that they are not expected to feel. Nor are we really encouraged to expect that the real dog in *Something About Mary* has, indeed, been hurt. Nor will that dog on the magazine cover likely get shot.

But how can that inform our performance? How does the audience "know that they're not expected to feel?" Is it possible to take the exact same speech and play it in a comic versus a tragic vein? Could we get laughs with *Hamlet* or *King Lear*? Could *Tartuffe* be played "straight?" And, if it does live in the style of our performance, how might that *Tartuffe* speech be performed to maximize the laughs?

Some have suggested that *exaggeration* is the secret to playing comedy. If I am bigger, grander, more outrageous or ridiculous, then the audience is supplied that necessary "distance." They are told "this is not real," and it is okay to laugh.

Certainly we want actors to reach beyond the mundane, to take chances, to be big, to be seen and to be heard. But we would want that almost as much in a tragedy as in a comedy. And even as we encourage the actors to exaggerate, we still want them to play their objectives seriously.

Theatre is about change. Plays are built upon expectations of a beginning, middle and end. We establish a status quo. We shake the status quo, and we wind up with a new situation, the result of whatever element was added to the mix. Thus we have change, and we understand a reason for the change. (Or, a reason for the *lack* of change in the Theatre of the Absurd.)

The difference is in the manner that those changes arise. To be specific: *in their rhythm.*

Old Yeller takes the entire movie to prepare us for the killing of the dog. Realizations gradually evolve and we are impacted by the change in circumstances that makes the action necessary. *Something About Mary* abuses the dog in ninety different ways in the course of ninety minutes. Something has been seriously altered in the *rhythm* of change.

"Oh, what a falling off was there."

In *Hamlet* Ophelia makes the above observation as the result of a long, involved development. "Oh, how the mighty hath fallen!" is another such serious-play observation. I think we see these remarks in serious drama in order to alert the audience that change has, in fact, happened! At such a moment, we are invited to gaze backwards over the landscape of the action of the play and appreciate just how far the hero has come, to understand the depth of character that has evolved, strand by strand, into a new human being, ever more complex, and profoundly moving.

In a comedy, expectations, status developments, new discoveries and resolutions happen much more sharply.

"You're just not the man I thought I knew."

This is the sort of comment we hear in a comedy… more often as the result of a misunderstanding. We, in the audience, all want to call out, "Oh, no, he's no different than he was before. He just had to do a few things to handle those *circumstances* that arose."

There's another clue: Comedy is more about circumstances and situations. Tragedy is more about character.

Humor lies in the sharpness of the fall. If a character in a *comedy* were to say "Oh, what a falling off was there," she would most likely talking about the change "*from the guy I thought you were five seconds ago!*"

Think of a roller coaster with its gradual inclines, as well as its sharp rises and falls. A tragedy might well describe a single rising and falling action, with a lot of level paths in between. A comedy would hit the same highs and lows that a tragedy explores, but with virtually no level space. A comedy is almost constantly rising and falling, going from the highest highs to the lowest lows, and reaching each extreme twenty to thirty times during the course of the action.

Some actors will instinctively try to smooth out those changes, perhaps to make them more "believable" or "consistent." Those are serious actors who struggle when they try to play comedy.

Have you ever heard a sudden laugh in the middle of the most serious action? As an audience we seek out these moments to laugh if only to relieve the relentless tension. How often do we actors hear this and complain that the audience somehow hasn't "gotten it?" That they have failed the play in some manner?

The audience, like the customer, is always right. Don't waste your breath complaining about them. Look, instead, for what is encouraging their reaction.

Much Ado About Nothing finds the reluctant lovers Beatrice and Benedick finally confessing to their love for each other. The actors may commit with intensity and passion. The scene plays out:

BENEDICK
... I protest I love thee.

BEATRICE
Why then, God forgive me!

BENEDICK
What offence, sweet Beatrice?

BEATRICE
You have stayed me in a happy hour: I was about to protest I loved you.

BENEDICK
And do it with all thy heart.

BEATRICE
I love you with so much of my heart that none is left to protest.

BENEDICK
Come, bid me do any thing for thee.

BEATRICE
Kill Claudio.

I have yet to hear this last line delivered in such a way that it does not get a laugh. However "serious" the actors may be in playing the scene, however dead on, however cold the actress may be in delivering her pronouncement, "Kill Claudio" always gets a laugh.

Is the audience wrong? Shakespeare, in his genius, built the scene with a crescendo that he resolves with a rimshot. He wants us to laugh there, and all attempts to kill that laugh are just so much spitting into the face of the wind.

Characters evolve in tragedy. Characters flip in comedy.

Go back to our *Tartuffe* monologue (page 105) and try it two different ways. Play it once as Tragedy, and play it once as Comedy. The comic Tartuffe makes sudden, sharp discoveries. The serious Tartuffe has gradual inclines and extended falls. The same monologue, two different worlds.

Forget for the moment that this is drawn from a comedy. Read it through without "winking," and without any awareness that this should be funny. Read it as an honest pursuit of what Tartuffe wants. If you can imagine the intensity of the monologue on a ten-point scale, almost as if it were the volume knob on an amplifier, let there be no increase or decrease of intensity greater than a half of a point as you move from one line of verse to the next.

It may well be sufficient for the audience to be aware of the ironic distance between who Tartuffe says he is in public, to how he acts in private to give us all the comedy that this monologue might need.

Now go back and read it again. This time, jump. Try a different tactic in the course of every line. Charge ahead. Retreat. Blurt it out. Downplay. Arbitrarily, put a change of gears into the middle of a line. Let your character choose a word in the instant before you speak it, or make a conscious choice to manipulate that word in a particular way, halfway through the process of speaking it, and let the action of that choice launch you into your next tactic.

In the comic reading, we are aware of sudden changes, not gradual realizations. The comic actor "works" the material more actively, more instantaneously. We see tactics playing out, shifting, adjusting, realigning. It is not the slow erosion of the tide which might ultimately wear its way through a rock wall. It is a series of sharp, sudden strokes, which may not be as powerful in the long run. Each individual stroke alerts us that it is all right to laugh at life viewed through this lens.

And, while we may have dismissed "exaggeration" as the key component of comedy above, none of this is to suggest that the comic variation might not also be more exaggerated, or outrageous. As we block the show, we find Tartuffe falling to his knees, ripping open his shirt, sniffing Elmire's perfume, touching her hair, or licking his lips. We may choose to "punch it up" with higher highs, lower lows, and sharper distinctions between the two, making the laughs more overt and predictable.

But underneath it all, it is the rhythm with which the event plays out that spells the difference between our laughter and our tears.

Chapter 44

Commedia, Caricature, and the Super-Objective

The more the subject chases the object of his desire, the further driven from its achievement he finds himself.

How many of you can do an impression of a member of the faculty?

(...)

Okay, if I ask your teacher, here, to close her eyes, and ask again – with the assurance that I'm not actually going to ask any of you to do one here and now – how many of you can do an impression of a member of the faculty?

Okay, now we're up to about nine-tenths of the class. Don't be embarrassed. That's what young actors sitting around waiting to get cast naturally do. You develop characters. Those characters are your stock-in-trade. I'd be concerned if you did not have such a characterization handy.

Your impression of that particular faculty member may only be your impression of somebody else's impression of someone else's impression. It may, in fact, be an impression that has been handed down from one graduating class to the younger classes, gradually built over a period of a dozen years or more, but it is, for our purposes, a stock character, one which we may pull down off of the shelves of the "stock room," as it were. When I was a student, I think I was able to do impressions of teachers from whom I'd never actually taken a class, or even met!

As a *Commedia* performer in the 17th century, you may have made a living out of playing a single stock character for your entire career! You may well have learned Harlequino from your father, and you may play it until you can no longer execute the pratfalls and gymnastics that Harlequino demands, at which point you pass the role on to your son, who by this time has learned all of your moves, and can improvise around Harlequino's antics for any of the dozen or more scenarios that the company may perform.

Does that happen today? Do people play the same stock character through an entire lifetime?

(...)

No?

Okay, take a look at Hollywood. Who can you name from the movies who plays essentially the same character, in every movie in which they appear?

"Rodney Dangerfield."

"Mae West."

"Groucho Marx."

"Marilyn Monroe."

"Woody Allen."

"Sylvester Stallone."

"Jennifer Anniston."

"Bruce Willis."

Okay, so actually it's probably harder to come up with names of actors who play substantially DIFFERENT characters in every performance! But we can see that certain performers have tapped into something special inside them, and they bring that special quality to everything they do. That's not to say that they're bad actors, so much as that they've found the one thing inside themselves that resonates with audiences, and they've found a way to portray that... to make it available to an audience.

Rodney Dangerfield is the perfect example. Everyone knows that he's the guy who "never gets no respect." He futzes with his tie. He's uncomfortable inside of his clothes. He shrugs and rotates his shoulders. His voice has a particular lilt to it, a predictable rise and fall. In *Commedia* terms, we would say he has a specific vocabulary of *lazzi* (also known as "comic business," or "bits" or "shtick") that effectively communicates his character.

We generally aren't particularly aware of Rodney Dangerfield "playing" this character or this attitude. Somehow it seems to be "who he is" down inside, and yet sharper, more distinct, articulated... "played up." Somewhere along the line, he made a discovery about himself that he was able to bring to everything that he did.

We each of us have that special quality within ourselves that is waiting to supply us an endless stream of comic *lazzi*. It is possible to recreate ourselves as a caricature, a theatricalized variation of our own personality.

Caricature and Currency

To explore how caricature may give us new insight into *Commedia*, we look with greater detail at our most successful *Commedia*-influenced playwright.

Molière created characters dominated by a single character trait. In fact, the titles of most of these plays were reflective of the dominant trait of the lead character. It is what I refer to as their "***Currency***" the thing in their life that carries the greatest emotional *value* against which all other value and worth is measured.

***The Miser*:** Harpagon's "currency" is the most obvious of them all: **money**. He wants more of it. He hoards what he has. He buries it out in the back yard. He thinks his children are spying on him, trying to get the money that he has. He assumes that they are simply waiting for him to die, in order to inherit his fortune. But to their faces, he insists that he is broke. He will not buy new uniforms for his staff. He will not throw elaborate parties. He will invite people over, but refuse to feed them anything but soup. He plans to marry his children off to rich spouses, so that he can enjoy their money. He's a bad tipper.

***The Bourgeois Gentleman*:** Monsieur Jourdain wants nothing but to make a brilliant **impression**. He wants everyone looking at him. He hires all of the acknowledged masters in their fields to teach him how to think, how to dress, dance, fence, and act. He was born to merchant-class parents, but aspires to nobility. He *is* a nobleman (…if only all of the rest of the world knew it). As such he is thrown into a conflict of wanting to display his beautiful façade while struggling to hide the reality of his merchant-class life.

***The Misanthrope*:** Alceste wants the world to know that he is the best... a transcendent human being. The greatest thinker, moralist, ethicist. He wants to be revered for his brilliance and his honesty. And yet, in the process of "just being honest," he insults everyone. Even when they know he is right, they conspire against him because his brand of honesty can be brutal. Of course, "If they can't take it, that is their problem," he supposes. He simply wants to be **recognized** for who he is, and if the world is not ready for him, then he must shun the world. He would rather live as a hermit than accept an embarrassment or a rejection. He desires romantic love, but he kills it every time with his relentless critique of his lover. He holds his head high.

***The Imaginary Invalid*:** Argan wants your **sympathy** more than anything else. He wants to be coddled and cuddled. He wants the attention of everyone around him, and to get it, he has convinced himself that he is terribly sick. He inflates every sensation he has to the level of sickness, and consequently gets to be cared for, again and again. He takes great offense, even at offhand compliments that suggest that he is "looking well" on a given day!

Molière has constructed a series of caricatures… character sketches dominated by a single unmistakable trait.

> Think of a caricature that you have seen in the editorial page of a newspaper. There we see the President, drawn in such a manner in which a single physical characteristic dominates. It may emphasize the overlarge size of his ears, or his bulbous nose, or his squinty eyes, and the presence of that single feature is enough to tell you that the person we are meant to see in this situation is, in fact, "The President." We know that it is not a literal

representation of the President, but we still, instinctively, see the president in that portrayal of him.

Why do you suppose a political cartoonist draws a caricature rather than a portrait?

"Because, he's drawing under a deadline?"

"Because it's not worth the effort?"

"Because the idea is more important?"

"Because it would kill the joke?"

Yes. It would kill the joke, and ***the joke lives in the idea***. Viewing a portrait, people study the details, the texture, the subtle nuances of the environment or the perfection of the expression, and admire the handsomeness of the subject, or the talent of the artist. Their emotional sympathies get involved and they lose the intellectual conceit of whatever political statement the cartoonist is trying to make.

A portrait encourages us to feel. A caricature leads us to think. When we observe a character twisted out of realistic shape, we seek to understand the source of the twisting.

In the theatre, we might go this same route: to develop a caricature though the effective contortion of physical characteristics: our bodies, the use of makeup, masks or our own "rubber faces."

More impactfully, though, a theatrical "twisting" of caricature lives in the exaggerations of the character's central *desire*, a single-minded obsession at the heart of a character, from which plot developments and complications may spiral outward. In our theatrical terminology, we have come to refer to this as the character's "super-objective." In psychological terms, I think of it as "***Currency***:" a kind of "gold standard," where true value is determined by a very specific kind of emotional gratification.

Building his characters around a single point of obsession, Molière led us to think more than we empathize... to exaggerate a human desire out of proportions, leading us to question just what might distort a human being to such a degree, and what the impact that distortion might have when taken to its most outrageous conclusion. Amid that thinking and questioning, he enabled us to laugh.

Molière took his observations from the real world: people whose desire for money, impressiveness, recognition, or sympathy led to bad choices, alienated their families, or disrupted the community, and made vivid statements about them by focusing, integrating and pointing up those super-objectives so fully that the distortion was unmistakable. No one could miss the issue driving a character so evidently beyond the edges of reason.

And while "super-objective," is our conceptual framework for the stage, when we think of it as "Currency," we may also turn our attention inwards, to see traces of this in our own lives, the desire for that special something that motivates us more than all others.

For some, that desire, or currency, may be for something so obvious as money, yet we may just as well find ourselves driven by the need for attention (common in actors) or affection, power, sex, respect, food, popularity...

And in that grasp of our own inner drives, we may also find the roots of a caricature that is very personal to us... a commedia character, of sorts, that comes with our own particular stamp.

If you want a clue about where to look for Currency in your own life, start with your expectations around your closest loved ones.

Here's the secret. Are you ready?

Our "Currency" is the thing that we use as a substitute for love!

"Love" is one of life's great unprovables.

We may be fairly confident that we are loved, but love is not a thing that we can posses. It needs to be backed by a "gold standard," that thing that will demonstrate its value to the owner. I may be fairly sure that you love me, but when you... fix me breakfast/spend time with me/come to my play/kiss me warmly/share my interests... then, I know.

Speak the following sentence aloud. How would you complete it? "If you really loved me you would ___________________________." (Don't ignore whatever the first thing was that came to mind!)

When you find out *what that thing is*, whether it is money, attention, affection, sex, power, or something else, you will know your Currency... and perhaps also unravel that Commedia caricature that lives inside of us, much as Rodney Dangerfield, Mae West or Groucho Marx each, individually, discovered their own.

Think of it this way: If Rodney Dangerfield's caricature was confident that he was loved... would he have been so desperate for respect?

Get to the heart of what your character wants above all else. More than what they say they want, look to where their actions take them. What is "love" to them?

Harpagon, Molière's "Miser," is faced with a choice between the girl he says that he loves, and a box of money.

Guess which he chooses?

Chapter 45

The Secret Commedia Formula

...the "geometric complexity" of a scene.

Things go from bad to worse...

Your objective may be to fix things, or to make things better, but every step that you take to improve things either leaves you right where you began or in a worse position than when you started.

- The more the subject chases the object of his stated desire, the further driven from its achievement he finds himself.
- This is often because people and characters may chase the loves that they think they want, but the actions that they actually pursue rarely match their *stated desires*. Harpagon gets the money, but not the girl; Monsieur Jourdain gets his brilliant impression, but not his Marquise; Alceste gets his big, self-righteous gestures, but not Celimene.

Let us explore a caricature of a man who wants to avoid attention, humiliated under the slightest glare of the spotlight. He wants to disappear into the background and would rather the world pass him by unnoticed. We'll improvise with this particular obsession for a bit to see it play out.

As we assume the character of this new being, our overriding super-objective stimulates our eyes to widen and our mouth to shrink. As we perceive the world going by, our shoulder blades pinch towards each other, and the shoulders creep upwards. Our mouth tightens when we speak, and the voice that emerges does not resonate in the chest, or even the throat. It lives mostly in the cheeks and the nose. The knees pull together as the torso leans back. We are, all at once, fragile, pathetic and yet, kind of charming. Everything that we are suggests, "Let me just keep out of the way, here." We'll call the character "Don'tMindMe."

In our new persona, we give Don'tMindMe a situation which will put his super-objective into danger, my favorite scenario:

What to do with the dead body...?!

Don'tMindMe has been drinking coffee with a companion at an outdoor cafe. Perhaps, after years of going-along-to-get-along, Don'tMindMe has put his foot down and made a demand. "I want a raise." Or "I refuse to do your work for you." The shock of this unheard-of demand has startled the companion to the point of choking on a biscotti and dying.

Don'tMindMe, horrified, fears that if anyone notices, he will be implicated in the death. His *objective* may be to sink into the background and go unnoticed, but his *situation* makes him highly vulnerable to being noticed, and the issue of "What to do with the dead body?" rises to an urgency.

As Don'tMindMe, what might your strategy be in this situation?

"I would try to make it look like he's not really dead."

Great! What are five tactics that you might take to pursue this strategy in this desperate situation?

"Prop the other guy up to look casual."

"Close the guy's eyes, to make him look like he's sleeping."

"Put a newspaper in his hands to make it look like he's reading a story."

"He can pretend to read the paper over the dead guy's shoulder, and help the dead body wave at a friend passing by."

"Or, if somebody's coming by, Don'tMindMe can get interrupted, and pretend that they've been kissing."

Great! These five things could easily grow into ten or twenty things, and the other character, even though he is dead, will be played by a live actor, who will have his own ideas about how his "death" (and, perhaps, the comically exaggerated onset of rigor mortis) may inconvenience Don'tMindMe. But, as "Things go from bad to worse," at best, Don'tMindMe can only maintain the status quo.

With each attempt at going unnoticed, Don'tMindMe draws more and more attention to himself. A situation which could have been resolved easily by calling the police or shouting for an ambulance is now a matter for greater intrigue and further suspicion.

As such, this scene satisfies the formula we identified in Molière's plays: Don'tMindMe's single-minded obsession *is the very reason behind his failure.*

Commedia Wrinkle #1

Your words and your actions don't always agree.

Try doing something physically that reveals something that you wouldn't want to admit verbally.

It's the old joke in which someone shakes their head "no" while saying "yes," like the bride, amid her wedding vows, saying "I vow to love you for the rest of my life," even as her head wags left-to-right.

When first improvising stage business from *Don Juan*, for instance, I played the servant, Sganarelle, who says of his master, "He doesn't feel for Heaven or for Hell..." I gesture out ahead of myself on "Heaven," but distractedly gesture upwards on "Hell." I then proceed to look at my own hands and find myself shocked at the blasphemy of placing Heaven lower than I have placed Hell. I then awkwardly reverse the position of my hands. It reveals the absurdity of our value judgments, simply with the concept of "up" vs. "down." It gets a laugh every time.

Commedia Wrinkle #2
There is something that the audience knows that you do not.

Gerald Moon's play, *Corpse*, contains a similar "what to do with the dead body" sequence. This time the scene has taken place in the dead man's home, who has been mistakenly shot. Suddenly the shooter is faced with the desperate crisis of "how to eradicate the evidence?" This crisis sets up one of my favorite *lazzi*: "Removing the fingerprints from the bottle."

The two men have been pouring drinks from a whiskey bottle, and the presumptive "killer" realizes that his fingerprints are all over it. The brilliant improviser playing the role (Randy Craig) would, while grasping the bottle by its neck, wipe the belly of the bottle with his handkerchief before carefully setting it down. Randy would cross three steps away from the bottle before realizing his mistake (which the audience had realized the moment that the bottle was set down).

Randy returns, grasping the bottle by the belly, this time wiping the *neck* of the bottle with the handkerchief. He sets the bottle down, and gets two steps away before realizing that he has made the same mistake in reverse! He returns to the bottle, grasping the neck and wiping the belly, sets it down, takes one step, stops, returns, again grasping the belly and wiping the neck.

Finally, his thought process, always one step behind the audience, has caught up with his actions, and Randy must, at last, find some terribly awkward way of clasping the bottle between his knees and his mouth, while wiping it clean with both hands. As a "punch line," he later goes on to clean the table top, moving the bottle out of the way, without realizing that he has begun the entire process again.

Put this formula into a children's play, and before long the kids, who have far fewer inhibitions about this sort of thing, will be shouting out "You missed a spot!" or "Look behind you!"

Commedia Wrinkle #3
There is something you know that your fellow characters do not.

Imagine that you are playing the role of the dead body in our scenario. What might you know that your fellow characters do not?

"That you are really alive?"

Yes! What if you were really just pretending to be dead, if only to obtain some information, or to test how the other character might react?

This, by the way, is exactly what Argan does in *The Imaginary Invalid*, as Beline, his wife, discovering his "death," proceeds to rant about what a horrible man he was, all the while ransacking the room for his money, all of which Argan overhears.

In *Tartuffe*, we know that Orgon is hiding beneath the table, overhearing Tartuffe's attempted seduction of his wife. Even though we cannot see him, our attention is riveted by the reaction that we can only imagine that Orgon might be having, which heightens the interest in the scene well beyond the simple exchange between the hypocrite-lothario and his prey!

In both cases, the audience is now enjoying irony "squared." Not only do they know what the villains do not, but they know that Argan and Orgon know something that Beline and Tartuffe do not, and they get to witness this secondary irony "through the eyes" (or "ears") of Argan and Orgon.

The very simple wrinkle of someone stumbling onto the stage and overhearing a conversation will change the "geometric complexity" of a scene: A straight line from character A to character B now takes an unexpected pass through character C, and with every new revelation, activity or action, the audience' minds must detour through the listener's point of view, examining and re-examining what character C ought or ought not know, which essentially triples the complexity of the scene.

To review ...

- Our characters are guided by a single compelling super-objective (or obsession, or currency) which drives every decision that they make…

As a result of our character having this currency…

- Things go from bad to worse (We are never allowed to improve our situation, unless it improves entirely by accident.)

At which point, we generate lazzi, reinvigorated by these ironic wrinkles…[46]

- Our words and our actions don't always agree
- There is something the audience knows that we do not
- There is something we know that our fellow characters do not, or, conversely…
- There is something our fellow characters know that we do not…

Voila!

[46] In literary circles, these wrinkles are known as "dramatic irony," which may be the most underappreciated element of theatrical narrative.

Chapter 46

Chekhov

They are so busy trying to make Chekhov "realistic" that they forget to make him believable.

"Yes, but how much of this can you use for realistic plays? You couldn't apply this, for instance, to Chekhov?"

(Sigh.)

Yes, I would absolutely apply this to Chekhov.

And Ibsen.

And Shaw.

And Miller.

And Tennessee Williams.

And Sam Shepherd.

And so on.

Of course, Chekhov had characters turn their backs. He had characters pausing. He had characters speaking in "inside voices," and challenged the need to recite text in exaggerated, declamatory tones.

But that doesn't mean that he didn't want them to be heard and seen.

And that doesn't mean that the power of their emotional transformations was diminished in any way.

Chekhov stirred such a sensation when he had characters actually turn their backs to the audience because that turned back was the *opposite* of what the audiences of that time had come to expect and demand from capable actors.

That Chekhovian moment of the turned back was a sliver of a full-length play which signaled to that audience that anything was possible, and that they could look at the level of reality contained within this play in a new way. We could ask, seemingly for the first time – each successive generation thinks that they are the first generation to ask this – "What if this was ***reality*** we were looking at?"

Chekhov's plays were still hilarious. His characters were still vivid. His dialogue was crisp and necessary.

In fact, Chekhov himself had endless arguments with Stanislavsky about the comic nature of the action. Stanislavsky cited the passionate things that his character has to say, and the clear seriousness behind the drama.

Chekhov responded, obliquely, "Yes, but he says these things while wearing checkered trousers!"

Every ten-to-twenty years or so, the theatre has confronted the same question, as a new element of reality is introduced and incorporated, further cementing the illusion that what we are looking at is ***real***.

I once researched a paper on *Hamlet*, which looked at the many portrayals of *Hamlet*, dating back to the time of David Garrick, Shakespeare's own leading actor, playing the role.

With every new performance, the reviewers celebrate the *new, actual, believable*, "***real***" *Hamlet*. "This time they got it right!" the papers cry.

Each generation has its own schools of thought, its own fashions of belief and understanding. And each interprets and recreates *Hamlet* in its own image. (*Hamlet* is the Rorschach test of theatrical production.) And each declares in capital letters, "AT LAST, WE HAVE ARRIVED!"

They are saying, "This is, at last, ***reality*** on the stage!"

And yet, Hamlet, demanding that his actors not "out-Herod Herod" was responding to seventeenth century actors whose performances were so "over the top" that our audiences would barely recognize them as human! He was not projecting forward into what we think of as "realism."

> I have no problems with realism, until such time as we try to convince ourselves that realism is not a *style*. Or suggest that a given style is any better than any other style.
>
> The problem with most actors is that they are so busy trying to make Chekhov "realistic" that they forget to make him believable. Because, for them, "realism" is more about what they are going to ***leave out*** of their performance.

Chekhov painted unmistakably vivid characters. They aren't the "caricatures" that we have observed with Molière, but they aren't the bland depictions of everyday "reality" towards which most modern productions aim.

At the end of *The Seagull*, a man goes off and shoots himself! He picks up a gun as he exits, and moments later we hear the gun go off!

The seeds of that suicide lie in the action of the scene before it, when Treplev finds himself rejected utterly by the woman he loves. The ending of this play makes sense when we see Treplev pushed to the brink, when we see the devastating lightning strike of the scene beforehand.

When Nina tells Treplev of her eternal love for Trigorin, she does it knowing full well that Treplev is, indeed, in love with her.

The passion of her love is so furious and/or so self-centered, that it overrides the damage that she knows she is doing to Treplev (who has just expressed his love for her) in the process. It is driven by a pain and desperation which are as full and expressive to her as that of a Shakespearean heroine.

We can trace this back, one step at a time through the course of the play… frustrated loves, connections missed, aspirations frustrated, dreams shattered. It is a play full of hope and fury, occasionally expressed in a quiet realization, or a pause.

But when we pick up Chekhov, we go soft, sentimental, wistful… into a "Chekhovian" mood, as if this moment in time captured a bunch of quiet, self-indulgent, brooding wastrels.

We may even apply our notions of "Currency" to Chekhov. The irony that hovers thickly over his plays finds each one of these characters wanting something desperately, passionately… but always something slightly different from each other and, thereby, incapable of fulfilling each others' needs.

Love triangles emerge because Masha loves Treplev, who loves Nina, who loves Trigorin, who loves Madam Arkadina, each in a slightly different way and for a slightly different reason.

Treplev wants to earn respect and regard for the play he has written and produced, but finds it mocked by his mother, and barely hears or acknowledges that he is getting the very praise that he has been looking for, as the modest Dr. Dorn has truly appreciated the play, enthusiastically encouraging him to continue. Unfortunately, the adulation has not come from the source that would satisfy the currency he is looking to trade in.

These contrasting desires that fail to match up with each other give us the conflict, as well as the comedy, which rages and blunders just as fully as in Shakespeare or Molière. The details of these currencies, these values, obsessions and passions are simply hidden a little further behind the everyday domestic concerns that tighten the noose on each and every one of us.

Chekhov wrote people who stood at breaking points, and captured the moment in which their passions spilled out because they just couldn't hold them back any more. They commit suicide, they fight duels, they have affairs… and sometimes they admit to these things passionately, out loud, and sometimes they mask their secrets within scenes which do not actually even mention the suicides/duels/affairs into which they are about to plunge headlong. They engage in banal conversations, and then walk off to commit the "act" that calls them forth.

Most modern actors play the banality of the conversations, because that is "realistic." A good actor also plays the storms that are raging inside, because, given the *reality* of the acts that they are poised to commit… that is believable.

Chapter 47

Three Boards and a Passion

What is vague and abstract becomes concrete. The cosmic ether is shaped into meaning. The intransigent nature of human thought gains shape and reality.

If we take away all but what is absolutely necessary, we find that we may still do theatre without costumes, sets, lights, auditoria, director, playwright, producer and all that goes with those.

What we are left with… that which we cannot clear out of the way without disqualifying a given event as an act of theatre:

The Actor, the Idea, the Audience.

Or, as Lope de Vega once said "three boards, two actors and a passion."

But what if we took away one of those two actors?

The One-Person Play

Let us look, for a moment, at plays which keep the focus almost unflinchingly, relentlessly on the human element. The one-person play is an especially theatrical phenomenon.

Often, the one-person play celebrates a historical character. If that personality is captivating in its own right, the play resonates with an audience who otherwise would never have the chance to interact or to breathe the same air of an Abraham Lincoln, a Mark Twain, Emily Dickinson or Will Rogers. It takes the famous works, stories, accomplishments of these great people, and connects them with a living, breathing human being with honest, human desires and objectives, with whom we may now *identify*.

There are also strong fictional one-person shows which reveal a character working through an internal struggle, or autobiographical one-person plays which center around a particular story or series of stories, perhaps of a particular theme, or contributing to a given *statement*.

The very ***fact*** of the one-person play places the focus on the performance, and on the presence and potential of an individual human being. In the course of watching the play, an audience may, only with difficulty, divorce themselves from the train of thought that goes something like:

"Wow, he is doing it all by himself!"
"Wow, nobody else is going to enter onto the stage, for this whole play!"
"Wow, he memorized all of those lines!"

And while this is rarely the specific intent of the production, it is almost impossible to disregard this pattern of thought. Those feelings about the actor's performance inevitably transfer over to our feelings about the main character, and the irrepressible spirit, or spark of humanity that character represents.

If the theatre is unavoidably about humanity, life and its potential, then rarely is that more evident than in a well-executed one-person play. A single idea, a single actor, with no technical support, may take over the stage and hold our attention, with nothing but the performance to convey the idea. What is vague and abstract becomes concrete. The cosmic ether is shaped into meaning. The intransigent nature of human thought gains shape and reality.

Collectively, the audience is moved by something as tiny and vulnerable as an idea. Aware of the power of the individual, they are empowered into a vision of what is possible for themselves. The world and all of its possibilities are transferred to their fingertips.

The good news

Solo performers also have no "down time" during which they are waiting for somebody else to cast them.

They may be waiting on more bookings, or alternative gigs, but they don't need anyone else's go-ahead to dive into rehearsal on a role that is only limited by the reaches of their imagination.

We actors are often brimming with helplessness. And yet, we always have sufficient energy to complain about our lack of work, or the doltish ignorance of the director who failed to see our worth. Our default setting always leaves us living in anticipation of the next round of casting.

We learn passivity.

We give over our power to directors and producers and agencies and wait for the phone to ring. We place the power for our success and our growth and development into someone else's hands.

We can choose to be the victims of someone else's programming needs and whims. Or we can be the initiators/creators of our own cottage industries, forging material that makes *us* think, or makes *us* laugh, eagerly anticipating that the joy or the fascination or passion that it brings out in us, will one day catch fire with others.

More good news: I can gather the cast of my one-man play at a moment's notice.

The Major Trip-Wires of a One-Person Show

Pausing too little: Plays still need to breathe, and sometimes the most difficult thing is to force oneself to "take the moment," to let a bit of tension build, or to give the audience the opportunity to respond… especially when we are hyperconscious of the audience's relentless attention on ourselves, and ourselves alone! We are that lone plate spinner, constantly struggling to keep those plates from crashing to the ground. Sometimes, the audience needs the chance to catch up.

Pausing too much: More often than the actor with the foot on the throttle, we discover the *casual* actor, who, after completing a five or ten minute monologue, punctuated with some final witticism, wanders toward the back of the stage. There, he bends down to pick up a water bottle, diligently unscrews the cap, takes a long swig from the bottle and, after catching his breath, *rescrews* the cap onto the bottle, sets the bottle down, and works his way into the next monologue.

I have seen some actors actually ***leave the stage*** for 30-60 seconds, bring out a bit of furniture, set out a few props, change a costume and eventually resume the play.

The theatre is a time-based art form. When time passes without any real or implied action on stage… the audience feels abandoned. We may choose to play music, fill the bridge with pre-recorded dialogue, or even a video, but the performance "contract" is clear: ***it's the live stuff that counts!*** If we fill in the breaks with technology, we immediately see this as a device substituting for the real thing. When the play becomes more *device* than *live performance*, our minds leave the play. We wonder whether it mightn't work better on YouTube.

Leaning overmuch on the technology: Audiences do not go to one-person plays to see how technologically savvy we can be with videos and voiceovers. They are looking for that special human connection. All the work we do to make the play more technologically dazzling actually works in opposition to the impulse that feels most honest and natural to a live audience observing a live human being.

Technology also plants the seeds for disaster, sooner or later. The further we open that Pandora's box, the more dependent we become on the microphone, the underscoring, the CD, the DVD, the slide show, or the simultaneous film, the more signals that we send to our audience that contradict our unflinching, relentlessly human theatrical phenomenon.

Chapter 48

Born Actors

If they knew of the struggles that awaited them, the lack of money, lack of respect, the disappointments, the bad casting, the rude directors, the backstabbing... they would still act.

Thirty years of persistence have brought my passions in line with my abilities, and my abilities to meet the pitch of my passions, and somewhere, when I wasn't paying attention, I got better at this stuff.

None of it feels like a "choice." More like "compulsion" or... the feeling I've been doing this since before this particular lifetime began.

I would describe myself as a born actor who took thirty or forty years to fulfill on the challenge of what I was born to do.

The danger in designating such a thing as a "Born Actor, is that many actors already think of themselves as gifted by some special dispensation of God, and refuse to put out the effort to develop these natural instincts into abilities, nor do they have the vision to contribute to the production as a whole. In kindergarten, they scored low on "plays well with others."

"Born Actor" is more of a syndrome than a blessing.

Some of the symptoms:

- Born Actors know when they are being looked at, and respond to that fact. They are hyperconscious of the first responsibility of the actor: Being Seen.
- A Born Actor will often report getting sick after a show closes. They have a special relationship with their adrenaline, which keeps them healthy through the run of a show, and then quickly sidelines them once the show is past.
- The Born Actor may spend the majority of a performance day listless and tired, dragging through pre-show rituals. When that first entrance arrives, the Born Actor will find the burst of energy that was missing throughout the day. Subconsciously, they have been saving up all day long, surprising even themselves in the crucial moment. Their bodies instinctively prepare themselves to do the work.
- Most crucially, Born Actors cannot see themselves doing anything else with their lives. If they knew of the struggles that awaited them, the lack of money, lack of respect, the disappointments, the bad casting, the rude directors, the backstabbing… they would still act.

Chapter 49

An Actor Acts

Imperfection is the gift that we have all been given as a virtue of being alive.

I can't tell you what city to move to, where to go to school, where to audition, who to know, whether or not to work as a waiter or a temp. I refuse to hold forth on these matters, given my demonstrated inability to prognosticate about my own life.

But the relevant imperative that I suggest to directors, writers, painters, artists and craftsmen of all types... (You can rearrange this statement any way you like to leave the key career for last.)

A painter paints, a writer writes, a director directs, an actor ...

"... acts."

Repeatedly, I meet writers who will not write, painters who will not paint, directors who will not direct and actors who will not act.

As exceptionally talented as they are, they have developed writer's block, painter's block, director's block, or actor's block.

It may be the fear of the blank canvas and the empty page. They fear that they have "lost it," and that the new attempt will be not as good as in the past. They fear imperfection.

Imperfection is the gift we have all been given as a virtue of being alive.

There is no "perfect." There is better and worse. There is improvement and there is decay. There is the gradual development of dexterity, and there is the ongoing wear of entropy.

- Perhaps a recent attempt fell shy of the excellence once achieved.
- Perhaps we have grown into more discerning critics, and thus more aware of the unreachable height to which we aspire.
- Perhaps we begin to suspect that the former excellence was simply dumb luck: getting cast in just the right part, stumbling across a brilliant idea for a plot… Often we let this freeze us in our tracks. Some of us stay frozen for years… or the rest of our lives.

I can't tell whether your next painting, story, play, or role will be better than the last one you created.

I *can* tell you whatever you create will be better than doing nothing.

Yes, we will make mistakes along the way. Some of them may be really embarrassing. And we may waste bits of our lives with regret.

On balance, we will regret inaction more than action.

The pettiness of the mistakes we make will never outweigh the seriousness of stopping our process.

- For the actor, this means auditioning, performing, rehearsing.
- It means accepting roles in crappy little productions that nobody will come to see.
- It means playing tiny roles where the most we may do is hold some sort of a banner.
- It means working with some people we don't like.
- It means putting ourselves into an arena where people will come and judge our work, sometimes harshly.
- It means negotiating through a performance, listening to criticism, and changing our approach. Developing nuance and texture. Getting bigger, bolder, louder, subtler, sharper, friskier, wiser.
- It means growing.

We get better and worse, and then better again. We make headway, fail, and move forward again. We stink the place up, and then do something brilliant.

In a career that is going to span say twenty-five to fifty years, on balance we end up better than when we start out. I cannot tell you whether this show or that show will stimulate the improvement that will make you better than before. But on balance, in the process of doing fifty or a hundred plays, you end up much better than when you started out.

You cannot second-guess which will be the performance or the production that will stimulate the improvement. The show you do in an equity theatre may actually teach you bad habits, while that class project gives you your "eureka" moment.

Occasionally actors refuse roles that they are offered. Perhaps they never really wanted to get cast, or to do the work. Sometimes they blurt out that they just wanted to audition "for the experience." And in the process, they screw up the delicately balanced casting the director has built around the actor's pretense of commitment.

There will come a time that someone is uncertain about whether to take a chance on you or not. And that person will talk with someone else who has encountered you in the past.

Here's a backstage peek of how these conversations go, as related by a director-friend who knew I was working on this chapter, who carves out a particular exception to my "an actor acts" thesis…

TRUE STORY

"So, I was hired to direct a musical...

"And there we were sitting at the table... myself, the music director, the choreographer, the producer, the stage manager and the assistant director. And we'd have somebody come in and audition, and they'd sing a song, and I'd be sitting there listening, and thinking, "Hm, she's pretty good!"

"And then from out of nowhere... pffft! I would notice that a note had gotten slid down in front of me:

"'She's a real bitch. You do not want to work with her.'

"And then somebody else would come in to audition, and they'd start singing, and I'd think that they were sounding all right.

"And then, again.. pffft! Another note would come sliding towards me from the other end of the table...

"'He has pissed off everybody he's ever worked with!'

"And, so on! Again and again! Actors don't realize how much their reputation follows them wherever they go! Ultimately, I had to put my foot down to make the case for an actress that they were all up in arms about. I had to have a soprano in that part and her voice was perfect. And eventually, every one of them came up to me to say... 'You know, she wasn't that bad!'

"And the notion that I really walked away with out of that experience was that actors who want to learn about how to get cast... absolutely need to spend at least one show not trying to get cast, but ***watching other people trying to get cast!*** *They need to stage manage at least once in their lives! That's when you see all the stuff that you've been doing right there in your face... the stuff that really pisses people off! And that's when you start making a list of every little thing that you will never do again!"*

Your career may be filled with people who loved working with you, who know you as a generous, passionate, hard-working artist who makes every play you work on a better play. You may be the first one that they think of when that other actor screws them over. You may be the first one they call when they schedule auditions.

They may even *choose* a play knowing that it has a perfect part for you!

Or perhaps you are talented enough that people will want to cast you and work with you in spite of your temperament.

That's a chance you may be taking.

An actor acts.

Chapter 50

Dealing with Criticism

The best that we can do is sit back and admire life's great diversity. It is, after all, kind of cute.

Yes, all reviewers are idiots.

At least until such time as they recognize our special genius.

We will be criticized. We will receive negative *and* positive feedback. Critics will attack, not only what we do, but who we are, or who they assume we are, as suggested by what we do.

Somewhere there was an idea, and either that idea ends up being valued, or not. That value can be significantly influenced and improved by the discipline of our effort, but sometimes no amount of discipline or effort can bring the necessary spark to a particular project.

Bad work has many authors in the theatre. Usually, the reviewer will assign such authorship to very specific members of the production team. (When you write, direct, produce and act in your own one-person show, they don't have to look very far.)

We may make an issue out of the reviewer's lack of objectivity, or intelligence, or their scandalous prejudice. We can invest our energy arguing with the rightness of each review. Or we can look for the impulse that stimulated the response.

A reviewer or a friend, may have issues with the play's climax. But in their response we may notice that the seeds of the problem were buried in the play's opening moments. Perhaps we underplayed an important piece of exposition,

Our disappointment is natural and human, but let us still seek out what stimulated the reaction. What were the critics looking for that we are not providing? What led them to look for it? Is further work with that aspect within our scope, or would it violate our intent? Did the press releases promise something different?

Having said that…

There are occasions in which we read the negative review, and know that the reviewer was reviewing the play that he or she *wanted* to see. Not the play that he or she *actually saw*. That is when we discover...

"The review says more about them than it says about me."

It may well be that our play was actually wildly successful in pushing that particular reviewer's buttons, and, as much as he or she may need it, this reviewer hates to have his or her buttons pushed!

Two Contrasting Reviews from the Vancouver Fringe Festival...

"If Timothy Mooney hopes to reveal Jean Baptiste Molière's comic genius, he's not going to do it with this piece. Mooney recites speeches from his own translations of the French master's plays. In his deadeningly predetermined delivery, he illustrates everything he says, and all too often he hits his rhyming couplets – even when they don't end sentences – like rows of tacks, obliterating meaning. Even the most stylized forms of comedy rely on surprise and underlying emotional truth. Mooney only finds freedom in his final monologue, which, ironically sends up falsity in performance." *Colin Thomas*, *Georgia Straight*, 9/11/03

That review showed up on the very same day as:

"I do love eating my words, with a liberal sprinkling of crow. I had low expectations for this production and am delighted to say I am full of shit. Tim Mooney is one clever clog and there was a point to rendering the prose of Molière into verse. Fantastic show. Helps if you know something about Jean Baptiste Molière's work, but you don't need to. Mooney knows more than enough for all of us, but never gets clogged up in it. One of my faves this Fringe." *Alan Hindle, Terminal City*, 9/11/03

Two reviewers, the same performance, a world apart.

Every actor must ultimately accept the impossibility of satisfying everybody. The best we can do is to sit back and admire life's great diversity. It is, after all, kind of cute. Someone took a stand. That particular someone selected the ***currency*** of the art as, for instance, "surprise and underlying emotional truth."

The rules in art are fickle beasts, filled with assumptions and associations. We make legal tender out of them, forwarding an agenda and a set of principles. If I, the reviewer, shift priorities for a show that does not fit my vision, how can the public value the *currency* of my aesthetic judgment? Can I devalue myself in their eyes?

Bluffing is as much of a tool for the reviewer as the artist. The reviewer bluffs that she or he has the measuring stick By Which Art May Be Judged. That stick becomes the public currency, as long as the public chooses to value it.

To whom do we, who have to perform again tomorrow night, listen? The voice of the most recent reviewer continues to echo, even as I perform. A negative review has emerged and there are two routes I might take.

1. I edge away from the sort of acting that was the source of the critic's commentary. If the criticism chided my rhyming, I downplay the rhymes. If the critique balked at my broad gesticulation, I rein in my impulses. I hold back. I resist. Or...
2. I throw myself back into the work. I claim the very territory for which I was criticized. I point up the rhymes, I gesture fully. I

> exploit each and every moment and envision the audience responding warmly and enthusiastically.

I guarantee you that the audience for option number two is going to enjoy themselves much more.

If I look out into that cavern of audience and see judgment, criticism, skepticism and ridicule, then that is what I generate. If I look out and see encouragement, love, enthusiasm, and success, then those become present.

There will always be those predisposed to seeing something different. They will either reassert or reassess the currency of their predispositions.

Here is an actual performance experience, quoted from my blog:

> The audience reaction seemed muted at first, and I could feel myself struggling to keep my energy up. I was worried that this was a trend that had begun with the last show. Following a review that was mixed, I could see that my thoughts around the show had reshaped around a negative interpretation, and I was thinking about "just getting through it."
>
> And then something happened. I think it was with the second monologue, *The Bourgeois Gentleman*. I got a big laugh and a nice round of applause. I found myself thinking about the upcoming awards for the fringe, and imagining that perhaps I still had a chance of winning something. Perhaps one of the judges was in the audience now, and he had not, as yet, made up his mind. I could feel a surge of positive energy. There was action that I could take. I could do something.
>
> When my mind was focused on criticism I had received, I was left conscious of having to NOT do something, to AVOID performing badly. Which stifles creativity. But when I was focused on a vision of great success, I was set into action, into motion, and I could ACT.
>
> I recognized this even as it was happening, and realized that, in the process, my performance had improved one hundred percent. Our future (or what we anticipate that future to be) *gives us our present*. When I anticipate the possibility of success, it reshapes the action that I am taking in the now.

Whatever any critic may say, the important voice is the one in your own head.

If that voice is not convinced you have something of value to offer, you probably don't.

Convincing that voice is more important than convincing any individual reviewer.

It impacts and informs every instant of your performance.

It gives you your "presence."

Chapter 51

What I Declare

We can own who we are in the presence of other people.

Everything on stage is a bluff. And very much of life is a bluff. If we declare that we are attractive, for instance, and put the force of belief behind what we say, we become attractive. That has nothing to do with what gifts God may have given us to start out with. Everyone can create this belief.

Of course, it helps to take care of the issues in life that leave us feeling that the "burden of proof" is on us, such as those extra twenty pounds that we convince ourselves are getting in our way.

We are not the victims, but the *authors* of our selves. We want the audience to fall in love. Even villains want love. In a one-person show, the audience lives exclusively in our company. They may experience the author's message on an objective, intellectual level… or they may just fall in love.

Love lends emotional importance. People are moved. Everything is more impactful. We can't make an audience fall in love with us. But we can let them.

We can give them the opportunity to accept or to reject, by putting more of "us" out there, all the while throwing 100% of our commitment behind the play.

We can position ourselves to be seen.

We can adjust the angle of the head so that the brow does not throw a shadow over our eyes.

We can taste every consonant that teases upon our tongue.

We can fight every impulse to run away, to hide behind the furniture, to collapse and contract the body, to turn profile, to face upstage.

We can act from the assumption that the audience wants to see and hear *more* of us… and, thereby, have intimate knowledge of the play that we present.

We can *own* who we are, and what the play has to say, in the presence of other people, declaring from the echoing depths of our psyche, "This is important," and "I am worth your time and energy and enthusiasm and devotion."

We can own who we are in the presence of other people.

Index

If you enjoyed this book...

- You may want to share it with friends, teach it in your classes, or get copies for your library...
- You may want to share your own reactions, thoughts and stories with the author...
- You may want to follow the author's exploits, read his blog, or learn of other works available from Timothy Mooney, or the TMRT Press!

If so, please go to **www.timmooneyrep.com/aatsol** for lots of fun stuff, including the *Measure for Measure, Tempest, Othello* in-depth scene discussions, and links to blog, video, scripts and bookings for *Lot o' Shakespeare* and *Moliere than Thou!*

Or, you can fill out the form below, and send it with your order for more copies of the book to:

TMRT Press
c/o Timothy Mooney
P.O. Box 638
Prospect Heights, IL 60070

You can also send your thoughts, comments and stories to this address. We love reading your feedback, input and adventures!

Name ______________________________

Address ______________________________

City, State, Zip ______________________________

Telephone ______________________________

E-mail address ______________________________

I would like to order _____ copies of "Acting at the Speed of Life"!
I would like info for ordering multiple copies for school or library use! ☐
I would also like to be on the list for the AATSOL Blog! ☐
Other comments and thoughts (use additional pages, if necessary!):

____

____

____

____

____

Thank you for your enthusiasm!
Tim Mooney

Also by Timothy Mooney...

Adaptations of the Plays of Moliere

Available at Playscripts, Inc., www.playscripts.com.

Don Juan

The Doctor in Spite of Himself

The Doctor in Spite of Himself *(Short version*)*

The Imaginary Invalid

The Imaginary Invalid *(Short version)*

The Learned Ladies *(Short version)*

The Misanthrope

The Misanthrope *(Short version)*

The Miser

The Miser *(Short version)*

The Schemings of Scapin

The Schemings of Scapin *(Short version)*

The School for Husbands *(Short version)*

Tartuffe

Tartuffe *(Short version)*

More scripts available via www.moliere-in-english.com.

And... Coming Soon...

Moliere Monologues

150 Hilarious Performance Pieces
From the World's Greatest Comedian!

** "Short versions" of these plays are designed for High School contest use, each written to be performed in 40 minutes (for a cast that picks up their cues).*